My Wife Suggested Crete

Discovering the magic of the BIG Greek island

My Wife Suggested Crete

Discovering the magic of the BIG Greek island

Hugh Fernyhough

Published in 2022 by Stellium Flame,
Plymouth, Devon, UK
stelliumpub@gmail.com
Tel: +44 (0)1752 367 300

Copyright © 2022 Hugh Fernyhough
Hugh Fernyhough has asserted the moral right to be identified as the author of this work in accordance with sections 77 & 78 of The Copyright, Designs and Patents Act 1988

British Library Cataloguing in Publication Data: A catalogue record for this book is available from The British Library

Photographs and illustrations copyright © 2022 Hugh Fernyhough
Cover design by Mark Latter
ISBN: 978-1-912358-01-4

Typesetting by Zambezi Publishing Ltd, Plymouth UK
Stellium Flame is an imprint of Stellium Ltd

All rights reserved. No part of this publication may be reproduced, stored in a retrieval system, or transmitted in any form or by any means, electronic, mechanical, photocopying, recording or otherwise, whether currently existing or yet to be developed, without the prior written permission of the publishers.
This book is sold subject to the condition that it shall not, by way of trade or otherwise, be lent, resold, hired out or otherwise circulated without the publisher's prior written consent, in any form of binding, cover or format other than that in which it is originally published, and without a similar condition being imposed on the subsequent purchaser.
Disclaimer:- This book is intended to provide general information regarding the subject matter, and to entertain. The contents are not exhaustive and no warranty is given as to accuracy of content. The book is sold on the understanding that neither the publisher nor the author are thereby engaged in rendering professional services, in respect of the subject matter or any other field. If expert guidance is required, the services of a competent professional should be sought.
Readers are urged to access a range of other material on the book's subject matter, and to tailor the information to their individual needs. Neither the author nor the publisher shall have any responsibility to any person or entity regarding any loss or damage caused or alleged to be caused, directly or indirectly, by the use or misuse of information contained in this book. If you do not wish to be bound by the above, you may return this book in original condition to the publisher, with its receipt, for a refund of the purchase price.

About the Author

Hugh Fernyhough was born in East Devon and now in retirement lives with his wife near the town of Dawlish. A university degree course in Hotel and Catering Administration led to a short career in hotel and leisure management. This was followed by a complete change of direction: over thirty years in garden design, landscaping and restoration.

The origin of ***My Wife Suggested Crete*** was a week's package holiday to a Greek island at the southern edge of Europe in 2011.

A lifetime interest in history and landscapes, together with a grounding in the hospitality industry, all contributed to his growing fascination with the island of Crete and her people.

Having reached retirement age and now with numerous Cretan holidays happily remembered in countless photo albums, he felt it was time to put pen to paper.

Contents

Acknowledgements..3

Preface..5

A Note on Transliteration......................................8
And the use of Quotations

Introduction..11

Chapter One..18
The Package Experience - Our First Taste of Crete

A Cretan Interlude..34
"A Walk up to Knossós"

Chapter Two..36
Beginning to Find our Feet

Chapter Three...45
Easter and the Cretan Diet

Chapter Four...54
Seeking out the South Coast

Chapter Five..72
The Autumn of 2014 - Bittersweet Memories

Chapter Six..90
Iráklio - A City worthy of more than a one-night stopover

Contents

Chapter Seven 102
The Cretan Psyche - A Tentative Look

Chapter Eight 113
Heading West - Haniá and the North-West

Chapter Nine 128
The Far South-West - Sélino and Sphakiá

Chapter Ten 140
Fighting for Freedom - Again

Chapter Eleven 170
Rummaging about in Réthymno

A Cretan Interlude 183
"The Katzphur People"

Chapter Twelve 184
The Lasíthi Plateau

A Cretan Interlude 192
"Stories from the Lasíthi Plateau"

Chapter Thirteen 195
Heading back East - our Second Home

Chapter Fourteen 208
Saying Goodbye - a Conclusion is Required

Postscript 219

Glossary 221

Permissions and References 224

Bibliography 234

Index 239

Friday's Rush Hour, Southern Crete

For Jennie

Acknowledgements

In order for this book to have come to any sort of fruition, I am indebted to many people:

Caroline West, Tom Moore, Mike Gerrard, Lynn Warren, Chris Webber, and Neil Pulling for offering their technical advice, support and knowledge; and Mark Latter for designing the front and the back covers. My thanks go to Mrs Jacqueline Fox who managed to cleverly decipher my illegible hand written script, and thereby provided the first typed version.

I am particularly grateful to Felice Hardy for copy editing my initial draft text. She undoubtedly made it an easier read. Together with correcting punctuation and grammatical errors, she also focused my attention on avoiding repetition and the use of certain mundane words. However, I would like to make it clear that any errors in the final version of my text are entirely of my own making.

In Crete, I am most grateful to Constantinos Mamalakis, Curator of the Historical Museum of Crete based in Iráklio, who devoted several hours of his time to me one December morning. I would never have met him without the kindness of Eleni Kampouraki from the sales department of the Museum. I thank her most sincerely. I would also like to thank Sandy Tzagkaraki, Irene Foukaraki, and assistant director Agisilaos Kaloutsakis for their help.

In Réthymno I sincerely thank the Kokonas family. One day I hope to meet up with them in "The Cream Society". I would particularly like to thank Nikolaos Kokonas, great grandson of Alexandros Kokonas of Yerakári, for his time and effort on my behalf. My thanks to Chrisanthi Papathanasaki for allowing me to use her photograph of the white sea daffodils in Xerókambos.

In Haniá, Stelios Jackson's knowledge, generosity and kindness has been endless. It was through the Hellenic book service in London that I was fortunate to make the initial contact with him. His good natured bonhomie knows no bounds! It was through Stelios that I managed to make contact with various authors (and copyright holders) who have written about Crete, and with family relatives of other authors.

My Wife Suggested Crete

In Australia, I would like to thank Walter Burroughs, Editor of the Naval Historical Review, for his enormous help, and Keith McLeod at the Margaret River Bookshop. In New Zealand, my thanks go to Fiona Gray, Research Librarian at the Alexander Turnbull Library and the National Library of New Zealand. Her extensive research eventually came up trumps.

All permissions are listed at the end of my book, but I would particularly like to thank Charlotte Osment at Penguin Random House UK; Frances Faulkner at Penguin Random House New Zealand; Caroline Westmore Managing Editor at John Murray (Publishers); and Paul Dry of Paul Dry Books Inc. Various issues needed clarification, and these kind individuals did just that.

When I set out on this journey I wondered whether any authors – possessing far greater skills and knowledge than I – would ever correspond or communicate with me. I cannot convey the extent of my excitement when they did. To the following authors I express my heartfelt thanks:

James Angelos, Roderick Bailey, Adam Hopkins, Seán Damer and Ian Frazer. To David MacNeil Doren and his wife Barbro goes a particular thank you and sincere wishes for improving health. Special thanks are due to Richard Clark, Imogen Grundon, Colin Janes, and Christopher Somerville. To Christopher I add the message that should a cork be popped one day, you will be the first to know!

There are then relatives and descendants of other authors who are no longer with us. Here I want to thank Robert Rendel and the Rendel family; Jolyon and Di Wiren and Rhys Ferguson; Marilyn Sadleir, daughter of Geoffrey Edwards, for updating me with news of Prevelly in Western Australia, so far from Moní Préveli in Crete. Prevelly continues to tell an intensely emotional story in the island's history. Most importantly, I wish to thank Cassandra Verney, widow of Stephen Verney, with whom I had a lengthy chat on the phone one evening. She retold some of the stories in *Snakes and Ladders,* which of course made them all the more entertaining.

To Jan Budkowski and his wife Sasha Fenton at Stellium, goes a big thank you for putting it all together, with such patience and understanding.

Finally, I turn to my dear wife Jennie. She has spent endless hours typing, correcting, amending, emailing and chasing. Without her there would simply be no book – nor would there be a story to tell.

Preface

I have never been driven to write a book on any subject before now. The last serious writing that I attempted took the form of final examinations for a Batchelor of Science degree in Hotel and Catering Administration in the summer of 1975. I remember it being stressful, undoubtedly because I had not worked hard enough. Over a period of four years I had become completely enamoured with a particular form of student ideology which involved visiting as many country pubs as possible in order to consume vast quantities of real ale and play darts. It was an ideology that I adopted with relish, but which I must have abandoned just in time to get the necessary revisions done before the dreaded tests of knowledge took place. In complete contrast, the following effort has caused far less anxiety and little stress. Unlike the exams of 1975, this is something I have wanted to achieve for many reasons.

Firstly, I am well aware that my wife and I have been boring our friends and families to the point of distress whenever we mention the word 'Crete'. One or both of us will then set forth with streams of excited and probably exaggerated drivel concerning our most recent visit to the island. In particular – and I believe this was in 2014 – one of our friends exclaimed in utter dismay on hearing about our fourth visit to Crete that particular year, "Oh no – not again!" With this in mind I am reminded of the late – and great, in my opinion – Canadian actor, John Candy, in the film *Uncle Buck*, in a scene where he was desperately trying to get his young niece and nephew to be quiet by showing them, or rather pretending to show them, how to zip up their lips so that they couldn't speak. With our exasperated friend in mind, I hope what follows here will silence us on the subject of Crete – unless invited otherwise of course – so that all friends and family will feel comfortable in our presence and will not feel another Cretan moment coming on whenever they see us.

Secondly, and more importantly, it is my dearest wish that the following pages may inspire some of those who are brave enough to read them to consider a visit to Crete, or perhaps revisit if that is the case. This is not a travel guide although inevitably it may appear at times to be just

My Wife Suggested Crete

that. Among several guides available, I believe *The Rough Guide to Crete* is excellent – although I now know of the odd historical error, and, as ever, time has the habit of changing things. My aspiration is that my words will provide a taste of what Crete is like, past and present, and above all give a feeling of the nature of the wonderful people who live there, because it is undoubtedly the people of Crete who have inspired me to write.

You may find that I drift off the chosen subject from time to time and that I have the audacity to proclaim my thoughts on various worldly subjects. My excuse for this is that in doing so I will get the reader to the last page in case there is some juicy gossip to be had. Having said that, I wouldn't be the first to rush off to the bookie to put a bet on that.

Thirdly, and rather flippantly, I hope to convince my friends and family that I have not been totally idle in retirement.

The following pages are essentially our experiences since our first visit in 2011 and how we have gradually got to know the island and some of the islanders. I have also felt the need to attempt a separate chapter on the people themselves and what makes them tick, their character and particular strengths, their distinctive nature, and their individuality. The end result will probably leave a complex set of questions and confusion. But there it is! And throughout my storytelling, I have been unable to avoid Crete's history. It seems to me to be synonymous with enjoying the island as it is today.

This book is not designed to be a history lesson, but be warned that on most pages a Minoan palace or Dorian city may be mentioned; a Hellenic house or a Roman mosaic will suddenly take centre stage; a Byzantine church, Venetian mansion or Turkish bridge will become the focus of my attention. This island has been invaded and occupied time and again for millennia and reminders of the past are visible almost everywhere you care to go. The last invasion – not including tourism – took place in 1941. It is only this period, 1941 to 1945, which has driven me to write a separate chapter, not I hasten to add on strict military history, but because of the reaction of the Cretan people to this invasion, their constant and consistent resistance to it and because of the political aftermath. Whatever side of the political divide, I have come to realise that this period of the island's history is still intensely real and significant to the people. I think that it is important to be aware of the fact.

Finally, in order to interrupt any monotony in my own script, I have included one or two short stories, written by others. I am most grateful to those concerned for giving me permission to use them here. I have called them Cretan Interludes which I hope you will find amusing or moving or both.

Preface

Just as a mainline express train is unexpectedly diverted into a railway siding you will find that I suddenly mention a member of my family, a friend or acquaintance, without any apparently logical reason for doing so. Just as it is probably only the driver of that train who knows the reason for its abrupt halt in the journey, so it is probably only I who sees a reason for the inclusion of these people in my story. But as Jennie has so often heard me say: "That's the way it is."

My late Granny Joan would spend hours fiddling with empty cardboard boxes, deciding whether drawing pins or safety pins, or perhaps even balls of string, should fill them. After a time of careful consideration and with several other options still on the table, and without proclaiming any definite judgement on the matter, she would declare that, at any rate, these boxes would be 'awfully useful.' It is too late of course to know whether Granny Joan would have been sufficiently pleased to place a copy of my book somewhere in her bookcase, or to know whether it might have been graded in her 'awfully useful' category, but if that had been the outcome, I would of course have been delighted.

A Note on Transliteration

And the use of Quotations

Transliteration from Greek to English is not an exact science – the Greek language has an entirely separate alphabet. For instance, while airlines will choose Heraklion as a destination, I use the spelling Iráklio. While the same airlines can take you to Chaniá, I spell this city as Haniá. My reasoning has been affected chiefly by the way place names are spelt on maps and on the road signs, which usually show place names in both Greek and transliterated English. I hope it doesn't complicate the story.

My full bibliography appears at the end of this book. However, when using quotations from various writers I clearly wish to acknowledge them and identify their work. In order to avoid footnotes, I have simply identified the source of the quotation by the author's initials. Below is a list in alphabetical order according to surname, revealing their identity, which book the quotation came from and its year of publication. These quotations are also fully referenced at the end of this book under the heading: "Permissions and References".

JA   James Angelos. *The Full Catastrophe* (2015)
AB   Antony Beevor. *Crete. The Battle and the Resistance* (1991)
RB   Roderick Bailey. Foreword to *Abducting a General* (2014)
RC   Richard Clark. *Crete - A Notebook* (2012)
SD & IF Seán Damer & Ian Frazer. *On the Run* (2016)
DMDavin   D M Davin. *Official History of New Zealand in the Second World War. Crete* (1953)
DMD   David MacNeil Doren. *Winds of Crete* (1974)
TD   Tom Dunbabin. *Tom J Dunbabin. An Archaeologist at War* Society of Cretan Historical Studies (2015)
GE   Geoffrey Edwards. *The Road to Prevelly* (1989)
AHF   Alan Fernyhough. *A History of the Royal Army Ordnance Corps 1920 – 1945* (1967)
XF   Xan Fielding. *The Stronghold* (Paul Dry Books 2013)

A Note on Transliteration

	Hide and Seek (Paul Dry Books 2013)
IG	Imogen Grundon. *The Rash Adventurer. A Life of John Pendlebury* (2007)
AH	Adam Hopkins. *Crete, Its Past, Present and People* (1989)
CH & MF	C N Hadjipateras & M Fafalios. *Crete 1941 Eyewitnessed* (2016)
CJ	Colin Janes. *The Eagles of Crete* (2013)
	The Guerillas of Crete (2017)
NK	Nikos Kokonas. *The Cretan Resistance 1941 – 1945* (2004)
EL	Edward Lear. *The Cretan Journal* (1984)
PLF	Patrick Leigh Fermor. *Abducting a General* (2014)
	Dashing for the Post - The *Letters of Patrick Leigh Fermor* Ed Adam Sisman (2016)
	Words of Mercury (2004)
LL	Lew Lind. *Flowers of Réthymnon. Escape from Crete* (1991)
HM	Henry Miller. *The Colossus of Maroussi* (2010) (Originally 1941)
RP	Robert Pashley. *Travels in Crete* (1837)
JP	J D S Pendlebury. *The Archaeology of Crete* (1939) Norton Library (1965)
DP	Dilys Powell. *The Villa Ariadne* (1999)
GP	George Psychoundakis. *The Cretan Runner* (Penguin Edition 1998)
OR & JM	Oliver Rackham & Jennifer Moody. *The Making of the Cretan Landscape* (1996)
AMR	AM Rendel. *Appointment in Crete* (1953)
JEHS	John Edwin Hilary Skinner. *Roughing it in Crete in 1867* (1868)
CS	Christopher Somerville. *The Golden Step* (2007)
PS	Patricia Storace. *Dinner with Persephone* (1996)
TABS	Captain T.A.B. Spratt. *Travels and Researches in Crete* (1865)
RS	Reg Spurr. *To Have and to Lose* Society of Cretan Historical Studies. (2007)
RHT	R.H. Thomson. *Captive Kiwi* (1964)
PT	Peter Trudgill. *In Sfakiá* (2008)
GST	G S Thompson. *The Royal Artillery Commemoration Book 1939 – 1945.* (1950)
GAT	Georgios Tzitzikas. *Freedom and Glory* Society of Cretan Historical Studies (2012)
SV	Stephen Verney. *Snakes and Ladders* (2006)

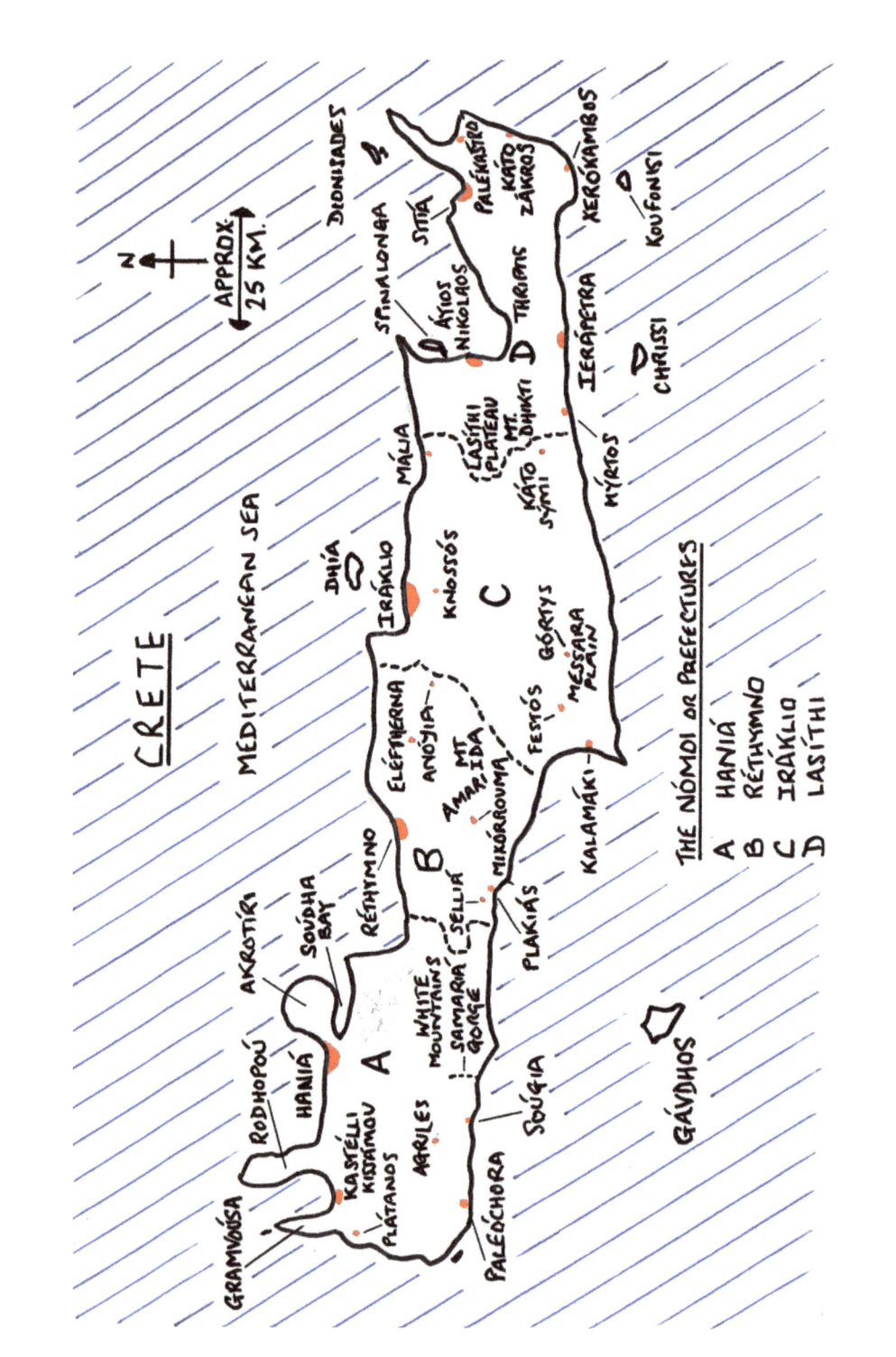

Introduction

In 2011 my dear wife Jennie suggested that we might try a holiday to Crete. Up to that point I had never set foot in Greece or on any of her islands. In fact, on consulting an atlas, the island of Malta and the city of Cairo are probably as close as I had ever been to Crete or Greece. Jennie is an accomplished astrologer and therefore it may be unsurprising to hear that she has an interest in locational astrology. I have thus been informed that my North Node (of the moon), my life's path, plies its way straight through Greece and is all about growth, destiny and development. It also usually represents a new direction for the individual to follow and a trip into the unknown.

Perhaps just as important for me is that my Uranian line passes just to the east of Crete. Many characteristics are apparently associated with this Uranian line and include excitement, eccentricity, inspiration, freedom, inventiveness, non-conformity and fellowship. It should become clear from the pages which follow that the east of the island has become a favourite part of Crete for me and all those characteristics link happily with the way I feel when I am there.

Since 2011, we have visited Crete many times and I continue to hope for more adventures on the island. My bookshelves now fill me with a sense of excitement as my list of authors who have written about the island gradually expands.

On our travels, we have visited about forty archaeological sites from Minoan, Dorian, Hellenic and Roman times. We have seen Venetian fortresses, villas and bridges, remains of Turkish houses, towers, bridges and mosques and visited many Orthodox Greek Christian cathedrals, churches, chapels and monasteries. Discoveries at all these sites are housed in a collection of museums throughout the island. We have had the pleasure of visiting at least a dozen of them, but I know there are probably another dozen or so which we have yet to explore.

We have walked up to ancient peak sanctuaries, clambered down one or two of the wonderful gorges and even strolled along small parts of the E4 Pan-European path which traverses the island. Swimming in the sea,

My Wife Suggested Crete

dawdling idly along the shoreline and gazing at the beauty of the mountains have been great joys, and at the end of each day we have sampled the wonders of Cretan cuisine.

One of the advantages which this island has, compared to other Greek islands, is its size. This is a large island. In fact, the Greeks have often called it 'Great Island' or 'Big Island'. To get some idea of its size, imagine a line drawn between Bristol and Bournemouth. All the land to the west of this line would roughly equate to the size of Crete. It is about one hundred and sixty miles in length and thirty-eight miles at its widest. It is divided into four provinces or prefectures – Haniá, Réthymno, Iráklio and Lasíthi – with three or four mountain ranges fairly equally spaced along the length of the island. Crete has three major cities and three or four other large towns. This island has a great diversity of landscape, and consequently the weather patterns can vary significantly from area to area, with plenty of microclimates to boot. There are several fertile plains and some equally fertile mountain plateaux. Put succinctly by the authors of a book about the Cretan landscape, "Crete is a miniature continent, and there are huge variations from place to place." (OR & JM)

Consequently I would like to suggest, even in the current state of climate change, that if you are going to see some of this fantastic landscape, you should hire a car. I always try to book with a local company. Alternatively, there is quite a good public bus service throughout the island, although it won't get you everywhere, but there are no trains. If you are fit and adventurous and have the time, there are many hiking trails and old mule-tracks called *kalderimi*. Whatever you decide, it doesn't take long to get away from the main tourist areas and then you will start to sample the real treasures of Crete.

As for driving a car, I was slightly nervous at the start but I now find it far less nerve-wracking than driving in the UK. There is one major road – dual carriageway in parts – stretching across the north coast of the island from east to west. Remember the local rule that you are supposed to drive with two wheels on the hard shoulder of this road so that other cars can overtake. With the exception of taxi-drivers in large Mercedes or Audis who drive as if there is no tomorrow and a few reckless young people, I find the general pace of travel is far more relaxed than in the UK. I would much prefer to be driving on this main road (the E75) than, for instance, the A38 to Plymouth. I can also report that the condition of Cretan roads is certainly no worse than in the UK. There are occasional potholes and on the minor roads there are plenty of hairpin bends, so a slower speed is essential in order to stay on the tarmac.

Introduction

I once watched Neil Oliver (of TV's *Coast* fame) being interviewed on *The One Show* on the BBC. He was passionately exclaiming that the British Isles were the best places on earth to live. Having strolled down to Dawlish beach from our home in south Devon, and having wandered along beside the typical red cliffs, I freely admit that I am so fortunate in retirement to be living here. I have also watched countless TV episodes of *A Place in the Sun* to a point where I realise that everyone who has travelled abroad will have their own dream destination, and nobody, let alone me, will be able to change their minds. This is probably just as well, and in any case it would be sentimental, unreal and in fact naïve of me to think that everyone could share the same passion for Crete as Jennie and I do. Crete is not Utopia and if I appear to be painting a picture of the perfect place on this planet, then please excuse my enthusiasm. However, it may surprise you that before I begin to tell my story, I am about to throw a spanner in the works and air a few issues which you could easily find disagreeable. I think it is best to do it now.

When Edward Lear travelled to Crete in 1864, the island was still under Turkish rule and he did not seem to enjoy himself much: "Little sleep: rats, nats, cats, bats; and toward morning a hurricane of wind and pouring rain again!" (EL) But once or twice apparently it stopped raining and Lear did admit: "wonderful view of Suda Bay, and Mount Ida beyond. I never saw anything finer or lovelier." (EL)

In the late 1920s and 1930s John Pendlebury, a fit and athletic English archaeologist, walked all over the island and in spite of some rough terrain and fiendishly difficult climbs he usually outpaced his Cretan colleagues. Even he, while staying one night in the eastern town of Sitía, felt compelled to write the following little ditty:

> *"Some talk of being bitten and some of being bit,*
> *By wasp or bee or hornet or by the humble "nit",*
> *But of all the world's best biters you can commend to me,*
> *The best of all is what we call the homely little flea." (IG)*

If – a century later – there are reasons for not visiting Crete then you will probably find them from the end of June through July and August. These are definitely the worst months to go: crowds of tourists from all over Europe descend upon crowded beaches and attempt to find a table in crowded tavernas, while high temperatures (and higher prices) and often extremely strong winds make life on the beach (and swimming) impossible. The culprit is the northerly wind: the Meltemi.

My Wife Suggested Crete

Although insecticides and insect repellents have instigated subtle changes in modern times, the high summer temperatures still appear to encourage the insect population especially when the wind drops. Biting sand flies and, in the evenings inland, mosquitoes can be troublesome and I would not recommend rummaging about in unkempt gardens as a scorpion can give you a vicious sting. Keeping to footpaths and tracks will avoid such a painful experience. Beware, too, of sea urchins which tend to congregate on rocks beneath the surface of the sea as they have nasty spikes; it is safer to swim away from rocky areas unless you wear suitable footwear.

In the 21st century I am well aware of the global problems of climate change, glaciers disappearing, sea levels and sea temperatures rising and all the expected horrors yet to come. You may be conscious of your carbon footprint as humankind continues to expand the use and frequency of air travel. It is after all a four-hour plane journey from the UK to Crete and consequently another four hours to return home. Using any other form of transport with the exception of a sailing yacht would, I suspect, still be considered unfriendly to the health of the planet and sailing to Crete would in any case take some considerable time, organisation and financial outlay. Having said that, I understand that the most pleasant way of arriving in Crete is by boat, gradually seeing the mountains beginning to rise above the horizon and then even experiencing a faint whiff of the island's flora as you approach the land. However, in practice most people journey here by plane.

Iráklio airport has difficulty in coping with the volume of traffic and although a new airport has been planned at Kastélli Pedhiádhos for some time, I doubt if it will ever happen. If you feel obliged to go on a package holiday, then you must expect queues. When it is time to go home, expect to be in a long queue outside the terminal building and an antiquated and complex check-in procedure. The toilets are not great either even though there has been significant modernisation of the shopping and eating areas once you have passed through security. You may have a rather better experience if you travel independently and Haniá airport (the other main hub) is certainly cleaner and by and large less tiresome.

The Cretan attitude towards dogs and cats is complex. You will witness tethered dogs used as guard dogs that have nothing to do except bark at anything that moves. Peter Trudgill's book offers some clarification: "…in rural Crete, dogs are not pets. Dogs help with locating sheep and with rounding them up, but up in the mountains their main purpose is to protect the shepherd's hut, his equipment, and especially his animals, and so they are required to act savage. They are appreciated for their bravery and other qualities, but people regard them as dirty and would not pet a dog or have

Introduction

one in their house. They may be treated with respect, but they are not usually treated with much obvious affection." (PT)

Occasionally I have come across dogs that are treated as pets by the Cretan people, but this is fairly rare. Furthermore, I have seen plenty of dogs on guard duty at builders' merchants on the edge of towns. It appears that electrical alarm systems are for the future.

You will also come across cats and kittens that appear to have no owner and may sometimes, but not always, look extremely thin. Expats from various European countries are trying to change attitudes and have had some success in neutering and sterilisation programmes. However, they are often up against stiff resistance from locals who believe, so I am told, that all animals should be allowed to have sexual intercourse – old customs are difficult to break and for now this is something to be aware of.

Festivals, weddings and christenings can be great fun and, if you happen to be in the right place at the right time, you will probably get a glass of wine thrust into your hand and be able to watch the celebrations. Religious festivals are most frequently linked to the particular saint of a local church. On the basis that about three hundred and thirty days can be classified as a 'saint' day, don't be surprised if you witness a party. These 'saint' days are also directly connected to 'name' days, which seem far more important than birthdays. So for example if your name is George you are going to have a big party on April 23rd, St George's Day. Don't worry if your name is not one linked to an obvious saint because your party will be held on All Saints Day! However, even if you have researched the days on which these festivals fall, you never know quite when a local party is going to happen – and Cretans can party often loudly and for hours on end.

One night we were kept awake by the combination of a nearby awning being hammered against a concrete wall due to the fierce wind and music from a party in the village. It continued until the early hours of the morning. We heard later that it had been a particularly vibrant christening. May I suggest some good quality ear plugs in your luggage.

I sense that many young Cretans are getting the message about plastic and of course this is a worldwide problem, but expect to see plastic waste and also large numbers of plastic greenhouses, mainly on the south coast. Nor is Crete immune to the building of more and more houses, hotels, villas and apartments. Occasionally building stops abruptly and the area is left with an unsightly concrete scar to blight the landscape. These soon fall easy prey to political graffiti artists whose skills leave much to be desired. Nevertheless, tourism has become a successful industry, providing a boost to the economy of the island which does not suffer the disadvantages of smaller Greek islands where water and food supplies are far greater concerns.

Some parts of Crete have succumbed to a version of tourism which is unattractive to many and may more typically be found in such places as Magaluf in Mallorca or San Antonio in Ibiza for example. In Crete, this kind of tourism is available at Málía and Hersónisos – or more precisely Límin Hersonísou – on the north coast. These small areas do not represent traditional Crete in any way, but fortunately in my opinion they are easily avoidable.

The island is sadly not without the curse of fly tipping and if you do see it, and you may well not, it actually seems worse because it mars the beauty of the surrounding landscape. Now and again you may spot the jagged scars of quarries where great quantities of sand and rock have been extracted for construction work. If it does rain and that does not usually happen between mid-May and October, it rains buckets to the point where rocks and boulders fall onto roads without notice. Driving in these conditions is perilous and should be avoided. Other pitfalls which can occur at any time include erratic electricity supply, hard mattresses – check out reviews of your accommodation before you book – and taxi strikes. Nor is Crete without its share of the wild fires, sometimes started deliberately, which seem to afflict the world more and more these days as the climate changes.

On a lighter if more delicate note, I ought to mention the subject of toilets. Don't worry, it has taken me nine years to find a taverna where the only option is a hole in the ground. Sanitary facilities are generally very good in all the buildings you are likely to visit – hotels, apartments, tavernas, museums and so on. But beware there are few public toilets and most importantly – which is why I dare to mention this subject at all – do not throw toilet paper or any other sanitary object into the toilet pan. Nowhere in Crete can the plumbing system cope with this. Bins are always provided instead.

I hope I have not put you off. I really can't think of anything else with which to alarm you. In any society there will always be the odd rotten apple and if crimes are committed these are often linked to *oikoyeniaka* or 'family matters', stemming from long-lasting vendettas or feuds between Cretan families. Honesty is the rule rather than the exception on this island, so visitors should have little to fear. One day I was so relaxed after consuming a lovely meal, eyes transfixed on the sea and the various comings and goings of the locals, that I left my worldly goods, cash, cards and all, on the empty seat beside me. It was only after strolling along the seafront that Jennie noticed that I was not carrying the rucksack. Having walked briskly back to the taverna, my anxious look inside was treated as

Introduction

a great joke. The kindly wrinkles on the owner's face led to a burst of laughter from him, as he handed back my worldly goods all safe and sound. A stupid old Englishman had evidently been the focus of some brief hilarity!

~ ~ ~ ~

I do not proclaim that I am in any way an expert on the island of Crete. I am still very much an apprentice, learning more as time passes as we explore areas which, even now, we have never seen before. This book might be adjudicated by the true experts as incomplete and inadequate, but I hope at least that it will provide an insight into what you may expect as a visitor. Above all else, I hope that what follows here will be taken as a tribute to all the wonderful people who live there.

Chapter One
The Package Experience - Our First Taste of Crete

"For us, it was one of those magic centres of joy and peace where you are standing at the very core of the universe, where you breathe happiness in great gulps, and where your faith in life in the world, in mankind is reaffirmed." (DMD)
FROM WINDS OF CRETE, DAVID MACNEIL DOREN, TALKING ABOUT THE CHURCH OF PANAYÍA KERÁ NEAR KRITSÁ, LASÍTHI PROVINCE.

Looking back, 2011 seems to have been an exciting year of travels for Jennie and me. Perhaps astrologically the planets were aligned in the most desirable way. I must ask the expert.

In January 2011 we spent a week on the island of La Gomera, one of the smaller and less visited of the Canary Islands. We had developed a soft spot for a resort complex of bungalow-type accommodation in the south of the island. Over time Fred Olsen has invested heavily in the Canaries, operating a network of ferries which connect the islands, as well as constructing this particular hotel and its golf course. 2011 marked our fourth visit – a welcome break in January from English weather and soggy and bedraggled gardens.

In February of that year we flew off on one of our biggest adventures – to Chile in South America. Courtesy of a Chilean friend living in the capital, Santiago, we enjoyed some of the wondrous landscapes from the Andes, the central valley and Pacific Ocean, to the wetlands and then to the desert-like country further north. We marvelled at the southern skies through giant telescopes and gazed intently at condors and eagles, vultures and owls through our binoculars. We bathed in warm thermal springs at the foot of the Andes and discovered enormous dinosaur footprints higher up. Perhaps a particular highlight was, by chance, to watch a giant hummingbird as it hovered, its wings in constant and extraordinary motion, sucking nectar from a favoured plant no more than ten metres in front of us. I still derive great joy from these wonderful memories and occasionally pinch myself that I have seen these glorious sights.

However, I freely admit to having the nasty habit, when returning from a holiday, of asking myself and my wife: "Where are we going next?" And you may well consider, understandably having read the above, that I might have been becoming a rather greedy traveller in 2011, but it was at this point in early spring that Jennie mentioned the island of Crete, where she had spent a week in May 2003. Thinking that I might be able to wangle a week away from work in September, I set off to my friends in Thomas Cook to investigate. Soon we had a week booked at the St Nicolas Bay Hotel near Áyios Nikólaos on the north coast, including a taxi transfer and four days' car hire once we had settled into our chosen lodgings. I began looking forward – greedily – to a warm and sunny week on one of the Greek islands.

Ignorant of all things Cretan, I acquired a copy of the *Rough Guide to Crete* in order to discover what was on offer. Book in hand, I was soon absorbed in the history, the varied landscape of the island and most importantly what we could expect to eat, (especially important as Jennie has a gluten intolerance). Perhaps above all I formed the impression that these people were going to be a friendly lot and that our own safety in a strange land was not something to be unduly worried about.

On Monday 5th September we drove to Cardiff airport, had a surprisingly comfortable and peaceful night at a brand new Holiday Inn, complete with a gluten-free evening meal for Jennie. An 8am flight to Iráklio the following morning took off on time and four hours later we set foot on the island of Crete.

I would be lying if I were to give you the impression that Iráklio airport or indeed its surroundings are in any way beautiful. The best that can be said is that it is located by the coast and you can look out to the substantial yet uninhabited island of Dhia. But I was consoled by the knowledge that our hotel must be about an hour's drive away and the excitement of it all took away any negative thoughts.

So began our package holiday and via a holiday rep we were introduced to Manoli Maniadakis, owner and driver of a large and swanky Mercedes taxi. At that time, of course, I had no idea how fast these taxis are driven. Since then I have discussed this experience with a friend who had holidayed in the same area. In my friend's soft Devonshire accent, words to his taxi driver which I won't attempt to write down but which were meant to convey that he wasn't in any hurry to reach his chosen hotel, had apparently fallen on stony ground.

My Wife Suggested Crete

Having reached his hotel in record-breaking time, I understand that the hotel bar's stock of draught beer took an immediate and sizeable hit. Luckily for me, Jennie seems to love speed as our own journey took no more than thirty-five minutes. Although our association with Mr Maniadakis only lasted for just over half an hour, he engaged with us in hearty conversation, pointing out towns, villages and places of interest, including his home village of Sísi on the coast, as we sped along the E75 highway heading east.

Gradually from the airport the landscape became more interesting as we bypassed most of the sprawling tourist resorts of Gournés, Goúves, Hersónisos and Mália. Not that I have any wish to chastise anyone for choosing to holiday along this stretch, far from it, and indeed if you are a party animal then Mália, as I understand it, should fit the bill nicely. Moreover I know a young family who enjoyed Piskopiáno (near Hersónisos) so much that they rebooked for the following year. Personally I was content that Mr Maniadakis kept his foot on the accelerator.

Mr M continued to point out where, for instance, you could turn off and head inland up to the Lasíthi plateau, home to old windmills, orchards and pastures and apparently a cave said to be the birthplace of Zeus. My research had taught me that there was also a lesser-known plateau named Katharó next to it and that you could drive to this by way of the village of Kritsá. I remember a rather surprised yet delighted interjection from Manoli: "You know this place? Ah Bravo!" when I had ventured forth tentatively with my recently-acquired guide book information. This was lesson number one, for here was my first experience of the convivial nature of the Cretans that tends to crescendo if you show interest in or knowledge of their island. So for the last fifteen minutes of our journey, we were inundated with information on chapels and churches and huge buildings used for wedding celebrations as we continued speedily past Neápoli, the former capital of this eastern province of Lasíthi. Finally we were told that our chosen hotel without a doubt was: "Very nice – yes – very nice hotel."

The St Nicolas Bay Hotel was perched on a small promontory just outside of town, complete with rather a grand gated entrance. We were greeted warmly in one of two reception areas by a Cretan woman in her 30s. Here I received my second Cretan lesson. This was the genuine warmth of the greeting to us, which was quite infectious and soon after I came to understand was part of Cretan nature. The receptionist spoke fluent English and in passing I said that Jennie and I would be celebrating our wedding anniversary during our stay. Coincidentally she told us that her own wedding anniversary occurred two days before ours, so there were smiles all round. Having been shown to our room I breathed a sigh of relief as it all looked clean and spacious, with a little balcony facing out to sea.

View towards the Thriptí Mountains from the St. Nicolas Bay Hotel

However, if you think that I am about to paint a picture of a hotel similar to the one that has been described to you many times by friends and family returning from their travels, who are seemingly infatuated with the place they have recently left behind – think again! Our evening meals were salted to the point of almost being inedible and the daytime snack menu was equally disappointing and none of it was cheap. Moreover, our backs began to moan about the unforgiving nature of the mattress on our bed.

On the positive side, the hotel was in a picturesque and peaceful location and had its own small sandy beach and swimming area. I embraced the warmth and clarity of the sea before we relaxed on loungers laid out along the rocky foreshore. Open-air buffet-style breakfasts were also appealing and included our first taste of the richly scented Cretan thyme honey, *thimárisio*, and outstanding fruit and yoghurt. In charge of the breakfast operation was a gruff-voiced man who in fact turned out to be quite charming. His main claims to fame were his facial features and hairstyle, which resembled those of a former American film star so closely that this had earned him – at least in the eyes of our fellow British residents – the nickname of Tony Curtis.

A twenty-minute stroll took us into the centre of Áyios Nikólaos, too touristy for our taste but nevertheless it was pleasant enough by the harbour, the marina and especially the supposedly bottomless lake. Our main reason for the walk was to find the archaeological museum which houses some extraordinary relics from past civilisations: notably the Minoans. This was our first insight into these people who had settled on the island as long ago as 2600 BC.

I would never describe myself as a museum enthusiast and previous visits to museums in the UK have usually been characterised by my uncontrollable yawning. Yet here I was totally absorbed by such articles as The Goddess of Mýrtos, a weird looking goose-necked Minoan clay jug (c.2500 BC) and the most intricate gold jewellery including an exquisite gold pin with a bramble motif. Also on display were some expertly decorated clay sarcophagi, (larnakes or coffins) and, as I mused over the craftsmanship involved in their making, I could not but help think that these people were far more advanced than the ancient Brits of that era.

The museum had given us an appetite, certainly to learn more about this island's history but more immediately to find some decent food. Courtesy of the *The Rough Guide to Crete* (which I will refer to from now on as the RGC), a taverna nearby called Pelágos proved to be a good one. At least now we knew that Cretan food could be wholesome and well cooked.

Our Cretan adventure only really took off with the arrival of a hired car. Luckily I have always felt comfortable driving a left-hand-drive car on the 'wrong' side of the road. It actually seems perfectly natural to me. Our next Cretan lesson was to discover that within ten minutes of the holiday resort you can be driving through countryside. In villages untouched by mass tourism traditional life carries on as it always has. I felt as though I was travelling back in time to my childhood when I remember my mother buying fruit, vegetables and other groceries from the village shop, all of which, after weighing, were deposited carefully into her shopping basket.

Conversely I find many modern inventions and practices rather depressing: supermarkets, plastic, bar-code scanning and computerised voices telling me not to forget my receipt. Often in my case the voice tells me that there is an unusual object in the bagging area. Although I would like to tell you that this object is my personal sledge-hammer carried at all times in case my frustration gets to the point when I destroy the voice, the fact that I still walk the streets as a free man will tell you that I haven't quite reached that stage. I guess you may suggest that I try an internet home delivery but this by its very nature requires someone who I don't know choosing my food. In these old Cretan villages I had no fear of hearing that disturbing noise: the bar-code being recognised.

With help from the RGC I had picked out a few places that we might visit courtesy of the hire car. The first was the historic church of Panayía Kerá near the village of Kritsá, which houses a wonderful and famous set of Byzantine frescos. Here I began to learn about the island's Byzantine and Venetian traditions of art and icon painting, examples of which I now know, as I write, are to be found throughout Crete in various stages of disrepair. I also now know that by visiting this particular church, we had stumbled on one of the finest examples of this art form in the whole of Crete. One expert has put it like this: "The scale is intimate, but here as much as in soaring cathedrals one can understand the meaning of medieval piety." (AH) Jennie sat on the cold stone floor for a while and began to absorb it all as our eyes adjusted to the sudden absence of direct sunlight.

Jennie and me outside the church of Panayía Kerá near Kritsá

My Wife Suggested Crete

Only a few kilometres from the church lies the ancient site of Lató, a Dorian city dating back to the 12th century BC. Half the fun for me was finding it even if the signposts to it were perfectly adequate. Now we were really out in the olive groves and after a 10-minute trudge uphill we found the old city on a saddle between two peaks. Even with a guide book it is often difficult to understand what is what at these historic settlements, but we found the gate to the city, an enormous cistern, the base of a temple complete with altar and an *exedra* which was a sort of public seating area.

Jennie was soon poking about amidst the shards of ceramics which were to be found all over the place while I sat in the *exedra* looking down and away towards Áyios Nikólaos, which was once the port of Lató. The far-reaching views were fabulous, reason enough I thought for those Dorians to choose this place as their home. We also glimpsed at Lató, by chance, the sight of our young waiter from Pelágos with his girlfriend. We decided not to interrupt their limited time off work, but it was nice to see Cretan people taking an interest in their ancestral history.

The Dorian city of Lató near Kritsá

Fellow visitors to Lató were few and far between, a fact which added to the magic of the place, but as always some fresh air and a degree of

The Package Experience

activity had brought on the need for nourishment. Opposite the Byzantine church I had taken note of the Taverna Paradisos with a pleasant looking road-side terrace. As the taverna's business card showed, they seemed keen to make the association with the church and were perhaps hinting that should paradise not yet be available there, it was actually always on offer at the taverna! So we had a go.

We were greeted warmly by Niko, a big, tall man with an enormous head and plenty of razor-sharp stubble on his Cretan face. At the time, I was acutely conscious of Jennie's gluten intolerance and courtesy of a member of staff at our hotel we had written down Greek words explaining what we needed. Niko appeared to understand and indicated that this was not a particular problem. Although we did not know it at that moment, we were about to engage in our love affair with traditional Cretan food.

From the menu we decided on stuffed vine leaves with lemon and yoghurt, small red pimentos containing a soft creamy cheese, stuffed red peppers and tomatoes and some fried courgettes, avoiding the courgette fritters as Niko told us they were coated in flour. This was all to be washed down with a Greek beer and a local Cretan white wine. Our next lesson was to learn that food arrives, or at least each particular dish arrives, when it is ready and not in any particular order; and hot dishes are never usually piping hot on the quite rational basis that if it's too hot your mouth gets burnt.

You might think that the food we chose was not particularly exciting, but I cannot adequately describe what joy we derived from this simple yet scrumptious meal when it was gradually delivered to our table set under an old olive tree. The textures and flavours and obvious freshness were complimented by Niko's attentiveness, especially in the way that he announced each dish he produced for us with a kind of quiet reverence which he believed was required to complete his task satisfactorily. All of it was truly wonderful and enjoyed in delightful surroundings as we watched more pilgrims across the road walking up the path to the church.

With our food now all consumed, we asked Niko for the bill: "To logariasmó, parakaló," we had learnt to say; to which the reply was: "One moment please." Our next lesson was to discover that often in Cretan tavernas you will be offered something extra at the end of your meal. That day Niko gave us some creamy Cretan yoghurt with a cherry preserve – sweet-spoon they call it. This, together with the fiery liquor made from grape musk called *raki* (or *tsikoudiá*), was delivered without charge and was, I suppose, our first taste of Cretan hospitality. To put the icing on the cake, the price of our meal was surprisingly modest. Back at the hotel we did not need to eat again, and were perfectly content as we watched the

My Wife Suggested Crete

sun go down. Glass of wine in hand, we reflected on our good fortune in finding three very different Cretan treasures: the church of the Panayía Kerá, the Dorian city of Lató and the Taverna Paradisos. It had been a truly memorable day.

Our week's holiday was now progressing at an alarming speed but my confidence in driving happily on the Cretan roads was increasing nicely. We journeyed for twenty minutes or so back to Mália, not I hasten to add in order to join the revellers who are intent on giving the UK a bad name, but to visit one of the great Minoan sites, the Palace of Mália. Jennie and I were now both poking about amongst the shards and also trying to work out the layout of the palace. We managed to identify the central court, altar, storage pits and covered storerooms. On the way back we stopped off at another site – Dríros, dating back to 800 BC and therefore much younger than the Palace of Mália. We found the Temple of Apollo Delphinios, together with an enormous cistern. However, we were alone here and Jennie thought it was rather a spooky place so we headed back for a refreshing swim and for Jennie at least, some sunbathing.

We had been blessed with fine, sunny weather all week and for our last day we drove further east along the coast road to visit the remains of the Minoan town of Gourniá, a place that began its history 3000 years BC. All you actually see here are the remaining lower floors of the buildings, all neatly connected by paths or streets. This was a working town with a small palace and a shrine nearby. Jennie's shard-poking continued in earnest.

Although it meant a slight detour, we couldn't resist another visit to Paradise! Niko gave us a warm welcome back which was endorsed by the owner's wife of this Paradise taverna – a return visit to a taverna, we soon realised, would always be greatly appreciated. With certain knowledge that the food would be just as good, we relaxed completely and started people watching. The Uncle, we decided, was in charge of supplies when required. This was performed in association with his slow and ageing scooter, which I fear would have succumbed to a failure rating if it had been subjected to an emissions test. Nevertheless, it did its duty and Uncle would usually reappear after a while, cigarette in one corner of his mouth and balancing carrier bags full of vegetables on each of the handlebars. I still have not been able to deduce how he managed to smoke his cigarette without injuring himself in any way.

As the light began to fade, we watched as the owner, Uncle and another man sat down to play cards. Niko was apparently left to do the work and one of his jobs was to put down a carafe of *raki* on their table. Although the owner and Uncle appeared to be modest drinkers, the other

The Package Experience

man noticeably needed his fill of the fiery stuff. We watched the emotions of this man intensify as the alcohol took hold. Having gone through the phases of sheer joy and laughter, his head began to roll and then finally drop. I got the feeling that owner and Uncle had seen it all before. We thanked Niko for everything and explained that we had to leave for home the following day. We had enjoyed another absorbing day complete with a little comic theatre at the end.

We bade farewell to Tony Curtis et al the following morning. Mr Maniadakis and his fellow taxi-drivers had chosen the 13th of September to go on strike, so a coach turned up instead. Thomson had apparently arranged all their flights to the UK on that particular day of the week and queuing outside the terminal building in the heat, as there was no room for us all inside, was an uncomfortable experience. This got no better when the antiquated and complicated check-in procedure seemed to take for ever. However, we left more or less on time and soon we were home.

As a good friend recently re-affirmed to me, air travel for many people is as easy as getting on and off a bus, but for us after any holiday, once back in our house complete with suitcases and having checked that basically our home is still in one piece, Jennie and I usually have a good old bear hug. This particular embrace has always signified to me our shared little triumph of visiting new places, meeting new people, learning a bit more about the world and getting back safe and sound. I usually say something stupid like: "We did it!"

Reality soon hit. Within twelve hours we were both back at work. There was no Tony Curtis to source my breakfast and I trundled off through the Devon lanes to my first customer at a speed far removed from that of Mr Maniadakis and his friends. My memories of the past week, however, were vividly fresh. There was something magical about this island we had just left but I could not as yet pinpoint what it was.

~ ~ ~ ~

One of the consequences of working as a gardener was that I often found plenty of time to daydream as much of the work had become second nature to me and I seemed to be able to complete some jobs with little mental effort. So my mind was easily diverted to the memory of that first Cretan adventure. It had been a happy week for both of us but routine life soon took control and Christmas week arrived, as usual, before I was ready for it.

In 2006 Jennie had been diagnosed with two forms of cancer but after nasty operations and treatment had come through it all and on Tuesday

My Wife Suggested Crete

20th December, after five years of it, she was 'signed off' by the specialist who had looked after her. It was an important milestone and we celebrated with a meal at our local Thai restaurant on the 23rd, when Jennie's children and grandchildren came to us for the Christmas weekend. 2011 had been quite a year and it finished on a high note.

Our travels in February 2012 did not turn out quite so happily. To celebrate Jennie's final visit to the specialist we had decided on an exotic holiday to southern Thailand at a seaside hotel south-west of the town of Trang. From the brochure the hotel looked luxurious and peaceful. Unbeknown to us, the brochure was out of date as in reality this hotel had been turned into a Thai version of Butlins, dedicated to families with young, very active and noisy children from Scandinavia. We made the most of it and later, after much perseverance, I obtained a reasonable refund from the holiday company.

It may well have been this experience that made us forget about the rather uncomfortable bed back in the Cretan town of Áyios Nikólaos, as three weeks after returning from Thailand I went again to my friends in Thomas Cook and rebooked the St Nicolas Bay Hotel for a week in September. Once again we had something to look forward to.

The afternoon of the 11th September found us being warmly welcomed back and upgraded to a larger room with two balconies, one facing the sea while the other looked over the approaches to the town and a small fishing inlet. With the exception of the first day when we simply relaxed in and by the sea, I had hired a car for the duration of our stay, this time from a local company. Greeted warmly, I was surprised at the casual nature of the contract. Some cash and a driving licence secured the deal and there was no checking of dents or scratches of which there were plenty. The man handed me the key and told me not to worry – so I didn't.

I persuaded Jennie that Dríros, her 'spooky site', was worth another visit and up above the main site there was plenty of evidence that this place had been a sizeable town and Jennie was again soon shard-poking. Gradually we made our way to the top of a hill and with views in all directions it was immediately obvious why the Dorians had chosen this location. Up here as well was a tiny whitewashed chapel, one of many which can be found throughout the island. Very often you can see them from a distance, perched precariously on top of a hill. I understand the theory is that for those people who have had them built, they will be closer to God when the hour of judgement arrives. I guess it's hard to prove whether the eventual benefits are worth the building efforts, but these chapels certainly add to the charm of the landscape.

The Package Experience

From here I took the opportunity of driving through some of the villages of the Ágios Ioánnis peninsula on which Dríros is situated, passing by the restored monastery – Moní Aretíou. The sleepy villages of Doriés, Skiniás and Vrouhás were typical of small agricultural settlements featuring little more than a church and a *kafenion* (café/bar), the residents going about their daily business as they have done for many a year.

I found the experience a real treat, especially when I spied the local mode of transport – a cultivator with attached trailer serving as both driver and passenger seats with enough room behind for animal fodder or vine and olive branches or the wife's shopping. With a top speed of approaching 5 mph this was my kind of machine! I imagined owning a fleet of these magnificent vehicles back in the UK and expanding my gardening business as a result, but my imagination occasionally goes haywire and I am afraid this was a classic example.

Spying the local mode of transport, Lasíthi prefecture

Soon we were down by the sea at the village of Pláka. Out in the bay is the island of Spinalónga, a former leper colony and a current hot spot for tourist boats from neighbouring Eloúnda which is home to the most expensive and upmarket hotels in Crete. Eloúnda's other claim to fame is historical because nearby is the site of the ancient 'sunken city' of Oloús. At this end of the island the sea level has risen (although not uniformly) over two millennia and so harbour buildings – or at least what's left of them are just about visible below the surface. Nearby, on dry land, we saw the preserved floor mosaic of a Roman basilica.

Before the Romans had arrived Oloús had in fact been the port of Dríros, so we had at least completed the story of Jennie's 'spooky site' by our visit to the ancient port. It was a peaceful spot in comparison with the bustle of Elounda's hotel complexes. We left the hotel guests to their paradise while we decided to journey back to ours – the Taverna Paradisos near Kritsá. The greeting from Niko was warmer still, including a little shriek of delight when he first caught sight of us and we chose to have our main meals here throughout the week.

The sunken city of Oloús near Eloúnda

Knossós is by far the best-known Minoan palace and town and is top of the list of tourist attractions in Crete. Generally speaking, if you have heard of Crete then you have probably heard of Knossós. Although a Cretan by the name of Kalokairinós had begun excavations in the 1880s, the wealthy Englishman Sir Arthur Evans had been the man responsible for excavating and 'restoring' Knossós at the start of the 20th century. He lorded over the excavations and determined exactly how his 'restorations' were to appear. Even though we knew it would be busy, Jennie and I felt we just had to pay a visit if we were going to advance our knowledge of the Minoans.

Armed with a packed lunch we set off, this being my first experience of driving on the E75 back to Iráklio, where we found the palace just outside the suburbs. Jennie didn't feel her best on that day and after queuing at the ladies' toilets for ages, discovered that she had to pay to use these overcrowded facilities. Unfortunately, I had not anticipated this financial transaction and she had no money on her. After that, Knossós and the coachloads of tourists that constantly arrived did little to change the mood. I was pleased to see the ancient drainage system and the grand stepped theatre area and royal road, but Arthur's controversial interpretations left me rather puzzled. However, we had seen it and in time we would be able to compare Knossós to other palaces and the treasures we saw later which came from Knossós justified our visit.

The most famous of all the Minoan Palaces of Crete: Knossós

My Wife Suggested Crete

On the following day in an attempt to restore Jennie's well-being or *keph* – a Turkish word which Cretans sometimes use meaning pleasure, high spirits, enjoyment and appetite – I suggested another visit to Lató, the Dorian site we had enjoyed the year before. This was followed by a drive up to the Katharó plateau. Lató definitely took care of the pleasure and enjoyment part of *keph* and we were certainly not the first English people to have enjoyed the delights of Lató. An English captain by the wonderful name of Thomas Abel Brimage Spratt had taken a tour of Lató on his travels in the 1850s and pronounced that: "The site and ruins are certainly the most remarkable in the island of Crete and a traveller through the island will no doubt find much interest in its exploration." (TABS)

Once up on the Katharó and surrounded only by a few houses, a seasonal taverna and the wide fertile upland plain, we stopped to watch some enormous vultures – griffons we thought – as they swirled and drifted above us. Jennie was now in high spirits, so part three of *keph* had been achieved. Fortunately, we had brought binoculars and we could make out the griffon's extraordinary head. We hoped to have a sighting of the endangered Lammergeier or Bearded Vulture with its three-metre wingspan, but it wasn't to be. I embraced the fresh and certainly cooler air up here (at over 1000 metres above sea level), the tilled fields, the mountain views and the absolute peace of the place. Soon part four of *keph* needed attending to. It was sorted out conveniently on the way back by Niko, with comic theatre again included in the price.

Jennie's *keph* was holding up nicely and towards the end of our week we drove further east, passing the clearly visible Gourniá site, and turned down towards the sea at the windswept village of Pahiá Ámmos. It was here just as we came over the crest of the hill from Gourniá that I spied the Thriptí mountain range for the first time, took a deep breath and stared at the dramatic shapes as these mountains hung over the narrow isthmus which at this point connects the north to the south coast of Crete. I felt that I could have sat there all day taking in all that I could see: the mountains, the sea with its white horses and the windswept village with its tiny harbour which attempts to protect its equally tiny collection of fishing boats. In terms of size and height, the Thriptí range pales into insignificance compared to the might of Mount Ida and the White Mountains further west, but on that day the landscape made me gape with pleasure.

Our goal was to visit the ancient site of Vasilikí which sits on a knoll a short distance across the isthmus heading south. Vasilikí is not big, nor is there a great deal to see, but my RGC explained to me that its importance lies in its age. It was in full swing in the millennium before

The Package Experience

the peak of Minoan civilisation. In a nutshell, it dates from 2,650 BC, so it is quite old! It also lends its name to a particular style of pottery with dark mottled decoration. It was a fenced site with no living soul around but the hole under the wire was big enough for us to get in. Having told Jennie about the Vasilikí ware, a wire fence was not going to stop her shard-poking pursuits. The reason that this location had been chosen by these people was again obvious as from this vantage point you have a clear 360-degree view. I was more than content just to stare in wonder at the awesome slopes of the Thriptís.

~ ~ ~ ~

By and large a week's holiday never seems long enough. We had enjoyed the location and the private beach at our hotel, but the bed this time seemed even less comfortable than the previous year and if we were going to return to this island we realised that we needed to do some research. By now I was confident enough to drive, so we didn't need to rely on a package. Why couldn't we find an apartment to rent with a decent bed?

At Niko's taverna one day we bumped into a British family. They now lived in the area, but who had rented an apartment by the sea not far away while in search of their dream. I remember their words to us: "You could do worse that the Vangelis apartments," and so we trundled off to find them and actually sat on one of the beds there which we thought might be comfortable enough. These apartments were tucked away below the main road by the sea and seemed perfectly peaceful, but access to the sea along a rocky shoreline was difficult. We never did book the Vangelis but our minds were now fully focused on this issue. From our two package holidays in Crete we had experienced enough to know that we wanted to see more of this island.

Swimming in the warm sea had been a delight, being able to walk amongst historic ruins of long-lost palaces and towns had been fascinating and the ever-changing Cretan landscape had provoked all sorts of positive emotions. We had by now begun to discover some of the delights of the Cretan kitchen and our final meal ended with a Cretan bear hug from Niko and fond farewells from the family who owned the Paradisos Taverna together with the gift of a jar of thyme honey to take home. It was, I am sure, this taste of Cretan hospitality, of their warm and generous nature which was beginning to seep into our souls.

A Cretan Interlude

"A Walk up to Knossós"

TAKEN FROM *CRETE – A NOTEBOOK* BY RICHARD CLARK

Our own visit to Knossós had not been the happiest of many other happy days on the island, but the following story is not really about Knossós at all. It is rather, an insight into Cretan hospitality which, when you first encounter it, can be a moving experience. Richard Clark, author of *Crete – A Notebook*, was a teacher in Iráklio in the 1980s. One Sunday morning he decided to walk out from the city to visit the famous Minoan site of Knossós:

"*Getting up at dawn, the whole of that late summer Sunday stretched out before me. Following Evans Street through the city walls to meet the dusty Leoforos Knosou, I climbed away from the clamour of Sunday bells waking the metropolis and into the hills. By 8 o'clock the sun was already finding its strength. The heat and the dust thrown up by the occasional vehicle made slow and steady progress the only option.*

Four miles might not be far, but an hour into my walk, as temperatures nudged into the thirties, my progress slowed to a halt outside a taverna. Apart from an elderly man savouring an early morning coffee, the place was deserted. The man glanced up from his newspaper and welcomed me with a staccato "ella" (come in). I needed little encouragement. By then the prospect of refreshment was most welcome.

As I sat down the man bellowed out a command. From the shadows inside the taverna emerged an elderly woman who I took to be his wife. She approached my table and I gave her my order for a lemonade in halting phrasebook Greek, at which she smiled and uttered a surprised "poli kala" (very good).

Although little less than a mile from Knossós, I suspect this taverna was not a haunt for tourists. By and large they would drive past en route to the Palace, and my few words of Greek singled me out as an object for my host's hospitality. The man came and sat at my table as his wife

A Cretan Interlude

produced not only the bottle of lemonade I had ordered but some cheese pies and stuffed vine leaves. Over the cold drink and mezzes, the owner was keen to talk and find out where I came from and what I did for a living. I could just about explain that I was English and that I was a school teacher.

On hearing where I worked, he exclaimed that his grandson was a pupil there. This was cause for raki to be called for and toasts of "yamas" and "eleftheria" (cheers and freedom) to be drunk.

Early in the morning on a sweltering day, the spirit began to take effect with undue haste. If I were to get to Knossós I would have to take my leave. Asking for the bill, my request was waved away. Any further attempt to insist on paying would have been futile. Indeed, to my truly hospitable Cretan hosts, it would have been offensive. Not for the first or last time, I was experiencing Cretan hospitality. What little they have, they will share with a stranger. I have found their generosity of spirit to be unmatched." (RC)

Chapter Two

Beginning to Find our Feet

"There is so much to discover that there is always something new to learn; always a new discovery around the corner in the alleys of a mountain village, a new view to glimpse between the peaks of a mountain pass."
RICHARD CLARK FROM CRETE – A NOTEBOOK. (RC)

I suppose I must have an inquisitive nature as when travelling I always want to know what's around the next corner and I really wanted to know what was further east in Crete. The Rough Guide clearly helped, but my needs were no doubt controlled by my Uranian line in the world of locational astrology! So when Jennie found on the internet an attractive set of two-storey apartments in the village of Angathiá on the eastern seaboard of Crete, we booked the necessary flights and the equally necessary hire car.

The apartment was situated on a minor road which apparently led to a beach about a kilometre away. I reckoned that I would have to drive for about two and a half hours from the airport to get there, but excitement rather than nervousness was the overriding emotion. We were finally going to do our own thing and not rely on Thomson, or the sadly now defunct Thomas Cook, to do anything for us. Apart from the services of easyJet and a very good B&B-cum-parking-place half a mile from Bristol Airport, we would be relying totally on Cretan people to look after us.

Our travelling had already continued in earnest in 2013 with a visit to Oman at Easter (courtesy of the refund from our unhappy Thai holiday the previous year), and a pleasant sojourn in Sicily. We marked the summer solstice with a climb up Mount Etna which was, luckily for us, smouldering rather than erupting at the time. I'm sure, having had these travels to beautiful Oman, engaging with the Sultan's courteous people and having seen the ancient ruins of Taormina, a stay which was consistently accompanied by the distinctive delights of Sicilian food and wine, many people would be glad to settle back down at home. For us though, our flight to Iráklio on the 7th of September couldn't have come soon enough. When EZY6287 hit the tarmac on touchdown, I leant over to Jennie and whispered with a smile: "Welcome to Crete!"

Our Skoda Roomster was an odd-looking car but it had some petrol and it started. I followed the route Mr Maniadakis had taken two years before, being careful to put two wheels onto the hard shoulder, when he or one of his colleagues suddenly appeared in my rear-view mirror. Having topped up with petrol nearby, we bypassed Áyiós Nikólaos, spotted the Vangelis apartments nestling by the sea below us, took note of the impressive site of Gourniá before weaving around a few hairpins and down into Pahiá Ámmos. The sight of the Thriptís still caused me to gasp, the turn to Vasilíki was fondly remembered, but then our next adventure began. From here on, it was all new.

We were still on the E75, the main east-west highway of the island and although a good road with some straight stretches it soon turned into what I would describe as a British B road. Nevertheless, it is the main route to connect with the substantial eastern town of Sitía and when eventually you get within ten kilometres of Sitía you come across an enormous road construction project, almost Swiss-style in its complexity. It is now complete, accompanied by signs advertising the involvement of EU funding.

The first village we drove through, Kavoúsi, has become one of my visual favourites as it is lined with rows of mulberry trees and oleanders – an ideal candidate for a picture postcard. Very quickly we were climbing on a straight section of road which had been hacked out of the hillside, this being on the lower slopes of the Ornó Mountains, neighbours of the Thriptís. From here you can look across the Gulf of Mirabello, back to Áyios Nikólaos and the Ágios Ioánnis peninsula. With plenty of twists and turns the road then took us through traditional old villages: Plátanos, Mirsíni, Moulianá (where grape vines were a big feature), and Hamézi.

I really wanted to stop and explore and also get down to the coast below where more Minoan remains could be found, but I knew that I had to keep motoring to arrive at Angathiá in good time. The countryside we drove through was also picture postcard material, and with car windows wound down we sometimes breathed in wafts of fragrant flowers and scented herbs. Fennel and sage seemed to grow like weeds, oleanders were everywhere and every now and again bougainvillea and campsis, plumbago and jasmine adorned the whitewashed village houses and gardens.

My Wife Suggested Crete

We were enjoying a feast of colour and aroma from our Skoda. We negotiated our way through the town of Sitía carefully but without incident and for a while the road hugged the coast, passing by a concrete monstrosity, the shell of which should have been a hotel. Someone must have had a financial disaster, I guess. Very soon, the road turned inland and almost due east to connect with the small town of Palékastro, about a kilometre or so from our destination.

We needed supplies and I spotted a mini market and a lane just before it which led to a parking area. Inside the shop we met Kostas, the owner, who found everything we would need and wished us a happy holiday. Not long after we found our apartment and were greeted warmly by the owner's father, Yiánnis, together with a fridge full of goodies, including some fresh fruit. The two-storey apartment was big and bright and Jennie spotted the washing machine which I came quickly to realise was, for her, paramount to the success of a self-catering holiday.

French windows from the upstairs bedroom led out onto a balcony – with a view. It seems a long time ago now, but I think as I looked out at that view I knew that we had found a part of the world that was going to be extremely precious to us. Away to our left was Palékastro, dominated by its traditionally domed church, then gradually casting my eye in a clockwise direction I could see a small group of villas and cottages set on the hill some two kilometres away, which soon was followed by a distinct and rather oddly shaped flat-topped hill called the Kastrí Bluff. Either side of this lay the turquoise sparkle of the sea and to the far right gentle hills supported an occasional barn for sheep or goats. This panorama was completed by row upon row of olive trees and, in spite of the minor road outside which led up to the village of Angathiá behind us and down to the beach called Hióna, the sense of peace and tranquillity was overwhelming.

Half of the fun of a do-it-yourself holiday comes from no restrictions and no set times, so tea on the balcony the following morning was eventually followed by breakfast, followed by a leisurely walk down to Hióna beach in the bright and warm September sunshine, passing smallholdings where healthy-looking fruit and vegetables seemed to be well-tended.

Just before the beach we arrived at the Taverna Kakávia, one of two down here, both highly recommended in the RGC. The smells from the open-air wood fired barbecue were tantalising. However, the beach was our priority, a mixture of sand and shingle but pure sand when we waded into the clear warm water. This was a blue flag beach and in time I was to discover the fact that virtually all beaches in Crete have been recognised in this way, a happy sign that pollution and dirt are not issues to be concerned about by those of us who love swimming in the sea.

Hióna suited us perfectly as our smiling faces would have confirmed had there been people about to notice, but this 500-metre stretch of beach was occupied by no more than fifteen people and this was a Sunday so half the occupants were locals on their day off. We dried off, as is our habit, by wandering along the beach looking at stones and shells before sighting a strange object protruding from the low crumbling cliff. With erosion, what was gradually protruding turned out to be a couple of old pottery *pithoi* from long ago. It seemed extraordinary but this area turned out to be the harbour road, (the harbour itself long gone), to the important Minoan town of Palékastro or Roussólakkos nearby. We went there next and pottered about. You usually have to pay €2 but the official had gone home and we had the place to ourselves – gratis.

Hióna beach near Palékastro, Lasíthi Prefecture

The scent of grilling fish, meat and spices emanating from Mr Kakávia's barbecue had pricked the senses but we had decided to try one of two RGC recommended tavernas in town. The Mythos Taverna was centrally located at one corner of the main square that in turn was dominated by the church and accompanied by a couple of *kafenions*, a more modern café/bar for young people, and the Hellas hotel and taverna. To get to anywhere else you had to pass through this area, so the Mythos Taverna with its roadside terrace was a great place to soak up the action.

We were warmly greeted in fluent English by the handsome Manoli and his pretty wife Rula and were soon completely at ease. To give you some idea of how laid back this place was, (and still is), Manoli casually pulled out a chair at our table, tossed down his notepad and pen, and sat down. There was no rush, no anxious look back to the kitchen, no irritation that we might need some help in choosing from his extensive menu. We were made to feel extraordinarily welcome and eventually, with the aid of a beer and some excellent house wine, we managed the decision making process. I do not recall exactly what we ordered, but I do remember that we both enthused about everything.

I am probably known amongst friends as a rather undemonstrative person but I remember that evening uttering some quite uncharacteristic chortles of delight and the words: "My God, that's good," as my jaded taste buds rallied to record the flavours of this Cretan food, which arrived at intervals (as in the Paradisos Taverna) when it was ready. Undoubtedly it was the intensity of the flavours which had awakened my taste buds. The courgettes here, for example, had a kind of rich earthiness. Sliced, fried in olive oil and sprinkled with a local clean-tasting parmesan-type cheese, they were accompanied by wedges of lemons from the garden. This was a totally different experience to eating a humble hard-skinned courgette at home. When all was done, they brought us some fresh fruit and a glass of *raki* each, a taste to which we gradually became accustomed as we soon realised that this fiery liquid acted as a great after-dinner digestif.

While all this was going on, we people watched. The locals began to take their evening stroll, old ladies dressed in black scurried about, extra supplies were delivered to the Hotel Hellas across the street, children played about near the church, the odd stray dog looked about for scraps, teenage boys looked about for teenage girls, drivers of enormous 4x4s shouted greetings at Manoli as they passed by. The old men of the town continued their deliberations about the world over cards or *tavli* (a form of backgammon) and *raki* at the *kafenions* nearby. There was a buzz in the air; it was simply quite intoxicating.

We went back to Manoli's taverna several times that week, and began to get to know the family. Manoli's mother, a strong-looking, substantially-built woman sat towards the back of the taverna. Mama, as we now fondly describe her to ourselves, ruled the roost, while her husband busied himself with clearing dishes and laying tables, occasionally being ordered out by Mama to fetch fresh herbs or whatever else the kitchen required.

Rula's father was also part of the team but seemed to decide for himself whether he was actually going to be of any use. Manoli and Rula had two young children who both came and went with friends and were occasionally firmly directed by Mama to sit and eat. This was a chore for the young boy that he found difficult as his time with friends in the village square was much more fun. The family had further help in the kitchen from a woman who seemed unable to stay in one place for more than a second, quite understandably I suppose, because this taverna was extremely popular with both tourists and locals alike and the kitchen must have been a most frenetic place in which to work. Mrs Frenetic, as we now call her, blended in well.

We spent the last evening of our week here and were given an affectionate Cretan farewell by Manoli and Rula. Mama's husband thanked us, clenching his fist to his heart with touching warmth, and Mama, from her director's chair, beamed a smile towards us with a little bow of her head. We promised to be back, a promise which we gladly fulfilled the following year.

Although it might appear so, we hadn't come to this part of the world just to swim and eat. A trip by car a little further north took us to the ancient Dorian city of Ítanos, which had started life as a Minoan town and had survived several eras including the Roman. Ancient walls and basilicas were perched on the clifftops with views along the coast both to the north towards Cape Sídheros, the most north-easterly point of the island and back to the south. Once again, we were virtually the only visitors.

There were some tempting beaches here too, but we journeyed back to the one we knew – Hióna – although we stopped halfway at a roadside stall selling bananas from the plantation behind. They were small, creamy and full of flavour and Mr and Mrs Banana (by which name we have been calling these good people ever since) also sold their fresh figs and other fruits together with their honey, olive oil, fig jam, passion fruit jam and banana marmalade. Breakfast then took on a whole new meaning and my chortling resumed even earlier in the day.

The Skoda Roomster continued to serve us well so we travelled to the nearby Monastery of Moní Toploú, steeped in history and resistance to invaders. It appeared more like a fortress than a monastery, and had withstood pirate raids in the Middle Ages as well as pillage and blackmail

My Wife Suggested Crete

The Monastery of Moní Toploú

by Turkish rulers. This was all fascinating stuff and the beauty of the place alone made it a worthwhile visit.

The other great site we wanted to see took our car about half an hour to reach from our base. The road to this – the Palace of Zákros – led us through open countryside, isolated villages, olive groves and rocky hillsides carpeted with wild herbs and dotted about here and there were more whitewashed chapels. If you ever want to forget your worldly troubles, breathe fresh air and gaze at natural earthly beauty for a while, look no further than here. To get to the Palace we drove through the small country town of Áno Zákros, but if you are fit you can reach the Palace on foot through a deep ravine – the Zákros Gorge. As we are yet to reach this degree of fitness, the car took us there by way of spectacular coastal views before descending to the seaside village of Káto Zákros and the remains of the Palace.

Memories of our visit to Knossós unerringly appeared on my radar but visiting the Palace and town of Zákros was a relaxing experience. The place had few visitors – perhaps a dozen others with us – the modern toilets were clean and free (!) and Arthur Evans hadn't managed to get here, so it was quite easy to work out the layout. Another Englishman,

Beginning to Find Our Feet

David Hogarth, had begun excavations here at about the same time as Arthur was occupying himself at Knossós. Hogarth's search proved rather fruitless and the palace wasn't found until the 1960s, this time by a Cretan archaeologist, Nikólaos Platon.

Amongst the momentous Minoan relics unearthed, Platon must have been amused to find a cup of olives preserved by well water for 3,500 years. I was content enough to hear Jennie quietly humming a little tune, a sure sign that she was in her element and we ended our excursion on the nearby beach under the canopy of some tamarisk trees, nibbling our way through cheese and tomatoes listening to the gentle sounds of the sea.

Further highlights of this week in Angathiá and Palékastro undoubtedly involved the meeting of various Cretan locals. Yianni brought his pleasant wife Drusulla to our apartment; she spoke better English than her husband and produced some fresh eggs and grapes. Their daughter Kapi, the owner, lived abroad but employed a lively local woman by the name of Evangelia, to look after the cleaning and change of bedding within the apartments. She spoke no English, so this was a kick start for us to try learning some basic Greek vocabulary. Evangelia cried "Bravo!" whenever our attempts at Greek were understood.

The village of Angathiá, a five-minute climb up behind us, supported a village shop run by another Yianni and his wife Maria with inconsistent but welcome help from one or two of their three sons. All spoke English and Maria soon started teaching Jennie a little more Greek. Yianni kept bees and wow was his honey good! He had also taken the trouble to pin up some signposts in English so that tourists could find their way to the local sights of interest. Some of the signs also indicated the way to his shop! There was also a popular taverna in the village run by yet another Yianni and his wife Stephania.

In Palékastro we renewed our acquaintance with Kostas in his shop, tried out some words in the bakery and enjoyed the smiles of Mr Milk (our name), who surprise, surprise sold us good milk, cheese and olives. All these people were kind to us and it was not difficult to be uplifted by their nature and to feel that human beings after all – or at least in this part of the world – could still be instinctively warm and friendly to strangers.

On the other side of the Kastrí Bluff from Hióna beach we found the long windswept beach of Kouremémos. To round off our week's experience of this area we had a wander along here. This is the home of windsurfing in Crete, as the land leading to the beach acts as a natural wind tunnel. It was great fun watching the experts charging through the surf at ridiculous speeds. We sat under a tamarisk tree in a quiet spot and gazed at their antics.

My Wife Suggested Crete

On the day of our wedding anniversary, we decided to have our celebratory evening meal at another recommended taverna right by the sea on the Hióna side of the Bluff. It happened to be a quietish evening for the taverna which suited us just fine, and the sea had become calm. Our meal of freshly grilled fish was excellent and gradually, as the night sky appeared with its array of twinkling stars, we clinked glasses together, lost in some of our own dreamy thoughts, listening to the sound of gentle waves lapping at the water's edge. What a joyous week!

Hióna fish taverna near Palékastro, Lasíthi Prefecture

Chapter Three

Easter and the Cretan Diet

"as we emerged into the early morning light, we were conscious of an atmosphere of jubilant release; and when we heard the words "Christ is risen!" acclaimed on all sides, it was as if we ourselves had just risen from the dead."
XAN FIELDING THE STRONGHOLD. (XF)

Our 2013 Cretan holiday had been so exciting that we could hardly wait to make plans to re-visit. We had been back in England barely a month when we booked flights for a six-day visit at Greek Orthodox Eastertide, which in 2014 unusually coincided with Easter at home. The Greek Orthodox calendar is different and their Easter can be up to three weeks before or after ours. A brief look at my RGC had quickly convinced me that Easter was the most important festival in Greek Orthodox Christianity.

Jennie and I take the subject of sleep quality seriously and the only thing to mar our previous stay in Angathiá had been the bed. While we were there we had introduced ourselves to our neighbour, a pleasant Frenchman, who invited us to see his apartment next door. Our bed was on a concrete base, his on wooden slats. He said it was reasonably comfortable if 'un peu 'ard.' The rest of the apartment was identical, but he certainly enjoyed a bigger and more private balcony with perhaps an even wider view. Adjacent was someone's allotment which, due to the nature of my employment, was destined to become a source of interest and amusement as we ended up booking the Frenchman's choice for Easter.

This eastern end of the island is historically linked to the French, who occupied it in the late 1890s, and to Italy, as Mussolini's troops took up residence here to assist their Nazi allies in the 1940s. Today the east sees plenty of French and Italian visitors and far fewer British, but hardly any

My Wife Suggested Crete

of us start arriving until May when the tourist season begins. With this thought in mind we asked ourselves if the shops and tavernas would be open. Jennie sent an email to our new friend Kostas, the Palékastro minimarket owner, whose reply told us not to worry. His shop was open every day apart from Easter Sunday and all the restaurants would be open. "Don't paniking … you will not starve!" So we stopped 'paniking' (as he spelt it) and certainly did not starve.

I was happily getting used to the local 'Club Cars' contract method of cash, driving licence, signature, keys and 'have a nice holiday' procedure, which took little time to complete as we and our Peugeot 207 set off from the airport on a warm April day, taking the same route as we had the previous year. New sights and smells greeted us en-route including the yellow-scented broom and larger *spartium junceum* growing along the roadside and the countryside was understandably greener after the winter rains, far-removed from September days when the vegetation has died back after the long summer heat.

In Palékastro Kostas greeted us with a big smiling: 'Welcome!' and a Cretan hug. Four doors down the main street, the Mythos Taverna beckoned us again and Jennie anxiously asked Manoli if we could book a table that evening. It was after all Good Friday. This was a moment I shall always fondly remember as Manoli raised his arms patiently and reassuringly with the words: "Don't worry! We will feed you! Don't worry!" while a few steps behind, his wife Rula tried to restrain her giggles. Welcomed back by Yianni at the Angathiá apartments, we were soon on our new balcony overlooking the olive groves. The typical stress of everyday life back in the UK seemed to miraculously disappear – as if my bald head had become a permeable structure capable of releasing the aforementioned stress and steam into the Cretan air.

We ended up eating at Manoli and Rula's taverna every night. I remember watching Mama on her director's chair in the shadows carefully peeling the potatoes before cutting them into chunky chips, ready for frying. I remember even more vividly the taste of those potatoes. So powerful was the flavour that even my overworked taste buds will never forget the moment. Had I been blindfolded, the ripe earthy sweetness and delicate crunchiness would still have confirmed a mouthful of the best potato I had ever enjoyed.

The location of their taverna by the village square and church meant that we could of course watch the Easter proceedings. As we poked our heads through the open doors of the packed church we could hear some of the solemn Good Friday intonations of the Papa, as the priest is called. Jennie and I find late nights difficult to do these days, so when Christ's triumphant return was celebrated at midnight on the Saturday we were both safely tucked away amongst His Angathian olive groves. One day I would like to see all the candles ablaze and hear the locals greeting each other with the words "Khristós Anésti" (Christ is risen), but we managed to greet Evangelia, the cleaning lady, with those words on Easter Sunday morning, to which she replied "Alithós Anésti" (Truly He is risen).

While contentedly consuming Manoli's fare that evening, we watched as preparations were made in the square for the Easter feast, accompanied by music and dancing and all manner of excited Palékastro residents ready for a party. I had parked as normal in the convenient car park behind Kostas' shop without thinking that the square would be blocked off for our return journey. I suppose we could have walked back to our apartment, but I worked out a rather convoluted diversion via Moní Toploú, Mr and Mrs Banana's shed and the rough track along Koureménos beach which took us back via Mr Kakavia's taverna. Apart from a couple of startled rabbits, no damage was done. Evangelia had left us a dish of special Easter buns to celebrate the Resurrection and, unbeknown to her, our safe return to the apartment.

Vai beach, three or four kilometres out of Palékastro, is famous for its white sand and especially for its palm trees, Crete's indigenous wild date palm. Together with Knossós, the Lasíthi plateau and the Samariá gorge, Vai joins the top four in the list of travel agents' excursions. Easter was actually a great time to have a look at it because there was hardly anybody there. We both took the opportunity of using the toilets which, as Knossós, you will normally have to pay for. Nobody seemed to take any notice of us, so we departed without monetary loss, content that we had seen this picturesque place without rubbing shoulders with the heaving summer masses.

In complete contrast, about two kilometres away from Vai is a turning signposted to Maridhati beach and fish taverna. Having navigated our Peugeot over a very bumpy track for five minutes or so, we found the stony beach occupied at the far end by two semi-naked ladies who took no notice of our sudden intrusion. The sea was a tad too cold for Jennie, although I knew she would be content to sit and poke about amongst the pebbles while I took a bracing dip in the clear, cool water, having the entire bay to myself.

My Wife Suggested Crete

Vai beach, a few kilometres north-east of Palékastro

Swimming in April was therefore – as far as I was concerned – just about doable, but there were other places that we wanted to visit, including an important historical site about an hour's drive away. To get to Minoan Présos we had to drive back to Sitía and take a left turn onto a road which eventually would have led to the south coast. Just south of Sitía, the road cuts straight through a Minoan villa dating back to 1500 BC near the village of Piskokéfalo. It was a sort of 'blink and you'll miss it' moment; I must have blinked on the way through but managed to get a sighting on the way back.

I remember it as a fresh windy day with not a cloud in the sky. As we drove through the village of Néa Présos we spotted a young woman tidying up her village churchyard, no doubt for the Easter celebrations, and we spontaneously waved greetings to each other. This was still very much olive country, but interspersed with fertile green valleys sporting all sorts of fruit trees and vegetables. A narrow track led through this greenery to a small parking area.

I had by now recognised that good visibility for the ancient people of this island was high on their list of priorities, and it was perhaps even more important here as this city was the last bastion of Minoan civilisation

Easter and the Cretan Diet

before its final demise. A signed path led to the highest point, the first acropolis, where we thought we could make out the base of an ancient temple, an altar and a big cistern, all surrounded by defensive tiered walls just about visible amongst the spring vegetation.

Above all, however, I remember the wonderful profusion of wild flowers, large yellow and white daisy heads closely resembling the *argyranthemums* or margarites which you can buy for the summer season in English garden centres – for a price! On reflection they may be more closely related to the annual *chrysanthemum segetum*, with its lance-shaped leaves. At this point I should have consulted my learned cousin, a superbly knowledgeable horticulturalist who I am sure could have told me the correct species and variety of this plant. Whatever its botanical name, it was like a magic carpet, and I have a delightful photograph above my desk of Jennie examining a section of the defensive wall engulfed up to her knees by those exquisite flowers with a backdrop of the Cretan hills beneath a blue sky. I often look at this photograph, and even when one of those gruelling days comes along when nothing appears to be going well, an upward glance to my snapshot, under which I have written the words: "Or we could go and live in Crete!" will usually distract me from opening up a packet of Diazepam. (I'm telling fibs – I don't really use them).

Minoan Présos – amidst the wild flowers at the first acropolis

My Wife Suggested Crete

We have been back to Présos twice more since, mainly because I was frustrated on this first visit that I could neither locate nor reach the later substantial Hellenistic house which apparently occupied the western slope of this hill. It was not until our third visit one September when the scrub had died back and someone had cut a path through, that we found it, Jennie taking several pictures of me standing triumphantly on a stairway of this Hellenistic settlement looking as if I had just conquered Everest.

On the intermediate visit, still frustrated, I had identified a little more in the shape of two further acropolises, but the dominant memory of this particular visit was the chance meeting with a Welsh couple in the parking area who had also decided to investigate Présos. Until then it had always been just Présos and us. Jennie, with her usual bonhomie, began to engage them in conversation, apparently taking on the role of archaeological guide and expert and explaining how easy it was to reach the first acropolis and what you could expect to see there. This was done after she had ascertained that these people spoke English. The astonishing conversation went something like this:

Jennie: "So where do you come from?"
Welshman: "Wales."
Jennie: "Oh, so you're English!"
Welshman: "No, I'm Welsh!"
Jennie: "That's great, so you speak English then."

I think the Welshman was becoming increasingly irritated, but Jennie's bonhomie just about won him over, although his expression of relief when I started the engine of the Peugeot was thinly veiled, as we finally left him and his partner to discover the joys of Présos.

~ ~ ~ ~

Although the Welsh language was definitely not on Jennie's list of language learning possibilities, the Greek language certainly was. I think we both feel that spoken Greek has a lovely ring to it and it was at about this time that Jennie enrolled in a Greek language course at home in Exeter, which was soon followed by some personal tutoring. It wasn't easy as she soon discovered; after all you have to learn a new alphabet and the grammar is difficult to understand. I believe it is always easier to learn a native tongue when you are actually in the country concerned.

Nowadays, within a few hours of returning to Crete, Jennie's studies soon start to pay dividends as the language is remembered. The

Easter and the Cretan Diet

encouragement which she receives from the Cretans is always genuine and generous and tends to elevate her status in their minds from ordinary tourist to a respected visitor who has made the effort to try to speak their language. By the Easter break even I had picked up some essential words and phrases, enough at least to get by in the bakery or supermarket and of course most importantly in the taverna.

Place names are often signed in both Greek and transliterated into English, so I now attempt to read the Greek version before falling back on the English. Jennie's evolving interest in the language coincided with my own increasing fascination about the island's history, ancient and modern, so my collection of books on anything Cretan began to grow. The RGC was a good help getting me started in my pursuit of knowledge.

As you may have gathered, by now we were thoroughly enjoying the delights of Cretan food and this Easter holiday was no exception; but the Easter Sunday feast – usually of lamb – is wholly unrepresentative of the Cretan diet. At this point I must thank my sister-in-law for sending me an American book: *The Truth about Statins*, after hearing that I had been prescribed these drugs "as a preventative" to quote my designated heart specialist. It was an interesting if rather disturbing read and, at the very least, I took on board some of the side effects which these nasty little pills can cause. Barbara Roberts, the author, went on to discuss alternatives which naturally enough included the adoption of a healthy diet. I read with delight – but not with a great deal of surprise – about the benefits of the Cretan diet.

In a local bookshop, I discovered a cookery book for Jennie: *Cretan Cooking* by Maria and Nikos Psilakis. Apart from the wonderful recipes, (complete with photographs designed to move the salivary glands into a frantic state of activity), here was proof that the traditional Cretan diet is the healthiest in the world. An American study which began in the 1950s and statistics from the World Health Organisation in 1987, both showed that the inhabitants of Crete rarely succumbed to heart disease.

Statistics also pointed out that Cretans have more fat in their diet than anyone else. This belies the fact that their animal fat content is extremely low. Olive oil – explicitly extra virgin olive oil – provided the answer to this statistic. The Cretans get through more olive oil than any other people in the world. Even compared with the rest of Greece, Cretans consume double the amount of olive oil. Much of this olive oil is used in its natural raw state, but when it is used in the cooking process, it withstands high temperatures far better than other oils and therefore resists oxidation for some time. Cretans eat more fruit than anyone else; they eat large amounts of pulses and vegetables and nuts when available; but they only eat small amounts of meat and a little fish. Don't be surprised to find snails on the menu in Crete. The islanders would be appalled to know that garden centres in the UK sell slug pellets to poison snails. In Crete, snails are collected after rain showers for the cooking pot. Moreover, the only man-made chemical likely to be used in traditional horticulture – and then only after a period of unseasonal rain – is copper sulphate, especially to protect vines.

Unfortunately, on a commercial level, the arrival of the plastic greenhouse culture – introduced to the island by a Dutchman – has led to the use of the inevitable chemicals to artificially protect the artificial crops. I hope that these chemicals do not find their way into the gardens, allotments and smallholdings of the ordinary Cretan people. I probably also ought to admit that Crete has now been influenced by the outside world: more meat and dairy produce has been added to the everyday diet. Pizzerias are becoming more commonplace, and I regret the experience of seeing a sign advertising the arrival of a worldwide burger chain in one of the big cities of the island. I sincerely hope that this trend will somehow be reversed and that the younger generation will again appreciate the healthy diet of their elders.

Wine production on the island is fast becoming a sophisticated operation. Although the barrelled or draught wine offered in tavernas is usually very good, reflecting the unique flavours of the island's well-established grape varieties that have been cultivated for centuries, new boutique wineries are appearing and introducing other grape varieties such as Syrah. Some of the resulting wine can be outstanding. Wine is usually taken with food, perhaps more red than white, while the sherry-like *retsina* is a popular alternative. A meal without wine is not unusual, but a meal without bread and olive oil in Crete is simply not a meal. Cretans eat vast quantities of bread. Until recently most of the bread was made with wholemeal flour and even today there seems to be little gluten in Cretan bread. The flat pita breads used for snacking have no raising agents and again little gluten.

As with all people with a gluten intolerance, Jennie suffers from appalling discomfort if she eats the wrong food, and there have been times when I instinctively know when trouble lies ahead after she consumes something which her 'insides' cannot deal with. So you can understand that it was with a good deal of trepidation as I first watched my wife consume a mouthful of Cretan bread and, being unable to resist, a baklavá from a cake shop called the *zaharoplastía*. Unbelievably, and with my thanks to the angels, there appeared to be little if any indigestion and gradually Jennie has been able to indulge in foods which are still a complete taboo for her in the UK – or anywhere else for that matter. The traditional Cretan diet for me is a total joy, but I hope you can appreciate that for Jennie it is pure culinary heaven, without repercussions!

~ ~ ~ ~

Of the remainder of this Easter visit I remember tranquil walks to Hióna beach and beyond where quiet coves looked ideal for summer swimming, while the aromatic shrubs and herbs covered the headland as far as the eye could see. We were alone in this landscape and totally at ease. Back at the apartment Mr Allotment next door (for want of knowing his name) came daily to inspect his ripening crops which, from my view on the balcony, seemed to include tomatoes, spinach, aubergines, courgettes, peppers, onions and potatoes and, I guessed, a good deal more. His olive and fruit trees all looked fresh and healthy, which is exactly how I felt as we headed home. On looking back at my 2014 diary I appear to have summarised those six April days in simple terms: "So Good!"

Chapter Four

Seeking out the South Coast

"Crete, with its infinite variety and its astonishing changes within a few miles, never becomes boring but leads one ever onwards, deeper into its labyrinth."
DAVID MACNEIL DOREN WINDS OF CRETE. (DMD)

By now, even before our Easter visit, our heads and probably our hearts were pulsating with all things Cretan. Eager to see more of the island and also conscious of Jennie's requirements for a happy Cretan holiday: washing-machine, beach, historical sites, good tavernas and a comfortable bed, we chose an apartment in the Alexander Beach Hotel situated in the unpretentious village of Kalamáki, just about midway along the south coast of the island. All our necessary travel arrangements were well in place before my miserable attempt at Christmas shopping got under way towards the end of 2013.

    A 10-kilometre drive away from Kalamáki lies the old hippy resort of Mátala, famous for its caves inhabited on and off by local people for centuries and allegedly – on a more short-term lease – by the likes of Cat Stevens, Bob Dylan and Joni Mitchell amongst others. Jennie is a self-confessed former hippie and I am sure we talked about Mátala beforehand, but as yet we still haven't paid a visit. Apart from the beach, the guide books don't appear to enthuse over the place. In any case, I know that sleeping rough in a cave at Mátala would not have appealed to my other half, although in reality these caves are fenced off at night so it wouldn't have happened, and we have old vinyl records at home of Joni Mitchell singing away in her extraordinary voice. (Her song *Carey,* which mentions Mátala, can be found on side 1, track 4, of her *Blue* album, a Reprise Record which was distributed by Wea Records Ltd in 1972).

    Our hotel apartment was far more comfortable with a balcony overlooking the sea, the vista stretching for miles out to the deserted

Seeking Out the South Coast

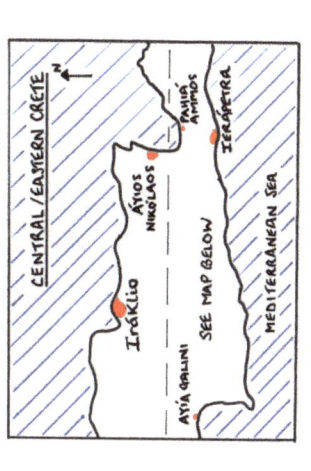
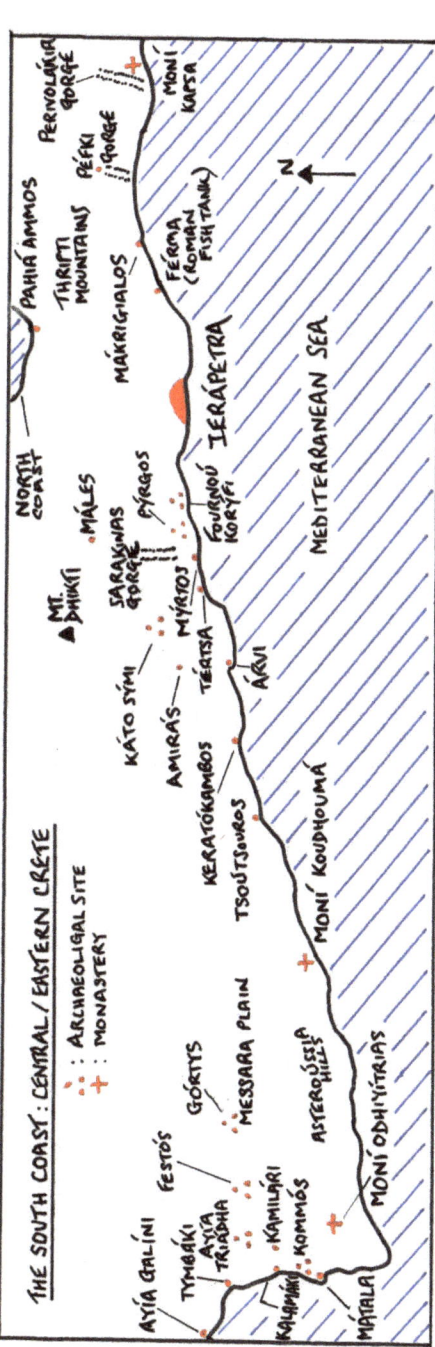

The south coast of central/eastern Crete

My Wife Suggested Crete

Paximadia Islands and across the bay to our right to the compact resort of Áyia Galíni, which shelters beneath the eastern edge of the Assiderato hills. Behind is a backdrop of the mighty Kédhros mountains. On a clear day and especially early in the evening even Edward Lear could have enthused, I thought, as I relaxed on the balcony on my birthday, with a cold Greek beer.

View from Kalamáki towards Ayía Galíni

I had wondered what Cretan welcome to expect in an area of the island well away from our eastern comfort zone. Alexi Tsafantakis, the owner, spoke no English apart from: "One moment!" but I realised later that he spoke good German, which was fortunate as this part of Crete seems to attract plenty of tourists from that country. It may again be an historical connection as the Tymbáki airfield nearby was a stronghold for German troops in WWII. Alexi's wife, Diamanti, soon arrived and we relaxed as her welcome in English could not have been warmer. As we had come to expect from Cretans, nothing was too much trouble. We strolled along the pleasant promenade to find our evening meal and soon happened upon the Taverna Delfinia where the friendliness of this village continued, the excellent seafood complemented by the gorgeous sunset over the Kédhros mountains.

Apart from the warm sea (which was slightly awkward to get into courtesy of a rocky shelf visible just below the surface), we had chosen this area because of several historical places of interest nearby. Although I understand that these sites are not for everyone, many of them are worth visiting for the scenery alone. The ancient Minoan port of Kommós was easy to find simply by walking along the beach from Kalamáki. Sadly, it was fenced off when we got there, even though a ticket office has been built, but you can still see quite a lot just by wandering around the perimeter – including one building containing an enormous length of Minoan wall. I hope it will be open to visitors one day as it looks tantalisingly fascinating from the wrong side of the fence.

Ayiá Triádha, a few kilometres away, is most definitely open and was the source of many Minoan artworks now in the museum in Iráklio. Archaeologists cannot agree about the purpose of this place: a royal villa, home to a wealthy merchant, or a local centre of administration? Whatever it was, it lies in a lovely setting underneath a canopy of pines with views to the sea (and the Tymbáki airfield). The easiest part of it to understand is a row of identical stores known as the market, although technically they probably belonged to the post-Minoan era. Another bonus here is that there are no crowds and you can poke your head into the small chapel which lends its name to the site.

If neither of the above appeals to you, I must draw your attention to the palace of Festos or Phaistos (or sometimes Faistos), which sits at the head of the great agricultural belt of the Messará plain and was excavated at about the same time as Arthur Evans was doing his damage at Knossós. Even if you are someone who tends to begrudgingly traipse about ancient ruins, I can recommend it as a far better experience than Knossós, with fewer visitors and yet it can claim almost as much historical importance. After a five-minute walk from the parking area the remains of the palace were suddenly before us. The grandeur of Festos was still evident, fully justifying its status in legend as home to the brother of King Minos. We hope to go there again one day, such was our enjoyment of this Minoan palace high above the fruits and vegetables and olives of the Messará.

In 1939 the American author Henry Miller enjoyed a visit to Festos, as described in his book, *The Colossus of Maroussi*: "God, it's incredible!" he shouted to his guide before his eyes were diverted towards the Messará: "Below me, stretching away like an infinite magic carpet, lay the plain of Messará, girdled by a majestic chain of mountain ranges. From this sublime, serene height it has all the appearance of the garden of Eden." (HM)

My Wife Suggested Crete

Jennie and I made a detour after leaving the palace and I drove through some of the villages below: Pómbia, Repi, Koussés and Sívas amongst others. The grand villa-style homes of the farmers testified to the wealth created by this large fertile plain for many a year. However, the people of the Messará have not always been allowed to enjoy the fruits of their labours. In the 1820s when the Turks sought the assistance of the Egyptians to brutally crush the islanders' resistance to their occupation, the Messará valley did not escape the Egyptian onslaught.

Thirty years later while surveying the coast and researching the island's historical wealth that Englishman with the wonderful name – Captain T.A.B. Spratt – found the area still in ruins: "In no part of Crete have the effects of the last revolution been less recovered from than in the Messará valley. Every village is in partial ruin still…The blackened walls and roofless hovels show still the brand of war; and ruined churches tell, too, of a religious as well as a domestic strife, with its horrors of violence and revengeful barbarity." (TABS) Nor did the Messará escape the attention of the next invaders, the Nazis, who fully realised that this area would provide much needed sustenance for their soldiers. As a result, there was an unusually large German garrison here to protect this food source. British spies avoided the area if at all possible, describing the Messará in coded form as Badlands.

The other big site of interest, quite close to Festos, is Górtys, or Górtyn (or even Gortyna). The fame of this place is due to its importance in Roman times as it was not only the capital city of Roman Crete but also the regional capital of Cyrenaica, and from about 67 BC it began to grow substantially, so that by the next century it had an estimated population of 20,000. I won't go into details of what you can see in the main site, but the ancient church of Áyios Títos and the Odeion (a covered theatre) and its law code dating from 500 BC are well worth a visit. Most importantly, whatever else you do here, make sure you cross the road and walk – without charge – into the olive groves with a map. Here you will find old Roman pillars and pieces of broken architrave strewn all over the place, and then you will stumble on the remains of the governor's palace and the Temple of Pythian Apollo complete with the altar, vast fallen masonry and a big headless statue. Walk a little further and you will be able to make out the shape of an amphitheatre still just about visible. It is a quite extraordinary experience as you gaze at all this Roman history tucked away in the olive groves. As the RGC intimates, you almost feel as if you are the first to discover the ruins of this once substantial city.

Wandering around the remains of this Roman city brought to my mind an Australian man to whom I had been recently introduced. In order to keep the bones of my back roughly in the positions in which they are supposed to be, and in order to keep bringing home some monetary reward for my gardening work, I had been recommended the services of this Australian chiropractor who worked out of his premises in Exeter. He had refreshingly bucked the trend and had emigrated to the UK. He had no doubt been obliged to tell his story many times to his new clients, but he seemed quite at ease to relate to me – as bones were clicked back into place – how the constant invitation to a 'barbie' to consume a few 'tinnies' at weekends had left him feeling that there must be more to life than what was on offer in the 'burbs' of Sydney.

It appeared that he was keen to see a bit of human history and did not rejoice in the fact that in order to do that from Sydney he had to spend six or seven hours on a plane to see the treasures of Angkor in Cambodia or the ruins of the former capital of Thailand at Ayutthaya. Now in Devon he felt that he had the history of Europe on his doorstep and he seemed particularly interested in Italy and ancient Rome. His 'piece de résistance', in order to reinforce his story, was undoubtedly when he flung open the window of his operational headquarters in Exeter's Southernhay, and with great delight pointed downwards with the accompanying words:

Roman Górtys near the village of Áyii Dhéka

"Hugh, that's a Roman wall, mate!" I feel it appropriate to mention him here because I hope, one day, he has the opportunity to stumble through the olive groves of Roman Górtys, as I am sure some classic Australian expletives would joyfully echo through the ruins.

In Manoli and Rula's taverna in Palékastro at Easter we had met, chatted and shared a meal with a retired German couple who, we discovered, had found their retirement dream in the village of Mixórrouma near Spíli in the province of Réthymno. They had moved from Frankfurt with all their possessions and bought an old property which needed some TLC. They had then decided to embrace the Greek Orthodox Christian faith and had both been officially baptised and given the names Yianni and Eleni. Although we have continued to call them by their German names, I will refer to them by their new Greek names in the pages that follow.

We had told them of our planned trip to Kalamáki and they had immediately invited us to their house for an overnight stay. So in the middle of our week in Kalamáki we grabbed an overnight bag and drove west for about an hour, our first experience of Réthymno province. They, and their two soft-natured dogs, greeted us like long-lost friends and their hospitality was such that it easily matched the typical Cretan version which we were enjoying so much. A drive of about twenty minutes from Mixórrouma will get you back to the south coast and we went swimming at a beach called Dhamnóni, near Plakiás, followed afterwards by a good meal at their favourite of several tavernas by the sandy beach. In the evening we sat outside under the stars in the summer warmth and the peace of the Cretan countryside, fortified by wine, beer and olives, dogs and all.

Yianni began asking why we didn't buy a house in Crete too. It was an option that we had vaguely considered ever since Drusulla back in Angathiá had mentioned that she had a property to sell in the village of Skordílo. On our second day in Mixórrouma our German friends took us to meet Agamemnon and his wife Ourania, proud owners of a spotless rural taverna in the village of Kendochori on the lower slopes of Mount Kédhros. Agamemnon, a big man with plenty of hair on both head and face and possessing the warmest of Cretan smiles, was also the owner of some land that he wanted to sell. Briefed by Yianni that we might be interested, Jennie and I were taken a short distance out of the village to have a look at what we now fondly call 'the goat house', as that was basically what it was. We were now completely in dream land, but although we wandered about the plot and hopefully gave Agamemnon the respect which he deserved, this particular fantasy was going to remain just that.

What was far more real and exciting was the lunch that they produced on the terrace of their delightful taverna. Expertly produced by Ourania and complemented by Agamemnon's attentive charm and jovial banter, this food fell quite naturally into the category of 'an exceptional meal experience'. Most of the ingredients – the meat, vegetables, cheese, fruit and olive oil – had come from their own land. We tasted the freshness, sensed the tenderness and ripeness, and marvelled at the explosion of fragrances and flavours created by the Cretan herbs. Having thanked Agamemnon and Ourania, and Yianni and Eleni, we said our goodbyes and vowed to meet again someday, before driving back to Kalamáki to continue our seaside holiday.

The 'goat house' above the village of Kendochori

We found a 1900 BC circular Minoan tomb in the olive groves near the neighbouring village of Kamilári; the walk to it and the views from it being just as much fun as the finding of it. On our last day we drove out to an isolated monastery, Moní Odhiyítrias, with a courtyard full of flowers – I particularly remember the orange campsis – a church full of icons and frescoes and a charming monk in all his solemn garb, who showed us around. We bought some honey and other bits and pieces from him at the end of our tour and managed to say 'Efharistó' several times, each of our thank yous being echoed by a little bow of the head and his 'Parakaló' – meaning: "You're welcome." Without a doubt we had felt most welcome in this quiet corner of the world where meditation, I would like to suggest, must have come easily to the monks who had chosen to practise it. That evening we again sampled the fare of the Taverna Delfinia and watched the sun go down in a kind of happy and meditative mood, perhaps induced by our friendly monk and the natural beauty of his monastic surroundings.

Moní Odhíyitrias, in the hills above the coastal village of Kali Limenes

Once again it was time to leave and we bade farewell to Diamanti and the staff of the Alexander Beach Hotel which had been a comfortable base from which to explore. On our flight home to Bristol we were joined in our row of three seats by a young English woman who had bought her particular 'goat house' near the seaside village of Arvi a little further east. Jennie and I spent most of the flight hearing all about it, and we asked who looked after it when she was in England. We discovered that her Cretan neighbours had gradually taught her how to grow various vegetables on her tiny plot of land and were helping her with a door and windows, neither of which she had at the start. Courtesy of these Cretan neighbours, who were the ones who kept an eye on her property when she returned to England, she had started to live out her Cretan dream.

~ ~ ~ ~

The south coast is just as long as the north, but made longer by the fact that in many areas the mountains plunge steeply into the sea and so travelling by vehicle means diversions inland and, in some cases, even back to the north coast in order to make any progress. There are certain sections of the south coast which are still only accessible on foot or by way of a boat. Exploration of these areas therefore takes on a whole new meaning.

Nevertheless, a coastal road covers a large length of the south coast from Góudhouras in the east to Mýrtos, Arvi and then on a minor road as far as Tsoútsouras, a distance of seventy-five kilometres or so. I cannot say whether, subconsciously, our recent English flight companion had focused our attention on her village of Arvi and the surrounding area close to the southern boundary between the Lasíthi and Iráklio prefectures but it was to the seaside village of Mýrtos nearby that we were drawn next, a picturesque village perched above a pleasant sand and pebble beach.

Naturally, Jennie's self-catering holiday requirements had to be met. Although the RGC had a range of good suggestions, it was Jennie who found on the internet the Mirtini apartments in a quiet side-street location. Marianna welcomed us to apartment number one having dealt with the paperwork in her basement office in an efficient and business-like manner. The sight of a walk-in-wardrobe, a good-sized bathroom, a comfortable bed and two separate outside terrace areas – one complete with a colourful shrubbery containing blue plumbago, hibiscus and overhanging purple bougainvilleas – all caused a yelp of delight from my wife. Within a short period of time she began to act as if this place was her very own, sweeping up the terrace areas and putting the washing on the line – as is her wont! Needless to say, we have ended up staying here more than once.

The village of Mýrtos is a likeable place and once you have worked out the one-way traffic system, initiated I guess because the old streets are so narrow, the white-washed houses, apartments, tavernas, minimarket, shops and seaside promenade all combine together to form a harmonious coastal community. Everything we needed was - almost literally – on our doorstep, including the beach and the sea for some refreshing swims.

My Wife Suggested Crete

The next village, six kilometres to the west, is Tértsa, reachable by the narrow coast road and we used the beach here too for our swimming and tried one of two beachside tavernas. Back in Mýrtos our favourite spot for an evening meal, having tried all the RGC suggestions, turned out to be the Mýrtos taverna, part of the Mýrtos hotel on the main village street, where we sat happily outside and where Jennie talked to the local cat population – as is also her wont. Fresh and juicy figs, good bread, local cheese and pine honey were my personal culinary highlights, all available from the shops in the village which is also large enough to warrant its own pharmacy and a most helpful pharmacist within.

Ancient history was as usual on our minds and Mýrtos has two important Minoan sites nearby, namely Mýrtos Pirgos and Fournoú Korýfi, both reached by scrambling uphill from the coast road. Both were also blessed with fine views and an absence of visitors, and it was at Fournoú Korýfi that archaeologists had discovered the goddess of Mýrtos, a peculiar female figurine with an elongated neck, holding a jug and made of clay. It was this weird looking object which we had spied back at the Áyios Nikólaos museum on our first visit to Crete.

In Mýrtos itself there is a small museum looked after by a British potter, John Atkinson, who has made an intricate and accurate clay model of the site at Fournoú Korýfi, with meticulous care. John is a charming and helpful curator and may give you a lesson in how to identify the age of pottery, which he did for us. He also dug out his copy of a book called *The Minoans* by Sinclair Hood. It contains many illustrations of various artefacts, which is why we now have a copy at home. John didn't look particularly well when we last popped in to see him, but we hope that he and the museum will continue to amuse and educate other visitors for years to come.

I liked to take an early-morning swim at the quiet western end of the beach, passing by some Roman-era ruins including a kind of circular brick construction at the side of the road leading to Tértsa. You can see other Roman bits and pieces at the back of the beach. Like so many places in Crete it is all sitting in front of you, waiting for the expert's analysis. I enjoy looking at these historical structures still standing – to some degree – after thousands of years. It is an easy way to get me smiling.

There is much to see along this stretch of the south coast, although beware the swathes of plastic greenhouses which, in places, rather detract from its otherwise natural beauty. The southernmost town in Europe, Ierápetra can be found here; a sprawling, busy place where parking a car (near the boat jetty) is difficult. Having eventually achieved that, a short walk took us to the archaeological museum housed in a former Turkish school. Although tourism has arrived here, Ierápetra thrives as the commercial centre for the agriculture which is at the heart of the local economy. The town sits behind a wide sweeping bay with views inland to the Thriptí mountains and provides a fine promenade walk with a couple of equally fine traditional tavernas to satisfy any pangs of hunger. We found that the Taverna Napoleon, evidently favoured by locals, was every bit as good as the RGC said it would be.

    Travelling east along the coast from Ierápetra, we eventually located a Roman fish tank carved from the rock near the village of Férma, still virtually intact and complete with a sluice gate. I expect the owner of the Roman villa at Makriyialós, a few kilometres further east, received a good share of 'the catch'. As for this villa, you can detect the outline of a former courtyard garden and bathing rooms which this wealthy owner must have enjoyed. Bits and pieces of his mosaic flooring are still visible here and there.

Roman fish tank on the south coast, not far from Ierápetra

    Further east, at the entrance to the Perivolákia gorge, stands another famous monastery, Moní Kápsa, whose buildings appear almost stuck onto the hillside adjacent to steep cliffs which plunge into the gorge. They have strict opening hours so our visit was limited to about forty minutes. We were guided into the monastery's chapel before being left to ourselves. Higher up the hillside, steps led towards the cave of Yerontoyiannis, a monk who is locally revered as a saint, courtesy of his reputation as a healer and philanthropist. The location of the cave is even more dramatic than the monastery itself, and I was particularly glad that reasonably solid railings had been placed to prevent us from joining the goats far below in the gorge.

By the time we got back down to the monastery, our host had joined his fellow monks for their lunchtime repast behind the closed doors of the refectory. We let ourselves out and sat on the pebbly beach below watching the waves and breathing in the sea air. Looking back, the orange and grey colours of the rocky cliffs forming the entrance to the Perivolákia gorge did not entice us to start walking. Just as well I think, as the RGC warned me of the significant challenge that this hike might pose. By all accounts, though, it is one of the most dramatic in this part of the island.

Moní Kápsa

Seeking Out the South Coast

On our way back, we turned off the main road and headed to the hillside village of Péfki from where you can hike down the gorge of that name. The RGC had informed me that this gorge was more straightforward, but we simply admired the views. Once back at our village base, however, we explored the Sarakinás gorge directly inland from Mýrtos at the village of Mýthi. There are some extraordinary rock formations in this area. From the gorge you can drive – or walk – up to the village of Máles which nestles in the foothills of the Dhíkti mountains. We gazed at the ominous and vast expanse of Mt. Dhíkti up above and the sea at Mýrtos down below us. The British wartime agent, Sandy Rendel, had a wireless base in the hills above Máles in the years of German occupation in the 1940s: "The days at Máles were so peaceful and beautiful, that I sometimes wished that time could stop." (AMR) It did not take me long to understand his sentiment.

Heading west from Mýrtos we took ourselves – uphill again – to the village of Káto Sými. It is home to the sanctuary of Hermes and Aphrodite, an original shrine dating back to pre-Minoan times, but adopted by Minoans, Greeks and Romans as time passed. Wandering around the perimeter of the fenced site we came across the spring that emerges here – the reason why this place has always been so important. Some super strong human being, or perhaps even Jaws himself from the James Bond films had been here, proof of which took the form of a misshapen iron bar, one of several engineered to provide the locked entrance gate. Jaws had obligingly twisted it so that Jennie and I could crawl through to gain access, and we wandered about inside, accompanied by a multitude of bees and wasps enjoying the nectar from the abundant pine trees and the water from this revered mountain spring. Of this holy place, so important to many people over so many centuries, only the archaeologists would be able to decipher the puzzling array of walls and mounds of organised rubble now left beneath and around a giant hollow plane tree, which itself must be incredibly old.

Dodging the bees and wasps, we got in our car to drive back down the hill, negotiating hairpin bends for a couple of kilometres or so, to the village of Káto Sými and the welcoming Taverna Afrodite in a serene setting underneath more giant plane trees and beside the now much larger stream that tumbles down from the sanctuary above. Wasps and bees had found it too, so we felt it prudent to seek our sanctuary inside the taverna.

It was one of those places where you are invited into the kitchen to see what is on offer in the cooking pots. The lady of the house seemed to be apologising for the lack of choice. She had three dishes available, so we had one of each! I particularly remember – although it was all very good

My Wife Suggested Crete

– the tastiest green beans I have ever demolished. I also remember a trio of other customers, from the Far East, who had decided to sit outside on the balcony and enjoy the ambience. A pesky wasp had decided otherwise and pestered one of the three so persistently that he eventually gave up on his kung fu method of defence and retreated indoors.

The only sounds we heard in the village came from the babbling stream, the buzzing of the bees and wasps and the occasional rustling of leaves as the wind forced its way through the branches of the trees. So the village of Káto Sými, in its isolated setting in the pine-clad hills of southern Crete, did not appear to be the sort of place that would have been inflicted by atrocities seventy-five years ago. A large war memorial in the village square confirms just the opposite. 1943 saw the destruction of the villages of Káto Sými, Áno Sými, Pefkos, Riza, Gdohia and Mýrtos itself. At least five hundred Cretans were put to death in reprisals for a senseless attack on a German infantry unit by one of the most influential of the Cretan gang leaders, *Kapetan* Manoli Bandouvas. He had his lair in the hills of this region at the time, and although his undoubted popularity amongst the Cretan people may have waned for a while as a result, it soon recovered.

Jack Smith-Hughes, who wrote an appendix to the official British report on the Cretan Resistance, concluded: "he was le beau chevalier sans peur et sans reproche, the man who had fought the hated German and defeated [him]". (NK) Several other British Liaison Officers thought him to be an odd sort of man, and wondered why his followers were so intensely loyal. Bo-Peep was his British code name based on the considerable number of flocks of sheep which he owned. Undoubtedly Bandouvas had become a Cretan hero in the eyes of many islanders, whilst British agents on the island at this time were less charitable in their opinions of this man, who certainly displayed plenty of self-esteem, but who was often incredibly difficult to deal with. It was at Kato Sými where Bo-Peep confronted this German unit, so I was not surprised to find a large photograph of the man with his brothers and his followers hanging behind the bar of the taverna. I pointed and asked the young man looking after us if this was indeed Manoli Bandouvas. I think his reaction was a mixture of surprise and curiosity that I should know his name, but I merely said that I had read about him, and left it like that.

~ ~ ~ ~

On our first visit to Crete we had witnessed a rather touristy, but nevertheless pleasant performance of traditional Cretan music and dance at the St Nicolas Bay Hotel. Not until our stay at Mýrtos did we come across any other live music. Here, towards the end of September every year the local civic dignitaries organise an evening fiesta for tourists and locals alike that takes place in the village square, not fifty metres away from the Mirtini apartments. So it made sense to attend, and it was our first direct experience of a Cretan party. The village tavernas and many individual households produced a mass of oven-baked dishes and sweet pastries, all laid out in the village hall, while trestle tables and chairs were arranged in rows outside. A significant space was left for musicians and for dancing.

Of the instruments used in traditional Cretan music, the lyre (or lyra) - a lap fiddle, and the *laúto*, like a mandolin or lute, are the most important. The Turkish *bouzoúki* or *sarangi* is also widely played. I am not a musician and as my wife so rightly says: "You can't dance!" Nevertheless I still enjoy what I like to think is a wide range of music, and one day I hope to visit the village of Houdhétsi, where a museum of musical instruments also organises a programme of concerts.

On a warm September evening in the village square of Mýrtos, having enjoyed our fill of fine local food, we waited in anticipation as four musicians arrived and eventually started playing some haunting music. David MacNeil Doren was someone noticeably captivated by the sound of the lyre: "I am hypnotised by it, as I am by the landscape of Crete, and ideally the two should be taken together, for I know of no instrument so suited to its country as lyre is to Crete… I never hear a lyre without cold chills playing up and down my spine, my heart beats faster; my breathing becomes more rapid; my feet move irresistibly to the rhythm. Wild atavistic images flood my brain; I am seized by indescribable impulses." (DMD) The music we heard in Mýrtos that day was indeed compelling, sometimes soulful, sometimes uplifting, and the dance steps merged seamlessly with the sounds of the instruments.

I noticed one man who, like David MacNeil Doren, appeared hypnotised by the sounds, although I also thought that a considerable quantity of *raki* might have contributed to his happy countenance. It was an evening full of fun, but it prompted me to realise that my knowledge of Cretan music and dance was really non-existent. A young boy – perhaps only nine or ten years old – had taken centre stage once or twice and performed the dance steps to the music with tremendous enthusiasm. His proud father had an enormous grin on his face as he praised his son's performance.

I now know that the *siganos* dances are slower and are often incorporated into wedding receptions when, eventually, everyone gets a

My Wife Suggested Crete

go, while the Cretan *pentozalis* are the fast, complicated and energetic dances performed mainly by men who need extraordinary stamina and resolute determination. Jennie's grandsons are both keen exponents of today's modern western music. I understand it's called Drum and Bass. It would be interesting to see what they made of the Cretan *pentozalis*. Having watched the boy's performance in Mýrtos, I think young Cretans could make a pretty good fist of Drum and Bass! We have yet to witness other folk traditions which include the Cretan *mantinades* – short poems of rhyming couplets sometimes recited with music and often spontaneously masterminded so that they never sound boring or antiquated. Neither do we know enough about Cretan poetry other than knowing the name of one of the most famous and extremely lengthy poems: *Erotokritos* written by Vitzentzos Kornaros in the 16th century.

Poetry can come in a variety of styles and I know the word itself can be used to describe a quality of beauty and emotional intensity. This I found as we walked inland from Mýrtos along a narrow road adjacent to the torrent bed of the Mýrtos river, a solitary road if ever there was one. It eventually turned into a track which led us past small orchards of oranges and loquats and an occasional owner's dwelling while vigorous bamboo-like grasses protected the riverbank. Suddenly an impressive sand-coloured Turkish bridge appeared. Dated 1884, with three symmetrical arches spanning the river, it was still paved with rather uneven stones. A more modern advisory sign warned of the weight capacity which this bridge could tolerate. It tolerated us as we stood on top of the central pier and gazed across the riverbed and up to that peaceful hill village of Máles above the Sarakinás gorge. Higher still, the Dhíkti mountains rose majestically towards the heavens.

Less poetically, improvements were apparently being made to the electricity supply in the area so there were rather frequent two-hour power cuts in the village during our stay, but hopefully this situation was of a temporary nature. The owners of the minimarket clearly thought differently as they had installed a generator which was permanently at the ready. It looked like it had seen plenty of action. The staff however were always courteous and helpful; in fact the people of Mýrtos had made us thoroughly welcome. The enormous woman at the village bakery, whom I had presumed to be the baker's wife, looked as if she must have devoured all remaining merchandise at the end of the working day, but her welcome to me was consistently friendly and kind.

The staff at the Mýrtos hotel taverna were headed by a rather eccentric, but nevertheless convivial couple who had a good-natured son with learning difficulties; meanwhile the quietly-spoken woman who

Seeking Out the South Coast

Walking inland from Mýrtos

looked after us all the time here, called Evey – I guess short for Evangelia – was a delightful person to have met, and we felt like friends by the time we left. She told us, if we ever returned, that she might not be working there in the future, but that we would be able to find her in the village if we asked. One day I hope we do.

Discoveries can be made all along this fascinating section of the south coast of Crete and if you require isolation then the remote monastery called Moní Koudhoumá, reachable only on foot, could fit the bill if you are agile enough to attempt the long walk as this place really is far away from the nearest village. For us the village of Mýrtos will always bring a smile to our faces, and the villagers themselves all sit happily in the memory of our sunny days along these southern shores.

Chapter Five

The Autumn of 2014 - Bittersweet Memories

"We should not forget to entertain strangers, lest we entertain angels unaware"
THE BIBLE: HEBREWS 13.2

If I have given you the impression that the hospitality shown to us was provided only by the older Cretan generation, then I ought to correct this because we have found many times that youngsters are also keen to please and help – they do indeed 'entertain strangers'. Whether they have discovered Hebrews, chapter 13, verse two is really neither here nor there. The teenage staff at the Delfinia taverna in Kalamáki provided a typical example when we spotted three of them chatting on the promenade one morning before their work began. Jennie was having difficulty with Wi-Fi connections and asked if they could help. With warm smiles they solved the problem and wished us a happy day. On another occasion a young boy directed us to a local museum not by pointing where to go, but by spending five minutes or so taking us there himself. Without a doubt, this hospitality is in their genes.

~ ~ ~ ~

Half a century ago most Cretan homes were comprised of only two rooms with limited sleeping space and few creature comforts. Mattresses of dubious quality and cleanliness were owned only by the wealthy. Shepherds would sleep on the floor of their huts if not in the open air, and in many of the poorer homes the only bedding to lie on would have been dried plant material. So it may be that Cretans have another genetic inheritance: their ability to sleep on beds which provide no comfort at all for the likes of us.

The Autumn of 2014

We had in fact been perfectly comfortable at both the Alexander Beach Hotel and the Mirtini apartments in Mýrtos, but back at the apartments in Angathiá – even in the Frenchman's apartment – we had by the end of a week become accustomed to rolling out of bed in the mornings in a stiff and aching heap. So began the episode of the mattress topper, the story which has since amused several of our friends who have no doubt questioned our degree of sanity, as we had decided to purchase a ten-kilogram mattress topper specifically to take to Crete in order to alleviate the nightly aches and pains. As you can imagine it requires significant luggage space, and its weight depletes our luggage allowance considerably. As a result, my holiday wardrobe suffered a drastic reduction. But it worked. When we returned to the Frenchman's apartment in the September of 2014, our 10-kilogram purchase not only fitted the bed but it provided sufficient comfort for the whole week.

With that particular issue now resolved, we began another week back in the far east of the island. In and around Palékastro and Angathía we made new discoveries and revisited previous favourites. We became acquainted with more local people and former acquaintances welcomed us back as friends. We used the Angathián village shop owned by Yianni and Maria referring to them between ourselves as Mr and Mrs Bee due to the exquisite taste of his thyme honey. Jennie practised her Greek with Maria and I tried to learn about beekeeping in this part of the world, as well as finding out about local walks. We began to explore the tracks through the olive groves which wound up into the surrounding foothills. From there the views back to the sea and the Kastri bluff are fabulous. We visited Hióna beach several times, with Jennie unjustifiably horrified one day when she counted another fourteen people enjoying the same long stretch of sand and shingle. When the wind blew too strongly for swimming, we drove off to visit Sitía, the biggest town in the east.

Having seen a fair number of the ancient towns and palaces on our travels, it was more fun now to visit an archaeological museum and see some of the finds which had been unearthed in places that were familiar to us. The star attraction as you enter the Sitía museum is the Palékastro Koúros, a little male figure dating from around 1500 BC, which was discovered no more than 300 metres from 'our' Hióna beach. Seals made from agate, carnelian and jasper, and jewellery thousands of years old were particularly attractive to Jennie. I was happy to peruse the tall wine jars and original terracotta grills. One excavated tripod pot held the remains of a rabbit stew. The 'best before' date had expired by some 3,000 years.

My Wife Suggested Crete

Many items in the museum came from the 1985 discovery of a Minoan Palace and town at Petrás, just out of town. The excavations are ongoing, so opening hours are erratic – and parking is awkward. As often happens when we visit archaeological sites, it was difficult to understand the exact layout of this palace, although signs had been put up. Nor is there much left to see of the buildings used by a large group of artisans who had worked nearby. We found all sorts of pottery pieces and stone jars jutting out of the scrub as we explored out of sight of the guardians.

Other options for visitors to Sitía include a good town beach, Roman fish tanks, and up on the hill the old Venetian fortress now used for open-air concerts and theatrical productions. Just east of the town lies the recently-discovered Hellenistic site of Trypítos, on a windswept headland in full view of the modern town and its bay. Trypítos, Jennie decided, was now her favourite site while I was intrigued by the dry-dock hammered out of the cliffs 300 years BC to enable people to haul their ships ashore. We also found some giant and beautiful green rocks which, with a little guidance from the *Field Guide to the Geology of Crete*, may well be andesites in the form and colour of metamorphic olivine, or possibly serpentine.

Trypítos Helenistic site – the dry-dock

The Autumn of 2014

For me, the highlight of this September week was our daytrip down to the far south eastern corner of the island, to the coastal hamlet of Xerókambos. It is certainly a rather straggly village with no clearly identifiable centre, but the RGC is quite correct in pointing out the isolation and peace which is the essence of Xerókambos. We had driven as far as the small country town of Áno Zákros once before, but onwards from there the road was new to us. It took us over windswept uplands where the Cretan scrub had been parched by the heat of summer. It was devoid of human activity, save for the few dwellings scattered about in a central swathe of olive groves. One of these, not far from the road, was a single-storey villa with a swimming pool; a roadside sign advertised it for rent. I imagined the joy of lying out on a lounger at night under the stars and hidden away amongst the olives, far from the madding crowd's ignoble strife, as Shelley might have once described it. We must all have our dreams, and should 'Ernie' ever choose the correct premium bond number and allocate a suitably large prize, then perhaps this dream could be fulfilled. At least we had the joy of seeing this magnificent scenery before we eventually descended to the coast.

Landscape above Xerókambos

My Wife Suggested Crete

From a vantage point just before the road finally drops down to sea level, we made out the grey and orange rocks defining the outline of a rugged gorge to the north west and looking ahead we could see several sandy beaches. Once in Xerókambos, we discovered even more before settling on a tiny cove complete with rows of white sea daffodils, (*Pancratium Maritimum*), equally white powdery sand and clear warm water to swim in. Once in the water, and looking back inland, the mighty boulder-rich hills can be seen towering above the village.

Sea daffodils at Xerókambos

Before swimming we had poked about amongst the scant remains of a Hellenistic site (according to the Blue Guide to Crete) or a Minoan site (according to the RGC). Arguments rage as to whether this was ancient Ambelos, although a local map suggests that Minoan Ambelos was located on a hill a few hundred metres away. Right in the middle of the Hellenistic site, as I will call it, is a whitewashed chapel with its roof painted a soft Grecian blue. The door was unlocked so in we went. At the time an old friend of my family was seriously ill at home in Devon, and I took the opportunity of saying a prayer for her. Kindly locals had lit two small candles, and those few quiet moments remain deeply etched in my memory.

I am pleased that guide books don't over-enthuse about the attractiveness of Xerókambos, as rather selfishly I like the village the way it is. Before we left, we found refreshments at a local taverna (which also has rooms and a small apartment to rent) called Liviko View where we were welcomed by a friendly couple. They provided some delightful fresh vegetables in the form of *briam* – ratatouille for want of a better description – and the sweetest orange juice I have every downed. It was one of those days that I never wish to forget and, as it turned out, we stayed in this village several times in the years that followed. As a result, we have now discovered all the sandy beaches on offer. A walk along the coast to the south with its tiny fishing inlet and the odd goat amongst the scrub have confirmed this feeling of isolation and peace. As a result Xerókambos will always remain close to my heart.

Xerókambos coastline on a windy day

Just as at Liviko View, we continued to be passionate about the food we found in the local tavernas. Once again, we spent a dreamy evening at the Hióna fish taverna by the sea; Manoli and Rula resumed their jovial banter in Palékastro, and one day after a short excursion we had a snack lunch there. Manoli decided that it was our breakfast and added: "Good idea!" The most wonderful local feta from Sitía baked in the oven with peppers and herbs arrived with a tomato salad and fresh bread. Whether it was lunch or breakfast it had definitely been a 'good idea'.

My Wife Suggested Crete

The other culinary discovery of the week was in the village of Angathiá where we tried the Vaios taverna (now called Elia), run by Yianni and Stephania. Jennie had by now abandoned any thoughts that she would be poisoned by wheat or gluten on this island and embraced their entire menu. In this Cretan taverna, guests are invited into the kitchen to look at the daily specials. Here the choice was extensive and it was difficult not to order too much. It was the inclusion of herbs and unusual spices and cheese which made all the dishes so appealing. Needless to say, we spent our last two evenings at Vaios and each night we left in raptures about the food.

It was sad leaving this corner of the world as we said goodbye to Evangelia who had again looked after the apartment during our stay. Back at home a far greater sadness engulfed me at the end of the month when two dear friends of mine, who I have known since the age of ten, told me that their mother had passed away. She had been a great friend of my own mother, and when my father died, I believe their friendship grew even closer. After my mum's death, Joyce – as this was her name – had made a point of keeping in touch with me by regular phone calls and occasional happy get-togethers. We often discussed Crete as she had stayed with her

The whitewashed chapel at Xerókambos

The Autumn of 2014

husband and two friends on the edge of Áyios Nikólaos many years before. I remember telling her that when Jennie and I walked by one day, her hotel looked as though it was still thriving.

The sea daffodils at Xerókambos would, I know, have given my mother great pleasure had she seen them. She had spent many hours in happy and industrious flower arranging and had always appreciated the natural beauty of the flowers that she displayed. These two friends both had great faith in their god, and I like to think that Joyce would have appreciated the little blue-roofed chapel on the ridge. Whenever we visit Xerókambos now my eyes are always drawn to the chapel, and my memories drawn to two friends who could spend the happiest of hours in a kitchen together, producing a multitude of tasty casseroles and puddings while constantly giggling and laughing at goodness knows what.

The magnetic attraction of the island pulled us back once more in the autumn of 2014, helped in no small way by a constant barrage of encouragement from our newly-found German friends, Yianni and Eleni, who had decided that we ought to rent one of the two villas owned by a friend of theirs called Lena. Her brochure looked appealing, with the properties tucked away behind the main Réthymno-Spíli road near our friends at Mixórrouma. The additional attraction was that Lena – a charismatic young housewife who somehow managed to juggle her various roles of looking after home and family, running a café in Spíli, helping her husband with their olive groves and managing the two villas – was offering us one of these villas for half of her normal summer letting price. So, we booked it.

The vagaries of modern air travel led to a two-hour delay, not this time because of the weather nor because of striking air traffic controllers; the problem, it appeared, was that pilot and crew were arguing with the easyJet Gatwick authorities as to which plane they were going to use. The first choice had apparently lost its hydraulics. I now firmly believe that the only chance of knowing if your flight is likely to be as scheduled is to wait until the flying machine is charging down the runway before it rises up into the sky. All too often I have seen the cabin crew 'arm' the doors for take-off, only for the pilot to come on air with the good news and the bad news.

On this particular day, November 8th, having been told that the weather in Crete was "interesting," the pilot was pleased to announce later in the flight that the thunderstorms had cleared away. On a sunny afternoon when we eventually hit the Irákilo tarmac, I voiced my usual 'Welcome to Crete' to Jennie, and we picked up the car from an extremely patient Club Cars rep. Even though easyJet had delayed him and his family from their Saturday lunch out, I hoped that is wasn't a particularly important family occasion, as they all seemed dressed up for a party. I thought it wise not to enquire.

A car journey from Iráklio to Spíli (Lena's villa) in Réthymno province actually takes no more than an hour and a half, so we still had some time on our hands. It was a fresh autumnal day and we took a detour inland by way of another important Minoan site: Týlissos. Unfortunately the gates were locked and it was obvious that further excavations were taking place. We waved at a young woman who we soon discovered was in charge of the research and she kindly walked over and let us in. Yet another example of Cretan goodwill had come our way and Týlissos was declared to be one of Jennie's favourites as I found difficulty in getting her back to the car. From here the road – with plenty of twists and turns which were not greeted with quite so much enthusiasm by my wife – travelled through delightful hilly countryside and near the village of Axós we stopped to watch a big bird of prey as it prowled the skies above us.

2014 was a year in which my collection of books about the island had happily grown in number including an excellent reference book, *Cretan Birds of Prey*. Armed with this and a pair of binoculars we might have had a better chance of identifying our sighting over Axós, but above all my modest Cretan library now began to include books about the island's occupation by Germany in WWII. From Axós we drove to the small town of Anóyia, which had a reputation as a centre of resistance to occupation and was known for its help to the British. It had been, as a result, completely destroyed by the Nazis so all the houses of the 2014 version of the town were made of modern concrete. It was, I suppose, ironic that we were about to spend some carefree days with our German friends in Mixórrouma. They are of my generation and are well aware of Hitler and his henchmen and do not wish to be associated with the evil that happened in the 1940s. As they had chosen to live in this part of the island associated so closely with resistance I doubt they could otherwise have lived a happy life in Crete.

We moved on to rendezvous with Lena at her villa. It turned out to be an attractive modern house and I believe everything – including the washing machine – could be ticked off on Jennie's holiday success list. What's more the bed was so comfortable that our recent mattress topper purchase proved, at least for this week, to be redundant! The swimming pool which separated the two villas had been emptied for the winter, but I hoped that the summer occupants of these two villas were happy with their close proximity and got along together as I contemplated the words of an American visitor: "Cretans live close-packed, and they have no concept of privacy;" (DMD)

By November most tourists have left the island, seasonal tavernas have closed and the islanders prepare to gather in their olives. The temperature at night falls sharply, especially in these inland hilly areas, so local cats welcomed the warmth of the wood burning stove in a taverna in Spíli where we took our evening meal. These November days, which were mostly fine and dry although with an occasional rain shower, seemed to evaporate in a flash. On reflection we spent half the time with our friends. They were still hopeful that we would buy a house nearby and although we had previously ruled out Agamemnon's 'goat house', their friend Manoli was keen to show us a house for sale in the nearby Assiderato hills.

We followed his 4x4 pick-up through open countryside and tiny villages which looked out across the Libyan Sea, far from the tourist trail, eventually arriving at the house in the isolated hamlet of Ayía Paraskeví. I hope we made all the right noises and we thanked Manoli and the owner, but there wasn't going to be a sale. Perhaps if we had discovered the island many years before, the thought of buying a little place here might have materialised, but on this particular subject our heads still ruled our hearts. Later that day Yianni cooked a barbecue supper which we consumed indoors with the help of Anka and Pontikos, two delightful four-legged friends. While feasting on his efforts, Yianni suggested a visit to Réthymno on market day.

The third of Crete's major cities, all of which are located along the north coast, Réthymno is often viewed as the cultural centre of the island by those who live here, but anything from shower mats to freshly picked aubergines were on sale in the bustling street market. Having purchased some honey, we wandered past old Turkish houses and mosques, as well as the Rimondi fountain, constructed in the 16th century. We were taken to a modern *estiatorio* (restaurant) popular with locals, old and young alike, and the food was just as good here as anywhere in Crete.

A great Venetian fortress – Fortezza – stands proudly above the city although there is more to see *from* it than *in* it. Réthymno's small archaeological museum nearby was left for another day, but the character of the city had made an impression on us. It didn't feel as big as a city, more as an easy-going provincial town, still with plenty of history to view together with a pleasant promenade on which to stroll along by the seashore.

Having walked along the north coast in Réthymno we were treated the following day to the south coast at Plakiás, which for Yianni and Eleni is their local seaside town. To get there the road took us through the dramatic Kourtaliótiko gorge, one of the many jaw-dropping ravines which are such great features of the island's landscape. Plakiás is a lively resort in summer, unusually attracting British tourists who otherwise tend to congregate in the package-holiday resorts of the north coast. It has a good beach, but there are better, less crowded ones within easy reach if you have transport or you like a good hike. Perched high above the town, the village houses of Mýrthios have spectacular views of the coastline and the naturally-curving bay of Plakiás.

Back in town we had lunch in a little eatery on the promenade much frequented by locals using it as a take-away, which boded well as our choices were served to us by the smiling Georgia. Her cheese pies with thyme honey would, I am certain, have led to the extraordinary facial expressions and unintelligible grunts of delight which the presenters of television's *Masterchef* produce from time to time. Thankfully their culinary orgasms were not about to spoil our moments of undiluted pleasure, and Jennie had no problem forcing me back here before the week was over.

We didn't spend all our time with Yianni and Eleni, after all they had their daily routines to attend to. Moreover, because this area is steeped in 1940s history relating to the resistance to Nazi occupation, I wanted to acquaint myself with some of the places which I had by now read about. It made sense to explore these on our own.

The Amari valley, a drive of about twenty minutes from our base, is a verdant area known for its fruit growing, especially cherries, pears and figs, and even in the drizzle of a November day its natural beauty was obvious, overshadowed as it is by the tallest mountain of the island: Psiloritis or Mount Ida. It is not without its ancient history and we hiked up to the acropolis of Sibritos (or Sývritos) founded in 1200 BC. You can see the shell of later Greek and Roman ruins, and even as the mist swirled about, the views down the valley were magnificent.

There is more ancient history to be found in the Amari, and we located two more remarkable Minoan sites, firstly near the village of Monastiráki and secondly near Apodoúlou which lies further down the eastern valley road. However, it is this valley's more recent history that reveals a rather chilling series of events. It was in the dark years of the 1940s when the inhabitants of these villages looked after stragglers from the battle of Crete and then provided shelter, food and friendship to the British secret agents and their companions in the four years of occupation that followed. No wonder the wartime code name for the Amari was Lotus Land. For assisting the allies these brave people of the Amari were rewarded by the systematic destruction of their villages and murder of their menfolk by the Nazis.

We had no time to drive down the road that connects the villages of the western Amari, but one day I hope to see the memorials. Each village has its own, dated one day apart from the next, reflecting the path of destruction that occurred. Nevertheless we did have time to stop in one such village, Thrónos, at the head of the valley and visited the church of the Panayía, outside of which are the remains of a decorative mosaic floor of the much larger original church. The RGC had informed me that if you take an interest in the church, someone will soon come along with the key. And so it was.

A little old lady appeared with an enormous key, let us in and promptly sat down. As we were admiring the ancient frescoes and icons, the woman suddenly asked in perfect English: "Are you German?" I have read stories of visitors being asked this question in the 1980s when many Cretans were still of an age to be able to remember the atrocities which took place here. In 2014, to hear the same question being asked of us came as quite a shock. Fortunately, we had both learned the Greek: "Ochi, emasti apo teen Anglia," (no we come from England) and having managed to splutter out these words the old lady broke into a broad and fairly toothless smile which was followed by an invitation to drink coffee with her next door. The horrors of Nazi destruction still appeared a sensitive issue in the Amari and this old woman may well have witnessed the atrocities when she was herself a child.

Mercifully, these days the Amari valley's natural beauty is the overriding theme and if you are fit enough there are organised walks up to the peak of Mount Ida. Here I cannot refrain from mentioning again Thomas Abel Brimage Spratt. What a wonderful name he had! In the 1850s, "on the last day of May, I found myself standing upon the summit of the Cretan Ida." He described his emotions at that moment: "Enthusiasm is however, hardly the appropriate term for one's feelings on such an occasion; for it was mixed with awe, with admiration, or with gratitude as the eye first reposes on the plunging descent beneath, upon the vast expanse and beautiful scene around, or reflectively peers into the ethereal space above." He was captivated by the hazy light of the setting sun: "and I sat watching its play of pink, purple and golden hues, tinting the mountain-tops." (TABS)

However, Captain Spratt made the mistake of camping on the mountain with insufficient protection and became dangerously cold overnight. Nowadays it is a far more organised affair and shelters are available should the weather suddenly turn. Guided ascents are available

My Wife Suggested Crete

Viewed from Monastiráki archaeological site, the summit of Mount Ida is lost in the clouds

from Thrónos, although they mostly begin from the Nídha plateau from where Spratt started his trek. I understand that on a crisp, clear morning as the sun rises, the views to east and west are quite staggering.

The monastery of St John the Theologian at Préveli perched on cliffs high above the sea near Plakiás is one of the best-known of the many monasteries of Crete. To get here, you pass an even older monastic version which was abandoned by the monks as being too dangerous – it was torched by the Turks in the 19th century. However, the Turks failed to destroy the newer version, known as Moní Préveli. The monastic buildings sit amidst cypress and palm trees, peacocks mingle with chickens and sheep in the grounds below. Only some of the old monks' living quarters hint at the history of the monastery, which has many seasonal visitors. We were virtually alone on this November day and guided tours were only available from two resident cats. One of these had more interesting plans as it jumped up and away over a wall.

Less than a kilometre before you reach Moní Préveli, as the road climbs up to run along the cliff edge, stands a prominent memorial

The Autumn of 2014

The monks' quarters at Moní Préveli

called the Shrine of Peace and Remembrance. The statues of an allied soldier with rifle, and a Cretan abbot also with rifle stand defiantly on either side of the memorial stone, honouring those Greeks, British, Australians and New Zealanders who lost their lives in 1941. Even the most hardened of you will be visually impressed and moved by what you see here.

The heroic abbot and his monks had fed and sheltered many allied soldiers as they waited to be evacuated by submarine from a nearby beach and in doing so they had faced great dangers from German patrols intent on wiping out anyone opposing them. Inscriptions on the memorial plaques in Greek and English within the grounds of the monastery tell the story. One Australian soldier was so moved by the experience, wanting to pay tribute to the abbot, monks and local villagers who had befriended him in 1941, that he made extraordinary efforts to get these memorial plaques put in place; he also donated funds for a water fountain and played a large part in the construction of the shrine nearby. His name was Geoff Edwards and he came from Western Australia.

My Wife Suggested Crete

The Shrine of Peace and Remembrance near Moní Préveli, the Paximadia islands behind

After the war, Edwards built a successful holiday business in an isolated coastal area near Margaret River, south of Perth, naming it Prevelly. Such was his passion that he also managed to build a chapel nearby, which was consecrated and blessed by the Greek Orthodox Archbishop of Australia in 1979. A photograph of the chapel sent to us in 2020 by a former work colleague of Jennie, who has emigrated with her young family to Western Australia, confirms that the chapel still stands proudly amongst the Australian scrub. It is called the Chapel of St John the Theologian at Prevelly. Geoff Edwards passed away on the 11th of April 2000, having never forgotten what the Cretans had done for him: "and what true friends they had proved to be." (GE)

On our way back we drove briefly out to the headland from where you can look down on Palm Beach, a small strand of fine sand which is crowded with tourists in summer. In 1941 it was called Limni beach and it was from here that Geoff Edwards and his colleagues were rescued by submarine and taken back to Egypt.

The Autumn of 2014

Limni beach, now known as Palm beach

On our final day of this eventful week we drove west through Mýrthios, Selliá and as far as Rodhákino. It was a scenic route to follow and we stopped from time to time to enjoy the panoramic views, east and west along the coast and out to sea towards the island of Gávdhos, a hazy silhouette on the horizon. Another Australian called Lew Lind had walked this way in August 1941 with his Cretan protectors. "I looked down upon a beautiful village glistening in the moonlight – a village like no other that I had yet seen." (LL) This was the village of Selliá, where "Kindness, you might say, peeped from every corner." (LL) I have a particular soft spot for Selliá, and not merely because it has a fantastically good restaurant.

The narrow alleyways which connect the village square to the church appear little changed from the way they would have been seventy-five years ago and, as it happens, I made some important decisions here about work and retirement. More research in the locational astrology department will no doubt provide the real reasons but the wind (and it can blow up here) certainly clears my mind while the unrestricted views and warm welcome no doubt help my decision-making process. From here these easterly views extend along a great length of the southern coastline. They are halted merely by the limitations of the human eye as the curve of the horizon eventually closes the curtain. I always look forward to revisiting Selliá and when Lind left the village "…there was a lot of weeping when I said goodbye, and truth to tell, I was not far from tears myself." (LL)

View towards Plakías from the roadside near Selliá

Before we knew it, it was time to put suitcases back in the car and tidy up Lena's villa. From the kitchen window we looked up to the straggling village of Frati, where Lind and twenty other fugitives were looked after prior to their evacuation from Palm Beach. I really shouldn't have moaned about the two-hour delay at Gatwick at the beginning of the week; it pales into utter insignificance compared to the experiences of Lind and his colleagues and, as I noted in my diary, we had a good journey back to England on November 15th.

~ ~ ~ ~

My mum's brother, Uncle Frank, had been sent to North Africa with the 1st Air Landing Light Regiment at about the same time as Lind was being evacuated from Crete. Frank had several lucky escapes during the war,

The Autumn of 2014

which included surviving the slaughter at Arnhem in Holland. After the war, his working life took him all over the world with agricultural machinery companies, including one by the name of 'Rotary Hoes' (later called 'Howard Rotavator'). He and his wife had always been kind to me, and it was with great sadness that, a month after we returned from Crete, my dear cousins told me that he had passed away. The 29th of December turned out to be a bright, crisp winter's day as Jennie and I drove over the South Downs from Petworth to Chichester where his service was held. Over the car radio came the sounds of Elgar's *Nimrod* from his *Enigma Variations*, my mum's favourite piece of music, and I knew that her soul was nearby; she and Frank had been close siblings throughout their lives.

In his later life Frank had developed the concept of a mower that, almost at the touch of a button, could convert from a rotary to a cylinder operation and was able to 'turn on a sixpence'. It would have been an ideal machine to manicure the grass at the Soúdha Bay Allied War Cemetery near Haniá. In spite of his worldwide travels, Frank never came to Crete but I like to think that he would have chuckled at seeing my favourite Cretan mode of transport, in whatever state of rusty disrepair, still smoking and rumbling slowly along the island's roads – the converted rotavator.

The autumn of 2014 had indeed, for me, been bittersweet.

Chapter Six

Iráklio - A City worthy of more than a one-night stopover

"I hope for nothing. I fear nothing. I am free"
NIKOS KAZANTZÁKIS.

Heraclium in Roman times, El Khandak to the Saracens, Candia to the Venetians, even Henry VIII of England knew the importance of this city. However, the importance that our famous king attached to Candia was thanks to the sweet Malmsey wine that he particularly liked, as this was produced in the Malevisi district a few kilometres south-west of the city. Hence a British consul was appointed to arrange shipment of large quantities of this strong wine back to England.

Today, in the transliteration process, the city is often called Heraklion by the outside world, but if you look at the Greek spelling, it is Iráklio which bears the closest resemblance to the Greek pronunciation, so I will stick with that. Whichever way you pronounce it or spell it, the present-day capital of Crete has a lot more to offer than most of us realise as we charge off to our holiday destination, even if we have managed to pay a fleeting visit to this bustling city.

Iráklio is a city – now the fifth largest in Greece – which continues to expand. It does so, naturally enough I suppose, with the dust and grime and traffic noise and fumes which always accompany expansion in the current age. If you stay in the city, an additional irritation may well emanate from aircraft noise as flights tend to include an appearance over the harbour area, most commonly when they are leaving the island. The palace of Knossós which lies just outside the city limits has become the customary reason for tourists to pause here, and we too had managed to avoid the city itself on our own rather turbulent visit to this great Minoan palace.

Irâklio

However, for several years we had been keeping an eye on the progress of a brand new archaeological museum which had been due to open in Irâklio. It was now fully open for business. Fascinated by the island's ancient history, as our visits to many of the ruined palaces and settlements can confirm, we were keen to see exactly what physical wonders had been unearthed and which were now on display. To achieve this, we stayed for two nights at the Galaxy Hotel in Democracy Street, negotiating a 15-minute journey from the airport with surprising ease. While registering at the reception desk, a concierge relieved me of my car keys and promptly drove off in my car into a dark side street somewhere, having assured me that there was nothing to worry about. Once again, my growing faith in Cretan kindness to visitors led me to believe that the car would turn up again when I needed it.

Car or no car, we soon discovered that the best way by which to explore the city is to walk. The urban sprawl of Democracy Street provided little to exclaim or rejoice about, but as we made our way towards the Archaeological Museum, parks and *platía* began to appear along with statues of heroic Cretan leaders of the past, notably of Eleftherios Venizélos, the man who led the struggle for Crete's union with Greece. We also caught our first glimpse of the vast Venetian city walls, the sea and the working port. After about 20 minutes we arrived at this city's star attraction – the museum itself – containing an incredible collection of art and all kinds of decorative and functional objects from Minoan culture, unearthed from the many archaeological sites on Crete. Again I emphasise that I am not a 'museumaholic' in any way, and yet I had already enjoyed our short visits to the museums at Áyios Nikólaos, Sitía, and Ierápetra. The one we entered in Irâklio was nothing short of spectacular. It is the only archaeological museum I have felt the need to visit more than once, but beware: the opening of this museum has not gone unnoticed, and I strongly suggest visiting early or late in the day to avoid the inevitable crowds.

Such wonders as the Festos disc with its strange hieroglyphics, a stone bull's head rhyton, another made from rock crystal, the ring of Minos, gold signet rings, and other intricate jewellery including the famous Maliá bee pendant, form just a minute fraction of what is on display. I have no doubt that if you miss the crowds you will come away breathless and awe-inspired.

Jennie is now the proud owner of a replica of the Maliá bee pendant. Hers was skilfully crafted on the island approximately 3,800 years after the original version. Two bees are depositing droplets of honey into their honeycomb in this artistic masterpiece.

My Wife Suggested Crete

Jennie's replica of the Maliá bee pendant

Afterwards, in celebration of all that we had seen, we headed the short distance into Korai Street to find a recommended taverna in time for Sunday lunch. The Peri Orexeos taverna opens daily at 1pm, which was precisely the time we arrived and consequently we were able to nab a table by the window. The food was as pleasant as the welcome and was topped up at the end by a chocolate mousse together with a prodigious and generous quantity of good *raki* on the house. Sunday lunches are Cretan affairs which we now know can last for hours, so there was absolutely no attempt to hurry us. Only after a while did we wander off, purchasing a large chunk of *baklava* en route to the Galaxy – the hotel rather than the Milky Way – for our evening's entertainment.

The Galaxy Hotel had proved a good choice and the bed was extremely comfortable so that our mattress topper again remained in the suitcase. This was not a hotel completely given over to tourists; business people used it too, and conference facilities were available, so the wide choice of breakfast foods included a good assortment of traditional Greek and Cretan dishes which we enjoyed. As we departed, the concierge found our car which still looked in reasonable condition and had apparently not suffered from its banishment to the side street.

Since this brief sojourn, we have become more familiar with the sights and sounds of Iráklio. The city deserves its fame courtesy of Knossós and that magical archaeological museum, but there is a great deal more to savour if you have the time. Having discovered that we could reach our chosen hotel no more than 15 minutes after leaving Iráklio's airport, we now often take the opportunity to relax in comfort as the rigours of a day's air transport from the UK take their toll on our ageing bodies.

Wherever you choose to stay, a warm welcome will greet you and you will be naturally drawn to the seafront. The inner harbour is home to Iráklio's fishing fleet, where Jennie and I have spent happy, idle moments, not only watching and listening to the fishermen, but also translating the Greek letters which form the names of their boats. Simple things please simple minds!

A few pleasure boats are moored to the floating jetties close by and fishing trips are advertised here and there, but instantly you will be aware of the enormous Venetian Arsenali, a series of dry-docks with vaulted roofs which line the modern road, as well as the Venetian fortress which stands guard on the harbour wall. This is called by its Turkish name: Koúles.

If you like, you can let your imagination rip, picturing the hive of activity and noise emanating from this substantial 15th century Venetian dockyard, or perhaps ponder the grim times of the Turkish war when the fortress was besieged for 20-odd years before the city fell to the Turks. Mainly promoted by the Catholic Church and often involving French and German troops, several attempts to stave off the final conquest of Crete by the Turks came to nothing. One of the last of these, in June 1668, involved a French force of 6,000 men. Among the French commanders was the Duke of Beaufort who died near the Koúles together with 500 of his men. The Duke of Beaufort Street (Dhoukos Bofor) which commemorates his name, may well be the street you choose to take from the Archaeological Museum as you walk down towards the inner harbour and the Koúles.

Once your eyes have focused on these buildings long enough they will probably be drawn, in complete contrast, to the modern ferry dock which is close by. These monsters frequently leave in the evening, once all the cars and lorries and passengers have been safely boarded, and we have often watched their lights disappear over the horizon as they make their way overnight to Athens's port of Pireás, sometimes by way of other Greek islands.

My Wife Suggested Crete

The inner harbour of Iráklio, the Koúles, and one of the Venetian Arsenali

There is a wide, pedestrianised street leading uphill from the sea: the 25th of August Martyrs Street. I had delved into my copy of the RGC to try to discover the origin of this name.

The 1890s continued the turbulent decades that had already afflicted the island. Although the Turks had been clinging onto sovereignty, the 'protecting powers' of Britain, Italy, Russia and France were attempting to keep rebellions at bay. Increasing violence between the Cretan Muslim and Cretan Christian populations had intensified as a Greek force under the command of a Colonel Vassos landed in the west.

Military and political decisions by the 'protectors' were often ill-judged. Eventually, on the 25th August 1898 in Iráklio, Muslims vented their rage. Over 800 people were killed, most of whom were Cretan Christians, when fighting, looting and burning erupted.

Importantly, from a historical point of view, 17 British servicemen had been killed. 17 Turkish Cretans were then sentenced to death by the British. A further 2 met a similar fate, courtesy of an Italian tribunal.

This violence prompted 'the protectors', especially the British, to demand and then to supervise the departure of all remaining Turkish Ottoman forces. November 1898 marked the end of Turkish rule in Crete.

Iráklio

The blood-soaked day of the 25th August had led to this dramatic turning point in Cretan history.

These days the street is lined with tourist shops, banks, travel and car hire agencies, and as we strolled uphill I noticed an austere-looking building proudly proclaiming the headquarters of Minoan Lines, one of the chief operators of those big ferries. Walking on uphill the mood gradually softens as the Venetian city hall comes into view with its fine loggia or gallery.

Just before we reached the city hall, a square beckoned us towards the Church of Áyios Títos. The symmetry of the Venetian architecture was pleasing enough, and two mature palm trees, either side of the entrance door, added to this organised splendour. Any evidence that the building had once been converted to a mosque by the Turks had long since disappeared. Included in the 'contents' of the church is the skull of St Títos, the first Bishop of Crete who was appointed by none other than St Paul. We glanced at him briefly – it wasn't that gruesome!

We then passed the picturesque church and one-time cathedral of San Marco, as the street widened a little more. At the top it merged with the great square: Platía Venizélou, complete with one of the city's notable Venetian fountains – the Morosini fountain with its guardian lions. Hence another name for the Platía is Lion Square. This place has become a focal point for us for several reasons. For me at least it represents the heart of the city, ringed as it is by lively tavernas and cafés and many of the main shopping streets lead off from here. This fact, although Jennie's knowledge of geography is not renowned, is now well-established in her mind. I have to admit, having been forced into various fashion outlets in Hándhakos street, Dhikeosinis street and Dedhálou street that the vibrant colours and styles are far more interesting than anything I usually glimpse in an English high street. The vibrant colours come with interesting aromas, too, when you venture into the bustling 1866 Street which is the market. Side streets can also be fun. Good Lord! I sound as if I actually enjoy shopping! We found some rope to repair a damaged suitcase and I spotted a wonderful array of kitchen sink plughole strainers in a hardware shop nearby. They came in all shapes and sizes; some had useful little handle knobs incorporated in the design and I chose three to take home. I suppose some recently consumed *raki* had overcome my logic.

Above all else, Lion Square is synonymous with a great Iráklio culinary tradition: *bougátsa*. I don't believe that there is a good enough way to describe this creamy filo pastry pie which is sometimes mixed with *mizithra* cheese and honey, sometimes just with cream, and sprinkled with sugar and cinnamon. We always wash it down with hot chocolate as we sit outside on the terrace of one of several cafés which dedicate themselves to serving this wonderful stuff, and watch the world go by.

Once you have got your bearings, and I think Lion Square is probably where this will happen, many more of the city's treasures will open up for you. There are, for starters, three other Venetian and Turkish fountains to investigate. I particularly enjoyed the Priouli fountain, built at the very end of the Venetian period – but you will need a map and a little patience to find it. Not to be outdone by the fountains, there are a further four museums in the city – leaving aside the great archaeological one – which all deserve a visit; and yes, the words are written by someone who normally enters these places with a sense of foreboding, if not dread, that another hour of life will be snatched away for no good reason.

The Natural History Museum is ingeniously housed in a converted power plant situated along the seaside promenade. Although geared towards the younger generation with an earthquake simulator and enormous dinosaur replicas, there is plenty to learn about Crete's flora and fauna and geology as well as environmental issues which are being taken more seriously these days.

By now we had realised the importance of churches, chapels and monasteries and their attendant priests, abbots and monks in the life of Crete. Wherever you go on the island you are rarely far away from some religious building however small it may be, the smallest being the roadside shrine which appears frequently amongst the general scenery. In the square of Ayías Ekaterínis, again only a short walk from Lion Square (in case another helping of *bougátsa* is required) stand another three including the cathedral of Áyios Mínas and its forerunner, the medieval version.

We happened to find ourselves here on the day when all the island's wonderful herbs were being blessed. Wow – what smells! Here too is the fabulous museum of Ayiá Ekateríni, dedicated to the Cretan School of Icon Painting, and originally part of the monastery of St. Catherine. Within the monastery there had been a monastic school where the study of Byzantine art and Venetian Renaissance art produced famous painters among the many pupils. The museum contains work by Dhamaskínos amongst others. Here too is a depiction of St Minas painted by George Kastrofylakas as late as 1738. So, when you find that church or chapel out in the wilds of Crete which appeals to you most, and when you see the icon paintings on the screen which separates the inner sanctuary from the nave, you will perhaps be drawn to examine them more closely if you have visited the Ayiá Ekateríni Museum.

Iráklio

For work by the most famous of Cretan painters – El Greco – you have to look elsewhere. Toledo springs to mind, as this was where El Greco (real name: Domenicos Theotokopolous and therefore unpronounceable after a few *rakis*) chose to live and work in Spain. The residents of the Cretan village of Fódhele, which can be found a few kilometres west of Iráklio claim that he was born there, but scholars apparently suggest Iráklio was his birthplace.

Down by the sea within the Historical Museum of Crete you can learn about all things historical from the time where the Archaeological Museum calls it a day. Included in the contents of this museum are the only two works by El Greco to be found in Crete. These were painted in 1567 and 1570. The museum highlights the Battle of Crete and the Resistance in WWII, and before this the Byzantine, Venetian and Turkish periods are also covered. The museum's curator, Constantinos Mamalakis, is a delightful man who I have been most fortunate to meet. Because this place has fascinated me, Jennie and I have often popped in for a chat with some of the staff. I understand from Jennie that the pomegranate juice available in the first-floor café is also "to die for!" This or other refreshments, can be enjoyed in the small rear garden, where surprise surprise, stands another fountain, this time the fountain of Idomeneus.

It would be remiss of me not to mention one more museum: the Museum of Ancient Greek Technology, housed in another Venetian building – the Palazzo d'Ittar – which opened to the public in the summer of 2019. Well-displayed with English descriptions and with demonstrations provided by the pleasant young lady who welcomed us, here we learned about the extraordinary inventions of the ancient Greeks – covering the period from 2000 BC until the end of the ancient Greek world. This really is a museum for all ages and without giving anything away, I can assure you it will raise a smile or two. Pistons and cylinders, gears, sprockets and roller chains, pulleys and belts, programmers, auto-pilots and hydraulics were invented rather earlier than you might have realised. It all very much appealed to my rather cynical views of 'modern' scientific discoveries and technological inventions.

To escape from the museums, churches and fountains, markets and shopping, and providing you have your own transport, there is plenty to amuse you if you decide to use Iráklio as a base. We introduced ourselves to one of the spectacular caves on the island – the Skotinó cave – which can be found in open countryside south of the inland village of Goúves. We enjoyed the eerie depths alone, and there is enough natural light to see most of it, but bring a torch if you are a real caveman. As with all the big caves on the island, this one comes with plenty of history, and has been considered a sacred place for millennia. These days Christian worship takes place at the chapel of Ayiá Paraskeví just above the cave.

If caves are not your thing, how about wine-making? This is a subject which intrigues me as a long-lost member of the hotel and catering community. Further archaeological sites less well known and less visited than Knossós can be found in the countryside south of Iráklio, including the remains of a large Minoan villa at Vathýpetro complete with its ancient winepress. Viniculture, therefore, has been practiced on the island for thousands of years and these days there are four French-style *appellation contrôlée* wine regions, two of which – Pezá and Arhánes – are located in the countryside south of the city. Cretan wine production is developing rapidly, with many small producers making sophisticated quality wines. Advice from the RGC led us to Stilianoú winery in the Pezá district, where father and son Stilianoú gave us a warm welcome, a guided tour and a tasting session. I have much to learn about this particular Cretan art, and although the names of the various traditional Cretan grape varieties are beginning to sink into my remaining brain cells, there is no doubt that I need to sample more Cretan wine to develop my knowledge – a tough job but someone's got to do it.

The Stilianoú vineyards at Kounavi in the Pezá district with views of the Dhíkti Mountains

Iráklio

To mark my 65th birthday, we treated ourselves to three nights in a luxurious hotel overlooking the Venetian Arsenali, the Koulés, the harbour and the port of Iráklio. I must admit that the Megaron Hotel also overlooks one of the city's main bus stations, and is close to the flight path of those departing from the airport. Apart from this my long forgotten hotel and catering background led me to conclude that I could not fault this hotel, nor could I find anything about the conduct of the staff which I would want to change as they all worked to the highest standard. I had to award top marks to this place in each analysed category. For my 65th, the angels had really given me a treat.

The day itself began with a hearty breakfast before heading off towards another of this historic city's finest attractions: the great Venetian city walls, bastions and gates. It's worth seeking out one of these gates, which appear as roads tunnelled through the wall to a length of about forty metres, to appreciate the sheer enormity of the construction. Near New Gate we found steps which led up onto the wall and a path which led us west and then north-west through various mighty bastions towards the sea. From up here vast swathes of this sprawling boisterous city, which is perhaps unkempt but certainly not unloved, can be viewed and savoured.

**The Martinengo Bastion, part of the great city walls.
Snow lies on Mount Ida in early June**

My Wife Suggested Crete

However, on this particular day my goal – which might appear rather ghoulish to you but wasn't in the least – was to visit the graves of Nikos Kazantzákis, Crete's greatest literary genius, and that of his wife, on the Martinengo bastion. Just before we reached our destination, we met a middle-aged man who asked if we needed any help. He was surprised and delighted when Jennie attempted to talk in Greek, and seizing the moment I tried a few words myself. The outcome confirmed that the graves were close by and our new friend wished us well and held a clenched fist to his heart. My mind returned to Manoli's father at the Mythos taverna in Palékastro where I had first experienced this genuine gesture of warmth to the visitor.

Many people have, I am sure, encountered the film, *Zorba the Greek*, inspired by a book of the same name by Kazantzákis. To my mind, *Freedom or Death* is even more powerful and equally melodramatic. This Cretan writer was a deeply spiritual man but, because of his religious views, there was a falling-out between him and the Greek Orthodox Church. Kazantzákis might well have argued that the Church fell out with him, rather than vice-versa. There were consequences: he lost the 1957 Nobel Prize for literature to Albert Camus. Influential figures in the Church had apparently been determined to prevent him from winning.

Even in death, he was denied burial in a cemetery, and so it was on the Martinengo bastion that his body was laid to rest. The graves and the surrounding area are well maintained and a pleasant place to wander amongst the various trees, shrubs and flowers. It is quite obvious to me that the residents of Iráklio have a great respect for their literary hero and I understand many come up here at the weekend to do just that – to pay their respects. The other reason for weekend visits up here is rather different, as nearby is a stadium used by the Ergotelis football team. The floodlights provide a good marker to find this particular bastion.

My Cretan birthday party ended with a meal at our favourite taverna in this capital city: Ippokampos on the seafront promenade. We feel the food here is sublime, and in time we have got to know the owner and his family a little, even though thousands of locals and tourists pass through their door every year. Photographic evidence shows me with a big happy smile and an expression on my face which I like to think reflects the contentment that I feel whenever we visit the city.

It cannot claim to be the most picturesque of the Cretan cities; in this category no doubt Haniá would be the clear winner, and the town of Réthymno may well see itself as the cultural capital of the island with traditional lyra-making at its heart. However I sense from the bubbly and welcoming people of Iráklio that they are proud of their city in a laid-back kind of way, a state of mind which I believe may stem from the words of one of their greatest citizens, Nikos Kazantzákis; words which now adorn his simple grave high above the city: "I hope for nothing, I fear nothing, I am free."

The resting place of Nikos Kazantzákis

Chapter Seven

The Cretan Psyche - A Tentative Look

"Crete differs from the rest of the world at many points and critics who try to evaluate cause and effect there, especially in military matters, are soon astray."
PATRICK LEIGH FERMOR FROM *ABDUCTING A GENERAL* (PLF)

I doubt very much if any outsider ever knew the Cretan mind better than Patrick Leigh Fermor. He had after all lived amongst these people in the wild hills of their island during the period of Nazi occupation, he spoke the language and he had come to understand their traditions and customs. I guess that in the end nothing about the Cretan psyche surprised or fazed him. On the other hand, most of us will probably never fully understand the workings of the Cretan mind or soul. A look at the books of Nikos Kazantzákis will introduce you to fiery, larger-than-life characters such as Captain Michales in *Freedom or Death*. You may well encounter this fierceness, especially in the less easily reached parts of the island such as Sphakiá, but it is a trait of character that should not worry visitors. David MacNeil Doren accepted as a fact that: "Ferocity and generosity co-exist in the breasts of these bewildering and paradoxical people." (DMD)

You may feel that I ought to have placed this chapter at one end of my book, as part of an introduction to the island or as part of my concluding thoughts. At least by slotting it in here, an attempt to examine the nature of these people will provide relief from my storytelling, although I realise that Leigh Fermor's ample warning about being "soon astray" will no doubt come to pass. Therefore, I need to emphasise that the last thing I want to do is criticise a people of whom I have become so fond. On the contrary, as Richard Clark has pointed out: "What makes so many people return time and again to this enchanted isle is surely the people." (RC) It is also important for me to remember the wise words of my own mother who suggested to me once that it is best to concentrate on the good traits of people, rather than focus on their weaknesses.

~ ~ ~ ~

I once enjoyed a theatrical performance at the Criterion theatre in London by The Reduced Shakespeare Company. They claimed that they were going to perform the complete works of the great bard in 90 minutes. It was of course totally humorous mimicry with all of Shakespeare's classic comedies and tragedies represented briefly by one or two famous lines. The result was a breathtaking, side-splitting, exhausting, hilarious hour and a half which, naturally enough, caused the audience to produce a standing ovation. I am not about to attempt a potted history in the style of The Reduced Shakespeare Company, but I am sure they could have developed another suitable 90-minute show about the modern history of Greece. The last 200 years of Greek history has indeed been spectacular.

Greece had been under Turkish rule since 1460. In the 1820s came the war of independence, slaughter of the Muslim population, the rise of Greek Orthodox Christianity, the involvement of sympathetic philhellenes from across Europe including Lord Byron. The great powers at the time – Britain, France and Germany – imposed their will and created a monarchy. King Otto of Greece came from Bavaria, King George I came from Denmark. Expansionist wars, including the Balkan wars of 1912-13, were followed by civil war. A revolutionary government was formed, Greek troops entered WWI and then something called the *katastrofi* occurred, an expansionist disaster which, by 1922, had caused a massacre of Greeks and Armenians by the Turks. The history of Greece continued at pace: the formation of the KKE (the Greek Communist Party), the Metaxás dictatorship, WWII, civil war, the coup of the colonels, Cyprus, democracy, politics, corruption. Is there time to pause for breath? In 1981 Greece joined the EU and entered the Eurozone in 2001. By 2008 Greece's economic crisis – the debt crisis – and riots in Athens caught the attention of the media.

The scale of corruption which took place in this modern period of Greek history is well documented in a book by James Angelos: *The Full Catastrophe, Travels Among the New Greek Ruins*. In his book you will discover the words *fakelaki*, (small envelope) and *rouspheti*, (a special reciprocated favour which often involved a politician and a voter – exchanging votes for favours). You can read about Zakynthos which became known as 'the island of the blind' because benefit fraud was so rife here that a preliminary police investigation discovered that 498 out of

680 people who requested a blindness benefit did not qualify for it. I continued to read that in Greece as a whole, apparently about 40,000 pensions were shown to be fraudulent. You can also learn from Mr Angelos that: "Tax evasion in Greece was a national preoccupation." (JA) Most interesting of all, it appears that Greeks differentiate between the word 'nation' or 'ethnos', as they call it, which has a racial, tribal connotation, and 'the republic' or 'state'. "Scamming the state therefore, was not the same as scamming the nation." (JA)

The complexity of Greek politics is one thing. The complexity of the Greek people is another. Henry Miller, a controversial American author, summed up the Greeks as: "an enthusiastic, curious-minded, passionate people." He continued: "Not only passion but contradictoriness, confusion, chaos." (HM) In a book back in 1953, a passage within it could have been written about Greece in 2015: " …there is much about the country today that is directly akin to ancient Greece. No people has ever been more individualistic. Good, even great, leaders there have been, yet no country remains more difficult to govern. A village cut off from its neighbour by a shoulder of mountain or an arm of the sea will choose its politics largely from the urgent desire to be unlike the village nearest to it." (AMR)

There is, however, humour within the Greek psyche. Apparently a 19th-century novelist had concluded: "Every nation has its cross to bear: In England, for example, it's the weather. In Greece, it's the Greeks". (PS) Moreover, "Someone recently asked a clever political cartoonist whether the country has a future. Well, he said, we have a past. You can't ask for everything." (PS) In any case from an outsider's viewpoint, as Henry Miller found, "marvelous things happen to one in Greece – marvelous good things which can happen to one nowhere else on earth." (HM)

~ ~ ~ ~

Crete's eventual union with Greece was not achieved until 1913, even though a Cretan by the name of Eleftherios Venizélos had become premier of Greece in 1910. Crete, too, had been keen to break away from the yoke of Ottoman rule and find independence, before her union with Greece. A century later Crete, as part of Greece, was also sucked into the debt crisis and all the demands which the EU imposed.

Although union with Greece was undoubtedly welcomed by the vast majority of Cretans, the reality is that the islanders very much have their own separate identity. I don't see much evidence that this instinctive feeling is ever likely to disappear. In language this manifests itself in the distinctive Cretan dialect, with local variations such as in Sphakiá. Our friend, Kostas, has performed amateur dance and drama productions in Sitía. He thoroughly enjoyed the fact that visitors from Athens could not understand the Lasíthi dialect, which he used on stage. He thought it was a great joke.

Cretans differ in other ways. Apparently a study carried out in 2013 on the Lasíthi plateau concluded that DNA samples from Minoan skeletons had a great similarity to the DNA of modern-day inhabitants. However, as Oliver Rackham and Jennifer Moody have pointed out: "Cretans are descended, to varying degrees, from Albanians, Argives, Armenians, Bulgars, Dorians, Eteocretans, French, Germans, Hebrews, Minoans, Negroes, Pelasgians, Romans, Saracens, Serbs, Spaniards, Spartans, Tartars, Turks, Venetians and Vlachs." (OR & JM) This enormous list is not altogether surprising given the continuity of invasion and occupation, revolts, piracy, sieges and resistance which has dogged the island for centuries. It should also provide a clue as to the complexities of the Cretan character.

Remembering one of Simon Reeve's travel programmes which involved a visit to Crete, I watched him talk of the fiery and passionate people of the Mediterranean region, and the especially fiery and passionate people of Greece, and then again the even more fiery and passionate people of Crete.

This fire and passion is not restricted to the Cretan civilian – you need to include the clergy too. Monasteries and churches together with their abbots, monks and priests have always been heavily involved in resistance to occupation and persecution. Persecutions of Christians began in Roman times when 'the Holy Ten' were martyred at Górtys.

Centuries later in Venetian Crete, rebellions against the Venetian overlords were often due to the infliction of heavy taxation. At least for a while the new regime operated a system of government that was more authoritarian and violent than even the Turkish brand that followed.

Long before this, in the year AD754, jurisdiction of the Cretan Church had been transferred from Rome to Constantinople. As a result, when the Venetians took control of the island some 450 years later, the Cretan people had already begun to find their unique identity. Part of this was their belief in the Orthodox Eastern version of Christianity.

There was an inevitable clash between Roman Catholic Venetians and the Orthodox Cretans. Eventually, Venetian policy aiming to suppress the Orthodox version failed. With outside help, notably from the Patriarch of Alexandria, many monasteries were founded. By the time of the Turkish invasion, the Greek Orthodox Church had become a significant part of Cretan life.

It was under Turkish occupation when Islam became the official religion and when the Turks inflicted heavy taxation on those Christian Cretans who refused to convert that the abbots, monks and priests became totally absorbed in the Cretan struggle for freedom.

There were many uprisings which were bloodily suppressed by the Turks. An English adventurer who witnessed the continuing struggle in Crete in 1867 commented: "Cretan priests were expected to take their full share in the affairs of the people, some by conducting business which required head work, others by downright fighting, rifle in hand." (JEHS) One of the priests encountered by this English visitor went by the name of Father Zelaios. "When there was a battle, Zelaios was among the skirmishers, firing and shouting with the boldest of them. He prided himself on his well-cleaned rifle, and would help others to keep their weapons bright." (JEHS)

It is quite clear that the Greek Orthodox Church in the shape of those abbots, monks and priests played a huge part in the island's struggle for independence from Turkey and eventual union with Greece. There is however a rather sinister end to this part of the island's history: As a result of Greece's disastrous attempt to conquer Istanbul in 1922, the great powers forced a massive exchange of populations in the 1923 peace settlement. 30,000 Muslims had to leave Crete for Turkey. Almost 34,000 Christian refugees from Turkey arrived in Crete. It is hard to imagine this brutality or indeed the scale of this ethnic cleansing.

In the 1940s when the next invader arrived, the abbots, monks and priests continued in their now traditional role of supporting the people's resistance, this time to the Nazis. I have already mentioned the destruction of the small hill town of Anóyia in 1944. At that time the name of the priest of Anóyia was John Skoulas. He had assisted British secret agents for months and eventually the Germans became suspicious of him. He was therefore quietly evacuated to the Middle East, obtained special permission from the Orthodox Church to shave off both beard and the bun of hair at the nape of the neck, and undertook parachute training. Unsurprisingly his codename back in Crete changed from Friar Tuck to the Flying Parson or the Parachute Priest. Papa Skoulas took the British agent Sandy Rendel (codenamed Alexis) to see the destruction of his town and the mound of rubble that had been his home. "Well, Mr Alexis, I always said that one day I would welcome you to my house. As you see, there's not much left, but at least we can offer you a glass" (AMR) as he pulled out a bottle of *ouzo* from his coat pocket. They toasted freedom, victory and the honour of the house.

Some 71 years later it was the turn of Simon Reeve to be introduced to the priest of Anóyia who in 2015 was Papa Andreas. Papa Andreas combined his pastoral role with presidency of the local gun club, and so his religious attire was complemented by a pistol tucked into his belt. Reeve was shown the memorial to the townsfolk who were killed in 1944, and the Papa kissed the Greek flag nearby, proclaiming that anyone daring to desecrate the flag would meet a grisly end. He then took Reeve to the local firing-range for some target practice, before a cold night was spent up in the hills with the shepherds, priest and all. While eating and drinking *raki*, the pistols were fired again for a bit of fun. Reeve's traditional expletives – "Bloody 'ell" and "Flippin'eck'" – could be clearly heard.

This is still the way it is in Crete where priest and parishioner, and monk and shepherd live on an island where they understand and respect one another. They all know the history of their island and are proud of their past. The men of the church are not aloof from recognising the rigours of life in the hills and mountains while down in the towns and villages it will only be the likes of you or I who may be surprised to see the local Papa tucking into some tasty morsel in a taverna with local farmers while toasting freedom with a glass or two of *raki*.

~ ~ ~ ~

In the political world, Cretans have often enjoyed standing up to central government in Athens and it has also often been the case that Cretans buck the trend of voters in other parts of Greece when there is a general election. Nevertheless, as in other parts of Greece, corruption tends to rear its ugly head, although as a visitor you are unlikely to notice it. Having met a few expats who have made Crete their home, we have been made aware that large sums of money are sometimes unexpectedly needed to complete transactions such as land transfers, and the speed at which these transactions are completed is often linked to further requests for payment. The Greek word *fakelaki* is no doubt used in Crete too.

On a lighter note Cretans can discuss politics for hours on end, arguing loudly and vehemently without conclusion. Talk is a great island pastime and not limited to politics. For instance, I remember Jennie debating the subject of stray cats with a woman called Yiotta who looked after our rented apartment. Without offering a solution Yiotta raised herself to her full height, hands on hips, took a deep breath and declared with some urgency: "This is a problem!" Heated debates are definitely not limited to politics. Just about any subject can cause an intense conversation. Only in Crete have I engaged in earnest discussions with petrol-pump attendants.

This intense – and sometimes even ferocious – vitality and enthusiasm for talk is probably the cause of insinuations by other Greeks that Cretans are liars! I understand that ancient Cretans assured anyone who wanted to listen that Zeus was buried under Mount Yioúhtas near Iráklio. However, Zeus was a god and therefore immortal, prompting this adage by other Greeks that 'all Cretans are liars.' The reality is that Cretan enthusiasm often leads to exaggeration, not in a wilful way, but stemming from the intensity of their thoughts. If they say it loudly enough, they can convince themselves that they are most definitely speaking the truth.

This is not a new Cretan trait. In the 1940s Lieutenant Mike Cumberlege, Commander of one of the small motor launches used in clandestine operations, noted that some of the Cretans were given to: "highly coloured accounts of their experiences." (DP) Xan Fielding found that: "…their friendship has infected me with their own uninhibited enthusiasm and tendency to exaggerate." (XF) This picture is confirmed in Imogen Grundon's biography of John Pendlebury in which she describes how "Over time they began to believe the stories that they told, with a little more elaboration each time. Each storyteller would weave himself into places, company and events in which he originally had no part. It was the tradition of the island…" (IG) Our friend Kostas from whom we often rent an apartment told us with great gusto once that his cleaning lady worked at his apartments "every day from ten 'til five, yes every day." In reality, she used to come along on Wednesdays between twelve and two. It didn't really bother us.

The Cretan pace of life, especially away from the cities, is far removed from the frenetic pace in the UK and most of northern Europe. Ex-pats returning for a family visit have told me how horrified they have been at the frightening speed of vehicles on the roads of the UK. As one American long-term visitor to Crete put it: "Above all there was a sense of limitless time. Movements were leisurely; an invitation for a cup of coffee or a glass of *tsikoudia* could turn into an affair lasting several hours." (DMD)

We have had similar experiences. Once we were trying to locate some apartments which were particularly recommended in the RGC. Having eventually found them, we enquired of the owner if we could have a look, perhaps on Tuesday? "Of course," he said. So on that Tuesday we were shown several of his apartments and then we were invited to take a seat on his balcony. We nicknamed this elderly couple Mr and Mrs

The Cretan Psyche

Kploureménos (which was the name of the villa complex that they also owned) and Mrs K soon arrived with fresh orange juice and cakes. After half an hour's leisurely conversation helped by a Greek-English dictionary, Mr K gave us a tour of his land, his olive and fruit trees, pointing out the local landmarks, and as we strolled he picked some loquats for us to take away. I feel a little shamefaced that we never booked with them – we felt it was more suited to families – but I console myself that they were almost always full. It was for us, however, a most delightful hour spent in the company of Mr and Mrs K, when we were led to believe that time was of no importance whatsoever.

The Cretan aversion to authority is just as obvious as it is in other parts of Greece. The concept of freedom is always high on the list of Cretan priorities, understandably so considering those centuries of occupation which the island's people have had to endure. "Nobody, not even the Turk, has ever succeeded in reducing Crete to discipline and order." (OR & JM) You may well hear the word *eleftheria* (freedom) as an alternative toast to *yiámas* (cheers) in the tavernas. "Freedom is the only ideal that means anything to a Cretan, the only reality he will fight for." (DMD) Hence I think their aversion to authority, to being told what and what not to do, means that their rebellious nature shines through. Even though, for example, the Cretans realise that it is probably sensible to wear a crash helmet when riding a motorcycle or moped, the fact that their government has ordered them to do so is not something that they can easily accept. Consequently you will see many motorcyclists with no helmet, or motorcyclists with a helmet carried on an arm or strapped to a handlebar, or helmeted motorcyclists with helmet-less passengers sitting behind them. To cap it all (if you will pardon the pun), you may see helmet-less riders using their mobile phone with one hand and attempting to operate the motorbike with the other.

I fully understand the health and safety logic for the use of helmets, but I have to admit that I have a chuckle to myself when I see this law being broken; it appeals to my rather warped sense of humour. The Cretans, of course, will often make you smile when you encounter their wonderful sense of humour. Peter Trudgill, an Englishman particularly fond of the rugged Sphakian region, wrote about his wife Jean in conversation with their Sphakian friend Andreás: " 'We hear you've had snow!' Jean said to Andreás, after he had welcomed us. 'Ah yes', he replied with a grin. 'It was very bad – worse than Murmansk. It stayed on the ground for at least an hour!' ". (PT)

More recently, after a burst of the unwelcome south-easterly Sirókos wind, friends in Réthymno province told us that their neighbour had been complaining bitterly that although the former Libyan leader, Colonel Gaddafi, was dead, he was still managing to send across the sea to Crete "his bloody Saharan dust!" I am reminded, too, of a conversation with a young receptionist at the Historical museum in Iráklio. We had been having a serious chat about the horrors of WWII in Crete and some of the atrocities that the Germans had committed. I commented that it must have been a frightening time for the people. "And we are still afraid of them!" she replied as her facial expression changed to a broad and fearless smile.

Meanwhile, when talking to our friends, Manoli and Rula, in their taverna in Palékastro the conversation usually begins with questions about the family. Their teenage daughter was being a particular concern to Manoli who complained to us that there were too many teenage boys swarming around his daughter. "But," he said with a raised forefinger and a knowing smile: "I have gun." On another occasion while hiring a car from a local company in Áyios Nikólaos for the first time, I was anxious to know whether all insurance was included in the very reasonable price. To reassure me, the man I was dealing with proceeded to quite vigorously kick the hire car I was about to be given and asked me if that was proof enough that all was well. When we travel in the east of the island I always use this company now. We often stop at the office in Áyios Nikólaos to pay the boss, George, and have a chat. Before leaving George tells us: "You know where to park it at the airport when you've finished – just try and drive it into the wall!"

Enough examples of the Cretans and their humour, I think. It would undoubtedly be better if you were to witness it yourself. It is, after all, much more fun to be there as it happens.

~ ~ ~ ~

There are two words in the Greek language which would probably sum up the Cretan psyche quite nicely if only they could be translated into the English language. The fact that no accurate translation exists confirms Leigh Fermor's adequate warning that I should not be delving into this subject at all.

The first word is *philodoxia* which, according to Xan Fielding, vaguely translates into 'ambition', but with a sense of 'love of glory.' This word may certainly help to explain the pride that Cretans feel concerning their noble and courageous ancestors. "More than any other place I have visited, Crete wears its heart on its sleeve, an unashamed product of its past and proud to be the cradle of civilization." (RC) Perhaps the ambition is to emulate their forefathers and certainly reason enough to show this pride in their past openly and unreservedly. Almost every day, somewhere on the island some piece of the jigsaw of their past will be slotted into place once again, when they celebrate a festival, or commemorate an event connected with their cultural heritage. This may be best observed in the exuberant displays of their music and dance.

It is at this point, too, that I should refer to another Greek word: *levendiá* or *leventeiá* (depending on your preference in the transliteration process). I am simply going to describe it as their love of life itself. From my experience it is almost as if these people are somehow connected to an invisible electric current. There is no need for them to take synthetic chemical drugs; amphetamines are surplus to requirements here. These people exhibit a natural excitement and enthusiasm for life. At any given moment they can laugh, shout, scold or cry. Nothing lingers long. Life needs to be lived bravely, generously and to the full.

The second untranslatable word is *philotimo* which according to Stephen Verney, who was in Crete in 1944, is "their outstanding national characteristic." (SV) The nearest English equivalent would be 'a love or a sense of honour', but with the additional connotation according to both Fielding and Verney of 'self-respect' or 'deep respect'. This *philotimo* must in some way explain or incorporate another outstanding characteristic: *philoxenia* which manifests itself in the hospitality offered to the stranger: 'the love of the stranger.'

However, there is a more sinister element to *philotimo*. In many a Cretan history book, you will come across tales of sheep-stealing. Today it may still happen, although it probably won't be admitted. Having identified the perpetrator, the victim would have to kill the thief, to satisfy his sense of honour. This provided the classic Cretan scenario of a vendetta between two families, which could last for years. This aggressive part of *philotimo* is naturally difficult for outsiders to understand.

There are plenty of Cretan customs and traditions, and further aspects of the Cretan psyche such as an unexpected sensitiveness which may suddenly appear, as a result of some act or action which has inadvertently caused offence. If I were to detail them now, this would probably merely add to the confusion and misunderstanding which I have already no doubt created. So I am not going to venture down that path. Suffice to say that there is a strong tradition when people meet that it is those who arrive who should first greet people already there. A simple greeting to your Cretan host: 'Kalimera!' or 'Kalispera!' (good morning or good evening), whether in a hotel, a shop or taverna, will get things going and that *philoxenia*, their love of the stranger, will automatically surface. Their warmth and incredible hospitality to the stranger has been described variously by others as "unmatched" and heading even "to the point of insanity."

These people are so kind, so generous and so welcoming that I find it impossible to believe that anyone visiting the island would not experience this in some shape or form, and, when you do, you may be staggered and moved by the open and enthusiastic way in which this hospitality is offered. It is then perhaps that you will forget the complexities of the Cretan psyche, take Patrick Leigh Fermor's advice as I should have done, and simply embrace the *philoxenia*. Savour it fully is my only advice because it is so special and will probably be the reason why you consider returning to this fascinating island and to these extraordinary people. In 1867, John Edwin Hilary Skinner had seen enough on his travels in Crete to conclude that: "There is stuff in such a people …that will win them a place among the nations." (JEHS)

Today, the spirit of the Cretan people lives on.

Chapter Eight

Heading West - Haniá and the North-West

"In looking towards the south from the bay or city of Khania, the peaks of the noble mass of the Madura Vouna, the ancient Leuci or White Mountains, rise most picturesquely before one in a serrated arch, whose summits, after midsummer, appear bald and grey, but in winter and spring are covered with snow."
FROM TRAVELS AND RESEARCHES IN CRETE 1865 BY THOMAS ABEL BRIMAGE SPRATT. (TABS)

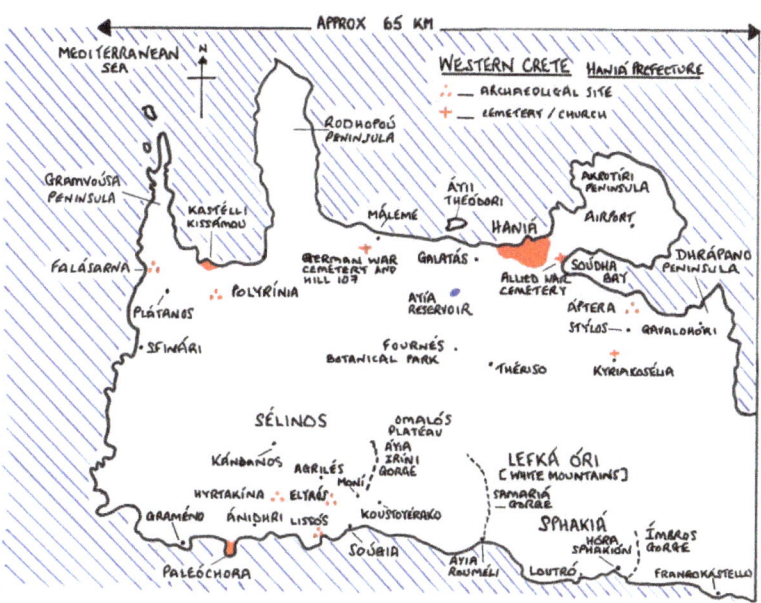

Map of Western Crete

My Wife Suggested Crete

I was all set to welcome Jennie to Crete in my usual fashion as our plane into Haniá airport descended to about 50 metres above the runway. At this point I heard the full thrust of the engines as the pilot lifted us up again for a scenic half-hour flight over the white horses of the Mediterranean. It was Easter again and I wondered whether it was all linked to the Resurrection, but we were told that the wind was gusting across the runway and at the second attempt the cabin crew welcomed us to western Crete.

Wind often plays an important part in the weather patterns of the island and the subject is taken seriously to the point where winds coming from different directions all have their own name. Our friend's neighbour in Mixórrouma, who I mentioned in the previous chapter, was quite justified when complaining about the Sirókos wind, because the Saharan dust that comes with it means that everything gets a good coating of fine sand. Even in 1865 the learned Captain Spratt had also complained about this particular wind: "There sprung up from the south-east a wind that for its heat was like the blast of a furnace." (TABS)

Nevertheless, windy weather does sometimes bring good news. It certainly powers the windmills, ancient and modern, and of course the windsurfers adore it down at Kouremének in the east. The many sailing boats that you see in harbours all around the island are evidence that this is a popular activity even though, having spoken to a serious yachtie, sailing in this part of the world is often restricted because the wind is too fierce, or there is no wind at all. Although I revel in warm, sunny days, the wind in Crete is often a blessing to cool the temperature a little – with the notable exception of the Sirókos – and it helps to keep the insect population away from the body. However, I was glad on our first visit to the west that the wind had abated enough for a successful landing.

I know there are many travellers who are devotees of this side of the island and it was high time to begin our quest to find out why. A coastal tourist strip stretching west from Haniá city certainly does not match the scale of the package tourist area in the east between Iráklio and Mália and the eye is soon drawn to the majestic White Mountains which dominate the backdrop to the city of Haniá. We drove through the outer streets to our immediate destination: the town beach at Néa Hóra, not on this occasion to swim but to rendezvous with a Cretan resident by the name of Stelios Jackson.

Although born in a town in Essex, which is probably known more for producing professional snooker players than historians, he has family links with Cyprus. However, it was his extensive historical knowledge of Crete, and especially of the 1941 Battle of Crete and the subsequent years

Heading West: Haniá and the North West

of resistance to occupation, which I was keen to investigate. He kindly invited us to his newly-acquired apartment around the corner from the beach and my mouth dropped in admiration at his enormous collection of books about the island, including the vast tomes of Arthur Evans and his beloved Knossós. Stelios, with typical Cretan kindness, lent me two books to read on holiday, one of which, *Appointment in Crete* by AM Rendel, has become one of my favourites to the extent that I am now the proud owner of my own copy.

Stelios, with further warm generosity, then presented us with two books to keep. I was given a book entitled *Crete 1941 – The Battle at Sea* by David Thomas and Jennie was given a book about the Minoans, *The Bull of Minos* by Leonard Cottrell. Thankfully I had photocopied the section on Crete which appears in my uncle's *History of the RAOC*, so at least we had something for Stelios, which he had not seen before.

On returning the borrowed books at the end of the week, I conveyed my thoughts about Rendel's book with enthusiasm: "What a great read!" and I detected a twinkle of delight in the eyes of Stelios – I think he thought so too.

From Stelios and his apartment we drove further west, in fact almost as far west as you can go, to the village of Plátanos, in the district of Kissamos, where we had booked an apartment. It turned out to be part of a barn conversion, a little cramped for my wife's liking but perfectly acceptable and it came with warm welcomes from Poppi and her son Basilios – and it had a washing machine! Poppi was a kind soul with a raucous, smoky laugh and clearly enjoyed Jennie's company. They discussed food above all else and often during the week we would find gifts of such wonders as *kolokythokeftedes* (courgette fritters) in the kitchen when we returned from our excursions.

There was a little flower-bedecked terrace outside and a few steps away a small olive grove where I spent happy times engrossed in Rendel's wartime stories. It was Easter and Easter Sunday turned out to be a showery day unsuitable for outdoor pleasures. Poppi had cooked the traditional Easter feast and she and her son and two Austrian holidaymakers, who were living next door, all crowded around our dining-table – much to Jennie's horror. Wine, *raki* and decorated hard-boiled eggs complemented the main meal. Apparently you have to crack the shell of other eggs while attempting to keep your own unblemished. Good luck befalls you if you succeed.

Walking 100 metres or so up the hill we came to a ridge from where you look down to the long sandy beach of Falásarna and beyond, the views marred in places by several plastic greenhouses. We had a good stroll along this ridge, being rewarded at the end with a fantastic view of the Rodhopoú peninsula, one of two which project northwards into the sea at this end of the island. On a map they look rather like the horns of some prehistoric creature.

View towards Falásarna

Ancient Falásarna was founded about 800 BC. It was a port city with an inner harbour and canal but these are now well above sea level. According to the RGC, this end of the island has apparently risen by 8 metres or so over 2,400 years. As it was Easter the fenced site was locked and we scrambled around the perimeter to get the gist of it all. I had not realised that Easter celebrations would mean the closure of archaeological sites, a rather idiotic complacency on my part considering that I knew the importance of Easter to the Cretan people. So with a shorter-than-planned visit to Falásarna, I drove further south for a while as far as the village of Sfínari, simply to take in the landscape. Stopping by the roadside there was a terrific view back towards the other 'horn' called Gramvoúsa, and we sat on a rock amidst the wild herbs; it was a sunny day but the wind was blowing again.

The other notable ancient site in the far north-west of the island is Polyrínia which the Dorians started to occupy in the eighth century BC.

Heading West: Haniá and the North West

Today the village of Polyrínia in which you can park before reaching the ancient sites is a classic example of Crete's many quaint and attractive rural settlements which fit the landscape as a hand fits a glove. We stopped for a mountain tea in the old *kafenion*, run by an English woman and her daughter, and here we were provided with a map of the locality. They invited us to a house nearby which they had restored in order to show how life was lived not many years ago; well worth visiting to understand the simplicity and lack of creature comforts of days gone by.

Venetian remains in the village of Polyrínia

Also before our trek, we paused to look at some magnificent Venetian arches. The acropolis, Hellenistic walls and towers, Roman cisterns, a more modern – but still old – chapel all stretched over a wide area and the whole mishmash of history was completed by far-reaching views over the countryside and out over the Gulf of Kissámou. An inquisitive, but thankfully tethered, billy-goat was feasting on the spring growth amongst the wild flowers, as we feasted on the views.

On the way back down to the village we stopped off at the workshop of George Tsichlakis who crafted all sorts of artworks from olive wood. George was quite a character, his brochure showing him as a rather younger man than the version who sat before us. Immediately a glass of *raki* was offered which I managed to down in one gulp much to his obvious delight as I received a chuckling "Bravo!" in recognition of my achievement. By the look of him, he may have downed a few too many *rakis* in his time but he hadn't lost his wood-turning skills. A small wooden owl and a delightful wooden goat are now proudly on display in our Dawlish home.

Patches of snow lingered on the tops of the mountains as we made a detour on the way back through small farming villages, stopping briefly at the village of Lousakies where the sweet brooms at the roadside wafted their scent towards us, while the village sign was undoubtedly a popular target for local shooting practice as it was peppered with the evidence.

The other big adventure of this week took us back and beyond Haniá city to visit the archaeological site of Áptera perched high above Soúdha Bay, but before that to the Soúdha Bay Allied War Cemetery. It was a magnificent spring day and I wish I was better able to describe the well-tended graves, the central memorial cross, the green lawns stretching down to the edge of the bay, the calmness and dignified ambience which befits a resting place of young people who have lost their lives and were

Entrance to the Soúdha Bay War Cemetery

Heading West: Haniá and the North West

therefore denied the opportunities of us who followed. In particular, I found the grave of Staff Sergeant Dudley Perkins from New Zealand who was killed in an ambush in February 1944 at the age of 29 while serving with the SOE. His name has become a legend in Crete for his courageous wartime endeavours; he was unsuccessfully recommended by Major Xan Fielding for the Victoria Cross, and he was known amongst his Cretan colleagues as *Kapetan* Vasili. A wreath laid on his grave five years after the end of the war included the words: "This man is honoured by all Cretans." I discovered these details – and many more – of the life of Dudley Perkins in a book by Murray Elliott: *Vasili The Lion of Crete*. To be standing by his headstone in the cemetery was therefore quite a moment.

Also here is the resting place of Captain John Pendlebury, the British archaeologist and a trusted friend to many Cretans. He was 36 when he was killed in the battle in May 1941. He had achieved a lot in his short life, some of which I will recount a little later but like so many others, this life had ended far too early.

Fellow visitors in the cemetery included a small Antipodean group, all smartly dressed. A few medals dangled from blazer jackets, and, here and there, the occasional military cap and regimental badge adorned an ageing warrior. Within the group I noticed an elderly woman, whose craggy facial lines reflected a tough existence, I thought, in some remote Australian farmstead amidst a harsh and difficult landscape. Gradually they all halted at one particular headstone. In sudden grief a flood of tears cascaded down the old lady's wizened face, at the recognition of a familiar name: a grandfather or a favourite great uncle, perhaps, who she had known only as a small child, or had never known. Here his body lay, thousands of miles away from a home to which he had never been allowed to return.

I know many Australians and New Zealanders have made this pilgrimage from the other side of the world. To witness the moment of this lady's outpouring of grief for a long-lost relation, was a moving experience in itself. Many of the graves here contain the remains of unknown soldiers, but on those where names appear, it was perhaps the tender ages of these young men which brought the inevitable tears to my own eyes, an awful and poignant reminder of how lucky I have been to reach my mid-60s.

We journeyed on a few miles to the village of Áptera – also known as Megála Horáfia – and before exploring the ancient site, we took much needed refreshment after the emotion of the cemetery at the Taverna Áptera. A cheerful middle-aged lady looked after us, asking in good English: "What can I get you, my dears?" She was unfortunately too busy for us to ask how she had picked up this expression; but we soon understood the reason why she was so busy as the various delicious vegetables which we consumed were being enjoyed by an increasing number of other customers. Her politeness to us was not matched by the obvious verbal abuse she gave to her husband, who eventually had to abandon his newspaper to lend a hand!

The ancient city of Áptera was probably founded in the 8th century BC although some say that it had been occupied 600 years earlier. It is clear though, as one of several city-states in Crete, that it had begun to reach its peak in the 4th century BC. The Easter celebrations unfortunately locked us out of the fenced site but there was still a lot to see including enormous Roman cisterns, remains of a Roman villa full of collapsed pillars and a big section of the ancient city wall with defensive tower and gate. We then drove to the end of the road where we found a big Turkish castle fortress with fine views over the whole of Soúdha Bay, before heading back to the tranquillity of Poppi's olive grove for an early evening glass of wine and reflection of what we had seen.

Kastélli Kissámou is the only town in the far north-west of any size and close to the central square is an interesting archaeological museum housing exhibits from Polyrínia and Falásarna. The star attraction is the collection of Roman mosaics, as the town had thrived in the Roman era. Mosaics have been discovered in many districts of Kastélli Kissámou, including at the nearby villa of Phidias, and hopefully one day they will all be on display. After our visit we just had time to buy some *baklavá* at a good zaharoplastía (or patisserie), where a young customer, recognising us as strangers, welcomed us to her town with a typical Cretan smile.

Unfortunately, time was running out and soon we were back at the airport and flying home. Sitting on the plane, I smiled to myself as I thought about Poppi's son Basilios, viciously stabbing his meat with a fork on Easter Sunday as if it was still alive. I remembered the reaction of the mini-market owner in Plátanos when all I had bought early one morning was a bottle of red wine and a bottle of *raki*. I had wanted to joke with him that the *raki* was my breakfast and the wine, my dinner; however, he saw the humour of the moment immediately as his large torso shook violently and uncontrollably in gay hilarity at my intended purchases. Above all else, I remembered our visit to the Allied War Cemetery and sitting in Poppi's olive grove reading about Dudley Perkins in my borrowed copy of the book by Sandy Rendel. His thoughts at the time of liberation had also turned to the sad demise of his colleague, the death of this young, brave and noble New Zealander.

Heading West: Haniá and the North West

Since that particular Easter visit we have returned to Áptera, determined to see all that is left of this ancient city. It was well worth paying two euros each – the entrance fee needed to get through the wire fence. A three-sectioned Roman barrel-vaulted cistern, still holding water, was quite magnificent; it really didn't look its age. A more recent addition (in 1082 AD!) was the monastery of St John the Theologian, whose last monks finally left in the 1960s, whereas back in the fifth century BC the Dorians had built their own temple, the base of which is still plain to see.

Notwithstanding all of this, the best part of our experience was seeing the ancient theatre, originally a Hellenistic construction which was later adapted by the Romans. My mind briefly recalled a visit to the Minack Theatre on top of cliffs near the village of Porthcurno in the far west of Cornwall. It must have been a wonderful experience to witness a production of Shakespeare's *The Tempest* on these wild cliffs, especially if one of those low pressure systems was galloping in from the Atlantic, heralded by thunder and lightning out to sea. Here at Áptera I could imagine a Greek or Roman tragedy being performed in the evening warmth amongst the olive groves. At this location it is the White Mountains that provide the dramatic theatrical scenery from where

The Byzantine church of Áyios Nikólaos, Kyriakosélia

perhaps the gods brooded over the performance with their own sound and light effects in the form of more thunderous echoes and lightning strikes.

We headed further into the foothills of these mountains on increasingly narrow and twisting roads before stopping at the isolated Byzantine church of Áyios Nikólaos nestling in a valley full of plane and chestnut trees, just outside of the village of Kyriakosélia. We used the water taps by the gates of the church to wash the dust off our hands and faces; as peaceful a spot as you could ever wish to find with only the occasional sound of a goat bell and the leaves of the plane trees rustling in the breeze. We spotted a rustic broom across the road which had been placed in one of the lower branches of a tree and Jennie decided that it was definitely a witch's broom left for her in case we came this way!

It was Sunday and after our explorations we stopped in the village of Stýlos where the Taverna Moustakia was in full swing providing a Cretan Sunday lunch to a whole host of local families, complete with grandmas and grandpas, small children and babies, as well as four tourists other than ourselves. It was great fun to watch the somewhat chaotic action which took place under a giant canopy of mature trees, ducks on the river and our hosts with a dangerous looking open air barbecue fire spit-roasting various meats. The food, which was all very good, could be washed down with free jugs of cool spring water, the same water which is sold everywhere else under the Samaria brand name. I took note of the large bottling plant in this sizeable village, the reason I deduced for the stylish modern houses in the adjoining hamlet of Provarma. Some of these Stýlosians had done rather well for themselves.

The manicured grounds of the Allied War Cemetery at Soúdha Bay had left images imprinted on my memory and had undoubtedly triggered a desire within me to learn more about the wartime history of the island. As a result, I now knew that it was at Stýlos where the Australians and New Zealanders had made their final stand against the conquering Nazis in 1941.

~ ~ ~ ~

Even with all the sights that we had seen on our Easter visit, in all honesty we had hardly scratched the surface in terms of acquainting ourselves with western Crete; the reality of the size of this island was by now well established in my mind and further visits to the west were most definitely required.

Unfortunately, five days before our next intended flight Jennie did not feel well. Shingles was confirmed by the doctor. In spite of this nasty rash

Heading West: Haniá and the North West

and pain, my wife seemed determined that this was not going to stop our proposed travel plans, so with the knowledge that if we needed help the Cretan people would always do their best for us, and armed with assorted creams, dressings and bandages, off we went.

The flight to Haniá arrived early – this particular aeroplane landing at the first attempt. The hire car arrived a little late, with profuse apologies from Victoria, the rep. There followed a warm and smiling welcome at the Kriti Hotel located in the Koum Kápi district of the former capital city of Haniá, together with a free upgrade to a suite overlooking those vast and imposing White Mountains. This was just what doctor ordered, as the additional space allowed my appalling nursing skills the extra room needed to attempt to look after the shingles patient.

View towards the White Mountains from our hotel balcony

My personal highlight of staying here was the success I achieved at the breakfast buffet when I managed to ask the young waitress – in Greek – whether they had any cold milk, and was pleasantly surprised that firstly she had understood me and secondly that I soon got some cold milk. Jennie felt well enough to explore and the walk into the heart of the old city took no more than 15 minutes. The angels had organised some great late September weather for us and it wasn't too hot to irritate the shingles.

Haniá is full of historic buildings, narrow cobbled streets, Venetian walls and arsenali, and an aesthetically-pleasing harbour and lighthouse. It is the most scenic of the Cretan cities without a doubt, a fact which has not eluded countless other tourists. Nevertheless, our fellow tourists did not detract from the fun. We saw the replica of a Minoan ship, this one having been rowed across to Athens for the 2004 Olympics. The Byzantine and archaeological museums were both worth visiting and we were fortunate that the former Mosque of the Janissaries down by the harbour was open to visitors, which is not always the case. Haniá's range of old buildings and ruins relate to the many different island rulers through the ages.

The outer harbour and lighthouse, city of Haniá

The harbour-side walk provides opportunities to sample the fare from numerous tavernas, or rest on a bench by the harbour wall and breathe in those cool, fresh saltwater aromas. We chose the second option. The back alleys, now housing many chic boutique hotels and apartments, have attracted the attention of American tourists amongst others, judging by the

Heading West: Haniá and the North West

usual "Ain't it cute" remarks which I could not help but hear amidst their constant camera-clicking. Haniá's other attractions include a quiet area in the old city known as the Jewish quarter where the ageing synagogue has been restored. The Roman Catholic Church, and a Cretan folklore museum next door are both worth a visit, as is the large indoor market in the new part of town where the choice of Cretan cheeses is quite staggering. I doubt too whether many cities can claim, amongst other attractions, a fine, clean, sandy beach as Haniá's Néa Hóra, with clear water (showers and changing huts too) and views across to one of those 'horns' – this one being the Rodhopoú peninsula, featuring Crete's most northerly cape: Akrotíri Spanda.

Jennie decided that I should purchase one of those 'silver' *taxímata* (ex-votos) which you often see hanging in a church or chapel, acting as a prayer for God to heal a wound or cure a disease. This one depicted my dodgy left leg, containing my even less reliable left hip. Having found one in a shop near the market, which I have to say doesn't seem to contain a great deal of silver, I am left to decide what on earth I am going to do with it. Perhaps a picturesque chapel will beckon me, or maybe a Minoan peak sanctuary, but I hope a suitable spot will be found on which to deposit my purchase before it's too late!

Another treat which Haniá provided for us was being able to meet up again with our historian friend, Stelios, near the town beach. Over coffee and a chat one day, Stelios advised me of several books to search for. He now conducts WWII tours for those interested in the 1941 Battle of Crete, as a lot of the fighting had taken place along this section of the coast. We finally managed to book him for one of these day tours so that I could get a better idea of the fateful days of May 1941 in this area between Haniá and Máleme and the famous Hill 107 which was so central to the eventual outcome of the conflict.

The Mediterraneo bookstore towards the western end of the harbour is the best I have found on the island for English titles, and I indulged in another four books including Edward Lear's *Cretan Journal*. Returning to our hotel, we passed through a riveting street market selling everything under the sun, bought some thyme honey and a wild herb known as *malotíra*, the ingredient for making mountain tea. Mix the two together and you have a most wonderfully refreshing and healthy hot drink. To this we greedily added a slice of *baklavá*, which we bought in one of the alleyway shops, and together with Haniá's late afternoon sunshine, we sat on our balcony looking up to the mountains. It was a great joy, as in fact the city of Haniá itself had proved to be.

My Wife Suggested Crete

If you have access to a car, there are plenty of possible itineraries to take if your base is the city. On the Akrotíri peninsula (where the airport lies) you can find several old monasteries as well as the grave of Crete's most famous statesman – Eleftherios Venizélos, and you may well feel at home if you visit the Dhrápano peninsula further east along the north coast, home to numerous British villa owners. These areas still await us but we have made some excursions inland from the city. Visiting the gorge of Thériso is the lazy way of seeing one of Crete's wonderful gorges, as the only way to do it is by motorised transport – there is no path. Unfortunately tourist 'trains' come up here too. Actually there are no trains in Crete; these open-air vehicles are simply supposed to look like them. I dislike them but recognise that they are useful for people who lack their own transport.

Once you reach Thériso itself there is a small museum – The Museum of National Resistance 1941–1945. The RGC had warned me of irregular opening hours, so I was not really surprised to find it locked. Thériso was an important village in many periods of the island's history; for instance it was home to the Revolutionary Assembly in 1905 which helped to achieve union with Greece, and it was here too in 1943 that a vital internal political pact was agreed.

In case my endless historical references are beginning to cause irritation, then please fear not. A great bird-watching spot can be found not far from the city – the Ayiá reservoir. It was delightfully peaceful and although we didn't see too much wildlife, as I understand it's best to come early or late in the day, there was enough to content us including half a dozen terrapins sunning themselves on a raised log. These reservoirs – and one natural lake – are few and far between in Crete and it is worthwhile searching one out if you need a rest from the city crowds or contrast from the mountains or the seaside.

Further out – on the same road as the Ayiá reservoir – we found Fournés Botanical Park. I rather felt, due to my previous existence, that I ought to pay a visit. It has become a popular attraction and justly so. Once in the gardens it is another tranquil and interesting place to be with plants and trees from all over the world. A disastrous fire had destroyed the owner's olive groves so the family had decided not to replace them but to turn their land into what it is today. Their café/taverna perched above the gardens is also worth a visit – wholesome cooking from an interesting menu even if some of the staff appear to need oxygen to keep them awake. Our waiter's excuse for his forgetfulness was that he was in love! "It was time," he said smilingly and also time I thought for him to produce the promised honey for Jennie's tea.

Heading West: Haniá and the North West

If in the end all you want to do is lie back on a beach and if the city beach is too crowded for you, there are others a little further west with great sand – one of these is called Áyii Apóstoli, where we found the water as clear and clean as ever. Admittedly, we also found more fellow tourists on this beach than we had ever experienced before. The reason became clear when I realised, heading west along the old coast road from here, that low-rise apartments and hotels mark the beginning of the package tourism sector of north-western Crete, stretching from Káto Stalós and Ayía Marina through Plataniás and a few kilometres beyond. However, head inland on minor roads and, almost within the blink of an eye, traditional Cretan villages reappear, undisturbed and seemingly unperturbed by life on the coastal strip below.

I cannot, in all honesty, declare that our times in this fascinating city of Haniá, its surrounds and our travels further away in the far north-west of the island ever affected us to the same degree as our dreamy, distracted young waiter in the Botanical Park, even if those ever present White Mountains can induce a trance-like state in anyone who admires the natural world. His distraction, after all, was caused by the natural beauty of another human being. However, I am sure few visitors could imagine Crete without this great city, nor without the mighty cliffs and wilderness and history which can be found in the area surrounding the town of Kastélli Kissámou, with those big 'horns' stretching out northwards into the Mediterranean Sea.

Chapter Nine

The Far South-West - Sélino and Sphakiá

"Again and again do I 'cast a longing, lingering look behind', as each step which I retrace towards the narrow glen, makes me lose sight of the lofty cypress-clad mountains of Samaría".
ROBERT PASHLEY TRAVELS IN CRETE 1837. (RP)

From the north coast of Haniá prefecture we headed for the far south-west by way of wild and empty hills and historically important villages such as Flória and Kándanos until we found views of the sea again, and the sizeable town of Paleóchora whose broken fortress sits on a headland which juts out into the Libyan Sea. It immediately appeared as a busy town and resort and not the easiest of places in which to drive a car, courtesy of one-way systems, nor was it easy to park, although gradually I got the hang of it. Views from the Venetian fortress were worth discovering – more so than the scant ruins – but the great wide (and popular) sandy beach on the western side of town is Paleóchora's star attraction. In an odd sort of way, Paleóchora gave me the same kind of feeling as Penzance had done many years ago when I travelled there from London by train – an end of the line feeling or, in Paleóchora's case, an end of the road feeling, even though, in both cases, land continues a little further west before the sea halts any further progress.

The apartment we had chosen, one of five or six in the same large building, was a 15-minute walk from the town, located on the opposite eastern pebbly shoreline. It was a peaceful spot, save sometimes for the barking of a neighbour's dog. The owners had thoughtfully cleared a way through the large boulders at the sea's edge so that swimming here was made quite easy when the sea was calm and a sun lounger and parasols provided all the comfort needed for relaxation, while our eyes could rest on the mountains to our left, the town and fortress to our right or simply on the ever-changing colours of the sea. To all intents and purposes, we

The Far South-West: Sélino and Sphakiá

Paleóchora with the White Mountains in the distance

had a private beach. You can walk east on a coastal track which after about an hour and a half will take you to the beach of Yialaskári. We spared our lazy legs the bother!

I knew that a sandy beach would suit Jennie better, so we explored a few kilometres west of town and found the lagoon-like waters of Graméno so sheltered that even on a windy day swimming would never have been a problem and it came complete with the requisite sandy beach. We dined one evening at the Taverna Graméno, conveniently located on the road behind the beach.

On another fine evening we decided to walk into town for our evening meal, being accompanied all the way by our apartment owner's elderly dog. This clever old canine had learned his tricks several years before our visit and promptly sat down by our table in the chosen taverna waiting for his reward for escorting us there. I remember advising the taverna's staff that the dog did not belong to us, but they had seen it all before and were not in the least bit bothered. Needless to say, Jennie decided that he was to have his reward – the left-overs from her plate – after which our new friend escorted us home.

My Wife Suggested Crete

Our favourite eatery in this area was soon discovered in the hill village of Ánidri some four or five kilometres from our apartment. Called Kafenio Sto Scolio, it had indeed been converted from the former village schoolhouse and came with a pleasant leafy terrace, which nicely represented the natural beauty of the wooded landscape in this part of Haniá prefecture. Although the food had a creative twist, it was still essentially full of all the goodness of traditional Cretan cuisine. The small Ánidri gorge provides a walk down to the coast at Yialaskári beach and from there back to our apartment and Paleóchora, but I need to admit that to date we have yet to accomplish this.

A few kilometres higher in the hills we found on the outskirts of the village of Teménia the quaintly picturesque church of Sotiris Christós, where a sign indicated the way to the ancient city of Hyrtákina. We took the path up to the top where hidden amongst the scrub lie the few remnants of what had been an important Dorian city, part of the confederation of Oreioi. Down below us we could see the village with its church, and further along I spied more isolated chapels before the land dropped away, concealing one of the island's great gorges, the Áyia Iríni gorge.

Just beyond, as the land began to rise again, I could faintly detect the villages of Livadás and Koustoyérako, both famous in the annuls of WWII history, having been burned to the ground by the Nazis in the 1940s. The latter was the home village of the Paterakis family, a name which will be familiar to anyone interested in those times. Above these villages, where only the shepherds and goatherds wander, the cloud and mist partially obscured the tops of the mountains, while almost offset the blue of the Libyan Sea was still just visible. All of this we witnessed alone and in complete silence save for an oddly tardy cockerel and the bell-ringing of an irascible goat. Perched on a rock within the bounds of Hyrtákina's long-deserted city I marvelled at the landscape laid out before me.

Western Crete, especially in the Sélino and Sphakián districts, has a different feel to other parts of the island. Perhaps the inhabitants are a tougher folk, their landscape is certainly rugged, more luxuriant in places and they experience more rainfall and snow than in the east. For many invaders this landscape was too harsh, too remote, too isolated to be successfully conquered. It often therefore became a centre of resistance to invasion throughout the ages. There are marked differences in the diet too, again probably due to the topography and weather patterns of the region. As a result, many different recipes exist: even cheese pies are prepared differently here. In Spakiá they are called *sphakianopites*.

What remains unchanged, however, is the warm and friendly welcome which you receive. For us this came from a young woman when

The Far South-West: Sélino and Sphakiá

we arrived at our apartment. It transpired that she was the owner's niece. Nothing was too much trouble, and once again this girl's mastery of the English language was first class. We gradually got to know her uncle through our stay and although the English language was not his specialist subject, his hospitality was. He showered us with gifts of grapes, wine and *raki*, apologising profusely for not being around all the time as he had work to do in the village and on his land. Often a family's land can be situated some distance from their home as a result of marriage and inheritance issues.

Back along the road to Haniá we stopped outside the village of Kándanos, where we bought home-made and outstanding orange marmalade, honey and *raki* from a young woman's roadside stall. She congratulated Jennie on her efforts at speaking Greek and insisted that we should take away a bag of her olives as a gift. We hoped that her enterprise would continue to thrive.

In contrast, ill fortune befell Kándanos in 1941 when the resistance fighters here determined to stop the advance of the invaders, and succeeded for two days, killing 25 German soldiers. The brutal Nazi response, which became typical all over the island, was the complete destruction of this village. The evidence is plain to see from plaques mounted in the village square. However, a few years later, Kándanos was rebuilt and is living proof of the steadfast resilience, courage and determination of these remarkable people.

~ ~ ~ ~

The distant view of Livadás and Koustoyérako, the knowledge that there was another ancient city – Elyrós – somewhere in the hills, and yet another – Lissós – on the coast near the modern seaside village of Soúgia (or Soúyia) no doubt influenced our decision to see more of this district of Sélino. Before long we were back on the same road towards Kándanos and halting our journey at the same roadside stall where we had met the young woman a year before. Now we know her name – Despina. She was looking after her two young children as well as promoting her home-made food and drink products, some of which we purchased. The tastes of her olive pâté and fig jam were extremely good, the memories of which still prompt my salivary glands into excessive production.

We had booked a two-bedroom apartment, (an Airbnb establishment, so therefore it felt very much like someone's home, which of course it was), in the tiny village of Agrilés which, with the exception of the *kafenio*, was tucked away from the main hill road and guarded at the entrance to the village by the Church of St George. If a professional photographer took a picture from this churchyard and its accompanying pair of tall Italian cypress trees with a backdrop of the lofty mountain peaks of Psilafi (1984m high) and Toumba, and yet failed to win an award, then I suggest a change of career might have been a good move. It really was a sight to behold and I hope it will always be there to provide such a visual treat. No need for an air-conditioning system up here – although there was one – as the cool clean night air was perfect for sleeping in.

So we had inched ourselves eastwards from Paleóchora and towards the villages of Livadás and Koustoyérako, both of which I had hazily glimpsed before, but which were now in better focus, as indeed was the outline of the Áyia Iríni gorge. How best to describe the view from our chosen lodgings? The lady next door diverted my attention for a while, simply because the routine of watering her garden in the morning and evening to ensure steady growth of her vegetables was itself pleasing enough. More importantly, from the set of large picture windows in our kitchen-cum-living room, we looked directly across to the western slopes of those White Mountains and gradually we watched the sun rising above them.

With the sunlight I could see the great wealth of pines clinging to the edge of the almost vertical rock faces like a series of circus trapeze artists deftly defying a tragic fall. How could these trees stay upright? The gentle Devon hills with their fields of patchwork quilt knitted together by the characteristic banks and hedges provide a truly harmonious picture, but what I was seeing here in south-western Crete was of a bolder nature, a more majestic landscape. This was magnificent scenery and yet as my gaze turned upwards the trees gradually thinned and disappeared, giving way to the barren wilderness. At the end of the day, even this high desert has incredible beauty as the sun turns the craggy grey heights into a wonderful hue of warm pink before night begins. All of this we spotted from our little den in the village of Agrilés.

One day we took the road which meandered up to the top of the Áyia Iríni gorge and walked a short distance to the head of the gorge on a path shaded by tall pines and cypress, planes and chestnuts, some of their mighty root systems twisting and turning into the rocky bed of the stream in search of water and nutrients. Jennie and I were up here primarily to investigate the possible nutrients which we might find in the small café-cum-taverna called Kri-Kri located amidst these trees at the start of the gorge. Here we met Yiorgos, a lively and industrious young man, who at the time was about to feed a local builder and his mate. We watched as Yiorgos prepared a typical salad with bread and olive oil, freshly cooked

The Far South-West: Sélino and Sphakiá

potatoes and a lamb stew for his guests. Jennie decided to do a bit of waitressing for our new friend. After a while he served us with olives, tomatoes, cheese and, to conclude, a couple of glasses of *raki*. I offered to pay for this but with typical Cretan generosity Yiorgos refused to let me.

Two dear friends – more casualties of my persistent pestering about visiting Crete – had succumbed and by chance they were staying in a village close by, so a couple of days later we arranged an early evening meal with them at the Kri-Kri. I always find it fun to meet up with friends in unlikely places far from home and this was a perfect spot for it to happen. Yiorgos provided a tasty spread, even if the wine had probably passed its best several months before. The last of the hikers had gone home as we had arrived and we had this peaceful forest glade all to ourselves as the light faded. Yiorgos then produced *raki* and joined us for the traditional toast of "Yamas" to conclude a most wonderful evening, the memory of which I shall always treasure.

Other gastronomic delights which we experienced this week included those provided by a taverna called *An to Petyxeis* in the village of Moní. The owner's wife, Monica, was quite charming and her cooking was excellent, her recipes including a pork casserole with apricots and dates. She was Romanian by birth, and had set off to travel the world. She had got no further than Soúgia where she had met and married Michali, a local man who spoke no English. He had inherited the taverna from his father whose main occupation had been farming and therefore only opened his *kafenion*, as it was then, from time to time. The name of the present-day taverna reflects this piece of local history, the name roughly translated meaning: "You are lucky to find it open."

In Soúgia we discovered the beach-front Taverna Livikon, which sold excellent fish served to us by the friendly staff, Ari and Yiorgi, and it proved a great spot to watch the colour of the cliffs turn to pink as the beach emptied and the sun set. To complete our rations, we used the two minimarkets in Soúgia, both selling good bread which Jennie had no problem in digesting, and they also sold mouth-watering fresh figs, while in the village of Tsiskiani, not far from our base, a roadside stall-seller tempted us to stop and buy an enormous hunk of Omalo sheep's cheese (Cretan Gruyere), which lasted us for the best part of two weeks, together with his sun-ripened tomatoes. Our taste buds had been royally treated.

It was a twenty-minute drive to the beach and coastal settlement of Soúgia: far quieter and more laid-back than Paleóchora in spite of the ferries which call at the small jetty at the western end two or three times a day. I immediately took a liking to this place with its wide and lengthy

My Wife Suggested Crete

pebble beach; there was plenty of room to spread out in spite of a large nudist camping community which occupied the eastern corner of the bay. I understand that the locals, with their delicious sense of humour, have named this stretch of their beach: 'The Bay of Pigs'! Jennie and I had a swim here – no, not in the Bay of Pigs – most days of our stay, floating easily in the salty water, soaking up the sun's rays and taking in the views of the pine-clad cliffs which plunge into the sea to the east. I wondered how these trees tolerated the salt spray which they must experience in winter storms.

Ancient cities thrived in this area from Dorian times, perhaps from 1000 BC, and they joined together in a confederation about 700 years later, Soúgia – then Syia – amongst them. Little remains of Syia on the east bank of the river bed, the modern sign directing you there being the only real survivor. Further west lies Lissós, which you can walk to in an hour and a half by way of a gorge and then up and over a hill. There is no road to Lissós, which is why it is so appealing, but you can catch the local boat from Soúgia's unassuming and sheltered harbour, this method of travel taking no more than 10 minutes. This was our chosen option. The sea was calm and having arrived we spent most of our time, accompanied

Lissós

The Far South-West: Sélino and Sphakiá

by the resident goats, wandering about in an area dominated by a big group of tombs which looked more like miniature houses with their barrel-vaulted roofs. A temple of healing and curative spring with a Roman mosaic floor, and two 13th-century churches complete the manmade remains of the ancient place. High up on the gentle western slopes you can look down on the sheltered bay and let your imagination describe the daily routines of the people who once lived here.

To complete my lesson in the ancient history of this area I merely had to glance ahead from the picture windows in Agrilés and gaze at a large mound-like hill no more than a kilometre or so away. This was Elyrós which had also been a member of the confederation in 300 BC. To be honest, when we took the walk through groves of seriously old olive trees there was little left to see, although a sign suddenly announced Roman cisterns and close by I spied small sections of Roman walls.

Our solitary walk under the canopy of these trees was unexpectedly interrupted by the arrival of three more Brits. I felt another 'Présos' moment coming on as Jennie was keen to point out the cisterns while ascertaining where these people had come from. Two of them apparently lived in Paleóchora, an hour's drive away, while the third member of the trio was staying with them on holiday. Hence their visit here, although the lady of the group was keen to point out to Jennie that they had naturally been to Elyrós before. Jennie, undeterred, continued bombarding her with questions, especially when she looked as though she desperately wanted to get away. They finally achieved their escape and we continued to explore alone.

The modern church at the start of the track had been built over the remains of a Greek basilica part of which was still clearly visible at one end. I understand that there is a bit more to see if you can negotiate your way through the farmer's fences and his olive nets. The views from Elyrós made up for our inability to find other remains of this important city. A 'wow' from Jennie as we walked through the parched grass confirmed these breathtaking vistas.

Roman Elyrós was important enough for the building of an aqueduct that fed water from a spring in the hills behind our Agrilés retreat down to Elyrós and from there all the way down to their port at Soúgia. Just before you reach Soúgia, on the right-hand side of the road, a sign indicates a small part of the aqueduct which still exists. Centuries later, the Turks also used Elyrós as evidenced by a watchtower up which I clambered, much against my better judgement as health and safety had not been incorporated into the spiral steps.

My Wife Suggested Crete

View of the White Mountains from Elyrós

In the 1940s, the Nazis came to this area realising that resistance to their occupation was especially strong in the three villages of Moní, Livadás and Koustoyérako. Their intelligence correctly sensed that a British clandestine operation was based somewhere in the hills above. In Koustoyérako the Nazis, having failed to find the menfolk, rounded up all the women and children and were about to kill them before Costas Paterakis fired a long-range shot from above the village which killed the German machine-gunner. The rest fled, but on 1st of October 1943, with air support, the Germans destroyed the three villages. You can still see some derelict roofless remains to this day. A triangular war memorial at the entrance to Koustoyérako remembers the three villages and the suffering of these people, but I felt it stood there high above the valley below as a symbol of stubborn defiance.

More memorials can be seen near the village square, while at the top of the village and reached by old pathways skirting the houses is the tiny Byzantine church of Áyios Yeóryios. We were guided to it by a cheerful man who was painting his gate. He omitted to say that the 'Papa' had the key, so we couldn't get inside, but his warm yet teasing smile when we came back down was enhanced by his admission about the keyholder. A bit of Cretan humour, me thinks!

The Far South-West: Sélino and Sphakiá

Turkish watchtower at Elyrós

These have been our experiences of the district of Sélino, and I feel blessed to have seen this powerful landscape and to have discovered some of its historical secrets. Sadly though, we have glimpsed few of the numerous church frescoes (with thanks partly to our friendly painter), which I know are particularly worth seeing in the churches and chapels of the far south-western hills. On the way home I drove up to the Omaló plateau where apple trees seem to fruit well in spite of the altitude; a picturesque sight towards the end of summer and yet I sensed that the people here live a tough life and have to retreat with their flocks to lower ground in winter.

A right turn would have taken us after four kilometres to the head of the famous Samariá gorge; we will be leaving the challenge of hiking down through it to the younger generation. It is after all a distance of at least 18 kilometres. Perhaps one day we will do the lazy route which involves getting the ferry to Ayía Rouméli which is where most people emerge from the gorge. We would then be able to walk in the opposite direction as far as the famous Iron Gates – Sideropórtes – where the two cliffs rise vertically to a thousand feet and almost touch each other. I can only imagine this dramatic sight which has impressed travellers for generations including

My Wife Suggested Crete

Robert Pashley in 1837. This is the heart of Sphakiá with the White Mountains aloft and the isolated village of Loutró, only accessible by boat or by a difficult four-hour slog on foot, further east along the coast.

We have at least now travelled to the main centre of Sphakiá, commonly called 'The village' by locals, but described on maps and in guide books as Hóra Sphakión, perched on the rugged coast close to the exit of another great gorge – the Ímbros. In 1941 it was down the Ímbros gorge that the retreating British army came to escape the conquering Germans, and many thousands of British, Australians and New Zealanders were evacuated from the village. The memorial to this event stands along the road to the ferry dock. Above it flutter the Greek, British, Australian and New Zealand national flags. From this point you get an idea of the limited size of Hóra Sphakión; you can see the zig-zag road heading up into the hills to the west where the villages of Anópoli, Aŕadena, Livanianá and – at the end of the road – Áyios Ioánnis, all still await our exploration; and you can watch the ferry boat approaching from the west in the late afternoon.

We bought a cheese and spinach filo pastry pie from the bakery and devoured it on the tiny Vríssi beach at the western end of the village.

Hóra Sphakión and the War Memorial

The Far South-West: Sélino and Sphakiá

Looking up, the hills above appear devoid of vegetation; altogether it seemed a rather desolate landscape which made it easy for me to understand a story about Hóra Sphakíón which implies that nothing grows here, "only stones." Above all other Cretans, the Sphakians are known for their fierceness, for their independence and aversion to authority, and yet for their astonishing hospitality. You can get a real taste of the region by reading Peter Trudgill's book, *In Sfakiá* – he and his wife were evidently addicted to the place and the people. In the preface to his book he quotes a great creation story about Sphakiá as told to a French traveller in the 1950s. I won't spoil it by repeating it here; reading it yourself will give you a pretty good idea of Sphakiá and the Sphakiáns.

We must all have our own favourites, and my fondest memories of Sélino and Sphakiá will always be associated with the long established villages nestling in the hills above Soúgia, blessed as they are with stupendous views towards some of those Sphakian mountains, and of course the people who live within the boundaries of this understated countryside. In particular, I will always remember the village of Agrilés where we found the little house in which we were allowed to rest, as, for a week at least, it became our happy home.

Chapter Ten

Fighting for Freedom - Again

A: THE BATTLE OF CRETE MAY 1941

"... to the great astonishment of both sides, all over the island bodies of Cretans – villagers, shepherds, old men, boys, monks and priests and even women, without any collusion between them or master plan or arms or guidance from the official combatants – rose up at once and threw themselves on the invaders...They had not had a second's doubt about what they should do."
From Abducting a General by Patrick Leigh Fermor. (PLF)

On television recently I was struck by an interview with Michael Morpurgo who was being questioned about the screenplay and film made from one of his books, *Waiting for Anya*. The subject concerned the sheltering of Jews in the Pyrenees during WWII and subsequent atrocities committed by the Nazis. What struck me most were his words: "Horrible things do happen in beautiful places." He could have been talking about Crete.

A package holiday to Crete will not necessarily lead you past any evidence or information concerning what happened to this island and her people between 1941 and 1945, but if you hire a car you will inevitably pass by war memorials, many with words in the English language. Your car may also take you to museums dedicated to this period of the island's history and perhaps even to old machine-gun posts and concrete bunkers dotted about here and there. I realise that I am about to write about events which happened over 75 years ago, so most of the survivors of this dreadful period have now passed away.

As I write, however, there are still people alive who will remember some of the horrors of this war and the occupation of their island, even if they were children at the time. The Cretans who experienced the brutality and beastliness of the war have passed on their first-hand knowledge

Fighting for Freedom - Again

down through the generations with the result that this period of the island's history is still fresh and significant in the minds of the current generation. They are justifiably proud of their parents, grandparents and now great-grandparents and of their atavistic reaction to the invasion and to the subsequent destruction and desecration of their land. They must surely be equally proud of these older generations for their kindness and generosity to those new friends and allies, at a time when they had little to give. This underlines the Cretan possession of certain human qualities which in other parts of the world, as Xan Fielding once suggested: "… went out of fashion with the advent of peace." (XF)

WWII concrete bunker outside a modern supermarket in Ierápetra, south-eastern Crete

The impact of the 1941 German Nazi invasion and subsequent occupation was such that I feel no need to apologise for including this chapter within my collection of traveller's tales. It is an important part of the island's story and had such dire consequences for her people.

There are a couple of reasons for my particular interest in the events of World War II even though I was born in 1953, eight years after the end of this cataclysmic conflict. Firstly, I suppose I could simply put it down to my genes as both my father (and his father before him) and my father's

My Wife Suggested Crete

Memorial near Galatas to men of the First Battalion, the Welch Regiment

twin brother had been professional soldiers for most of their working lives. In military terms they had done rather well. Both of them achieved the rank of brigadier; both were awarded the CBE (Commander of the British Empire) and both had earned medals of gallantry: to my father a DSO, to my uncle an MC (resulting from action at Dunkirk). In sharp contrast, the last thing I ever wanted to become was a soldier – I wouldn't have been any good at it as I quickly realised that official army dragooning was not for me. Nevertheless, it was undoubtedly my father's career and overhearing conversations with his army friends which soon made me aware of some of the horrors of WWII and I instinctively felt how fortunate I was to have been born after it was all over. Apart from the 'genes' argument, I soon developed an interest in history and thanks to a particularly good teacher it was this subject in which I eventually attained my best results at school.

In May 1941 my father was nowhere near the island of Crete. In fact, by 1942 he had been posted to the Staff College at Palmerston North on the north island of New Zealand. I remember hearing the story of his frustration when the ship by which he eventually returned to England had got stuck in the Panama Canal. Back in the UK he was then appointed Commanding

Fighting for Freedom - Again

Machine - gun post amongst the ruins of Áptera high above Soúdha Bay

Officer of the 53rd Medium Regiment of the Royal Artillery and took part in the Allied advance through France, Belgium and Holland in 1944.

While my father set off for New Zealand, other Regiments of the Royal Artillery had already seen action in Greece. The 64th Medium Regiment, which had originally been part of the 53rd, took part in the attempt to halt the advance of the Nazis before being evacuated from Porto Rafti (south of Athens) to Alexandria in Egypt at the end of April 1941. Meanwhile the remains of the 7th Medium Regiment of the Royal Artillery, having also fought in Greece, were transported to Crete rather than Egypt. It was these men who found themselves defending the rather flat and barren landscape between Iráklio's airfield and town in May 1941, 'transformed' into an untrained infantry unit. It was pure chance – or at least the will of his superiors – that took my father far away from Greece and the island of Crete.

~ ~ ~ ~

Many books recount the story of the 1941 Battle of Crete including one by Callum MacDonald called *The Lost Battle* which, according to a

My Wife Suggested Crete

knowledgeable friend of ours, is the best written book on the subject in spite of some factual errors. Another way to learn about the battle and its aftermath can be found at the Historical Museum on Iráklio's seafront where there is a permanent exhibition about the war as it affected the island. Here you can pick up a sizeable catalogue entitled *From Mercury to Ariadne. Crete 1941-1945* which incorporates some remarkable and graphic photographs as well as a thought-provoking history lesson.

A brief summary of the events and consequences may help to define the circumstances in which the British and Cretan participants found themselves. By October 1940 Hitler's forces had stormed through most of Europe, and Britain and her Commonwealth and Greece stood alone against the Axis powers. While the Italians failed to conquer Greece, the superior forces of the Nazis swept through mainland Greece in April 1941 forcing the Allies to retreat and evacuate their troops. Some were taken back to Egypt; others were stranded in Greece and became prisoners of war; the rest sailed to Crete.

By the beginning of May there were about 28,000 Allied and Greek troops of fighting strength on the island, although this figure becomes larger if you include *gendarmes* and Cretan irregulars and Greek solders with no weapons. It is also important to realise that many of the allied troops (including the remnants of the 7th Medium Regiment RA) were not properly formed infantrymen. Crete was attacked by fully equipped German forces totalling just over 22,000 men; in addition, their air force – the Luftwaffe – had complete air supremacy. Within a fortnight the Nazis had won the battle although they suffered huge casualties especially in their elite parachute regiment. There are 4,465 graves in the German war cemetery near Máleme. The Allies lost 1,742 men on land and 1,828 at sea, with the total loss of nine cruisers and destroyers.

I have, as I write, visited the Allied War Cemetery at Soúdha Bay near Haniá twice. As visits to all Allied War Cemeteries tend to be, these were moving experiences. There are emotional moments as the eye passes over row upon row of graves and then over the bay itself where there was so much carnage in 1941. On my second visit I particularly wanted to pay my respects to a Lieutenant AL Taylor who served in the RAOC and was killed on May 20th, 1941. In his book my uncle Alan paid tribute to the work he did both in Greece and Crete. "Throughout the operations in both countries from April 6th to May 20th he set a fine example." (AHF) He was 41 years old. Around the corner from the cemetery, a taverna called Pyrofani can be found in an equally beautiful setting at the edge of the bay. On the day we visited this taverna the sea was like a millpond and the Greek national flag on a pole at the water's edge drooped silently as if in solemn respect and quiet reflection. Jennie and I continued to nosh away contentedly, and yet I felt somehow that we were disturbing the peace of those who had been buried nearby so many years ago.

View across Soúdha Bay from the Pyrofani taverna

This is not the place to analyse why the Battle of Crete was lost by the Allies. The reasons are well documented and explanations are argued over in many books written by historians and by those who were actually present at the time. Antony Beevor's account is perhaps the most well-known, but there are many others of equal standing. *The Official History of New Zealand in WWII – Crete*, which consists of over 500 pages, also provides a succinct analysis. The author, DM Davin, concluded that the plight of the Allied forces was due largely to: "the concrete conditions of the battle: lack of artillery, lack of aircraft, and – perhaps most of all – lack of communications." (DMDavin) Allied Commanders on the ground have been blamed by many for disastrous decisions and futile delays, but Davin also concluded that: "No men ever held positions of responsibility in conditions more inimical to success than did the senior officers in Crete." (DMDavin)

If there is to be a 'blame game', then it ought to focus on the 'top brass' in GHQ (General Headquarters) Middle East based in Egypt. On

My Wife Suggested Crete

this subject I am sure my uncle Alan who was stationed there for a while could have enlightened me further. It seems clear that there were obvious excesses in the upper echelons of military society life in March 1941: gin drinking at Shepheard's Hotel and dancing late into the night at a time when the German invasion of mainland Greece (on April 6th) was imminent. In terms of organisation and decision-making here at headquarters, there seems to have been a lack of vision: "I judged them to have been petty and mean, ignorant and without insight," (IG) wrote Jack Hamson who worked in Crete in the early months of 1941. He talked about the old generals from the First World War, who were now the decision makers, in bitter terms citing: "the nastiness, the sloth, the nullity of Cairo." (IG) This was a different war and yet these ageing commanders were still living in a bygone age: "…so cossetted by the colonial life that they could never fully grasp what was happening in the field, or appreciate the difficulties that had to be overcome." (IG)

Even the Allied Commander in Crete, General Freyberg, was sometimes heard to recall after the war, that the authorities in both London and Cairo were completely unaware of the actualities that had to be faced at that time. British troops had first landed on the island in October 1940, and yet little had been done. In the six months that followed, seven successive commanders had been given neither time, nor clear orders, nor enough manpower to effect a solid defensive position.

My own understanding of the course of the battle has been greatly improved by a day spent with our historian friend Stelios in a part of the island near Haniá where Hitler lost thousands of his paratroopers and men from his airborne division, but also where the Battle of Crete began to go disastrously wrong for the Allies: Hill 107, the Tavronítis bridge, Máleme airfield and the village of Galatás are places which now mean something to me, as does the German War Cemetery near Hill 107. This cemetery has a totally different feeling to the Allied War Cemetery at Soúdha Bay. I can only describe it as typically teutonic, emotive simply by the sheer scale of it. It was indeed the scale of the casualties, particularly of the parachutists, which forced Hitler never again to launch a major airborne attack. So it was, that victory for the Nazis in this Battle of Crete had been won at great cost. Some have also argued that it delayed their offensive against Russia by at least a fortnight if not more, where in the end a harsh winter sealed their fate.

While recording these brief details of the 1941 Battle of Crete, I want, above all else, to mention the actions and reactions of the Cretan civilian population, especially as the entire Cretan division of the Greek army – the island's professional soldiers – had been abandoned to an uncertain fate on the mainland. Only a few had managed, by hook or by crook, to return to

Fighting for Freedom - Again

Allied bunker on Hill 107 above Máleme airfield

their island. It was just as Patrick Leigh Fermor described it, that the Cretan civilians came out to fight the invaders. Armed with nothing more than old and decrepit guns and rifles which had been hidden away since Turkish rule, or with kitchen knives and sticks, they attacked the might of the Nazis however they could.

Georgios Tzitzakes, a Cretan who had served on the Greco-Bulgarian border, had managed to return to Crete and fought in the Réthymno district in the battle. One night he saw a tall, slender woman in a long black dress holding and firing a gun with her right hand while holding a small child of about four or five in the other: "I've always believed that she was Crete herself with fire in one hand, revenge, and motherly love, devotion, in the other." (GAT) The Germans were incensed that Cretan civilians should have taken this attitude of confronting the invasion face to face. It was the first time they had experienced open civilian resistance in WWII, while their poor intelligence service had told them that the civilians would be mainly supportive. Nothing could have been further from the truth.

In the end when the battle was lost, almost 15,000 allied troops were evacuated from Crete courtesy of heroic efforts by the Royal Navy, but thousands were stranded on the island when it became too dangerous – in fact suicidal – for the navy to continue. What happened to those stranded

Memorial plaque at the German War Cemetery,
below Hill 107 near Máleme

men is a story in itself and is graphically pieced together by Seán Damer and Ian Frazer in their book, *On the Run*. Roughly 6,500 men became prisoners of war and were forced to trudge back from Hóra Sphakíon on the south coast to one of three main POW camps near Haniá. Conditions in these camps were atrocious. "Dysentery and kindred tummy troubles spared nobody. There was plenty of malaria, pneumonia, untended wounds and sore feet, all not helped by sand and heat and flies ……" (RHT) Once cases of infantile paralysis and malnutrition have been added to this list, it may be unsurprising to learn that many gradually escaped.

Wandering about in the hills and mountains of Crete were about 1,000 Allied servicemen, many who had decided to evade capture and surrender in the first place and others who had escaped the intolerable conditions of the POW camps. By May 1943 just over 850 of these men had made it back to Egypt including 254 Australians, 176 New Zealanders and 313 British (figures from SD and IF). Of these, 387 had been assisted by secret British military organisations (MI9 and SOE), while the rest had managed independently by repairing abandoned motor launches or small boats.

I mention the story of these abandoned Allied servicemen for the following reason: These wandering Australian, New Zealand and British soldiers found themselves in a precarious predicament. In published accounts they all, without exception, reflect on the kindness of the islanders who sheltered and fed them to the best of their ability as they roamed the hills trying to find ways of getting back to Egypt and safety. Most of these soldiers also understood how dangerous this situation was for the Cretans who would, with their families and in some cases whole villages, be punished by death if caught by the occupying Germans. However this incredible spirit of courage, unselfish protection of their allies, and hospitality was in their blood. This island had been invaded and occupied by Romans, Arabs, Venetians and Turks over so many centuries that: "In a way, of course, they were ready for all that was happening. They were brought up on powder and shot and on traditions of fighting against occupation;" (PLF)

In these wartime stories as told by Allied soldiers, it is this unique Cretan hospitality which stands out as the overwhelming sentiment. This resulted in lifelong bonds of friendship between Australians, New Zealand and British soldiers and the Cretan families who sheltered and fed them. Some of those soldiers who had been evacuated as the battle was being lost even wanted to return to drive the Germans out: "we hoped that we would be picked for the job" (RS) said Reg Spurr who was serving with the York and Lancaster Regiment's 2nd Battalion. It didn't happen, but nevertheless: "I can say quite honestly, that the seven months I spent on that lovely island had the biggest impact on my life." (RS)

For the professional soldiers caught up in defeat and surrender there were other emotions. They could not understand how it had been allowed to happen and they felt utterly deflated: "I was deeply disappointed; I felt frustrated and shamed – above all, ashamed." as one New Zealander put it. (RHT)

During the battle the big cities, Haniá and Iráklio as well as Réthymno, had been wrecked by the Luftwaffe. Large areas along the north coast had seen heavy fighting and the landscape was now a desolate scene. Soúdha Bay was like a ship's graveyard. Reprisals against the civilian population for their part in resisting the invasion began immediately with the destruction of villages. In June, 180 Cretan men were shot dead in the district of Sélino. Ralph Stockbridge was one Englishman intensely moved by what he saw as he was marched down to Iráklio's harbour in the early hours of May 28th to be evacuated to Alexandria: "I shall never forget the silence and desolation of the shattered town I knew so well. I took a vow at this moment to return to Crete as soon as possible and to help liberate its brave and wonderful people." (CH & MF) That, as it happened, is exactly what he did.

B: THE CRETAN RESISTANCE AND THE BRITISH SECRET SERVICE 1941-1945

"if anything of any value was achieved by the British in Crete, they owed this to the Cretans themselves, without whose protection and help of every kind no British officer could have survived more than twenty-four hours."
RALPH STOCKBRIDGE. FOREWORD TO THE CRETAN RESISTANCE 1941-1945 BY NA KOKONAS. (NK)

For the Cretan people the lost battle of May 1941 did not end things at all. Their fight to liberate their island continued until the German surrender four years later. From June 1941 it was with the considerable help of the Cretan people, as the official Allied evacuations ceased, that British and Commonwealth secret agents were gradually infiltrated into the island together with wireless operators who would be responsible for contact with Allied headquarters in Cairo, providing that their heavy batteries and charging engines were in working order – which was often not the case.

The objectives of this clandestine mission changed frequently as a result of military decisions made by the 'top brass' and the fortunes of the war as a whole. It began with attempts to organise the evacuation of those Allied stragglers. Gathering of intelligence concerning German troop movements, aircraft and shipping quickly became a priority and was undoubtedly one of the main achievements of this mission. For example, the Germans had a new airfield facility constructed at Tymbáki on the south coast. As one of the agents described: "their splendid new aerodrome at Tymbáki, on which we had been keeping a watchful eye, reporting back to Cairo each stage in its construction, had been successfully bombed by the RAF on the very day the runways were completed". (XF) The runways were of course repaired, but on another occasion the sighting of a whole contingent of transport planes leaving Tymbáki was reported just in time for RAF fighters to intercept them off the African coast before they were allowed to deliver essential supplies to Rommel before the battle of El Alamein.

Assisting with Allied sabotage operations, secret meetings with the Italians before whisking away their General Carta back to Egypt, and the capture of the German commander General Kreipe – the story of which was eventually turned into a film *Ill Met By Moonlight* starring Dirk Bogarde – were all on the job sheet. Stabilising island politics as best they could, liaising with the Cretan *Kapetans* who might provide some kind of military organisation should the need arise and the use of propaganda to undermine German morale – these were all in the brief - before they effectively supervised the gradual withdrawal of German troops to Haniá and the Akrotíri Peninsula in 1944. It is to their credit that this was achieved without a major incident considering the continued and understandable wrath of the Cretan people. Most importantly none of these objectives could have been attempted or achieved without the steadfast efforts of the Cretan population.

~ ~ ~ ~

The British Intelligence Service at this time appears extremely complex and it was evolving erratically. It was the SBS (Special Boat Service) which undertook the periodic sabotage operations on the island, and although MI9, formed essentially to aid escapers, was in theory operating by 1941, the mission which had constant presence on Crete came from two other organisations: The Special Operations Executive (SOE), and the Inter-Services Liaison Department (ISLD), the latter concerned strictly with intelligence gathering, basically the forerunner of MI6. In practice, and unlike the covert operations on mainland Greece, they both worked together, sometimes sharing wireless operators or wireless sets. In the four years of German occupation about 50 British Liaison Officers (as they were called) and wireless operators were surreptitiously landed on isolated beaches and in quiet island coves, although about half of these arrived once the fortunes of war had begun to favour the Allies towards the end of 1943. It should also be noted that as some officers were landed, others were taken back to Egypt by the same vessel.

Gradually this motley array of colourful, unconventional characters set foot on Crete. They were required to volunteer because essentially they were spies and therefore in danger of being shot if caught. For many, if not all, it was a chance to escape the drudgery of strict military discipline. As one of them, Xan Fielding, pointed out: "… I recognised in the offer a God-sent release, not only from the military dead-end I had reached, but from militarism itself." (XF) Tom Dunbabin, an Australian who eventually led this SOE mission, reflected: "I liked it because it was a completely free life: also, it was an unique opportunity to understand the Greeks and their way of life." (TD) He too (according to his nephew) found "little appeal in the tediousness of regular army life," (TD) and left commando training to join military intelligence. Sandy Rendel perhaps needed to convince himself that it was a good move to join this group: "and yet the more I thought of it, the more strange and also exhilarating it all seemed." (AMR)

My Wife Suggested Crete

For some, the island of Crete was familiar to them as they had been involved in the battle and had either been evacuated or had escaped and made it back to Egypt. They had already been on the receiving end of Cretan hospitality; they admired these people and wanted to help. Within this group of men, many shared a knowledge of the Greek language or had learned ancient Greek at school. Some were archaeologists, and academics – intellectuals who were a breed apart from traditional military minds. They were an alternative lot who were well suited to the irregular work of SOE and ISLD.

"Leigh Fermor does not submit willingly to discipline," (RB) wrote a staff officer prior to Leigh Fermor's posting to Crete, where, ironically, submitting to discipline is not regarded by many inhabitants as a positive trait! After the war these men were to follow careers in the top echelons of education, in the literary world, in journalism and the diplomatic service. They were a bright bunch. During their time on Crete, respect for – and admiration of – these islanders led to the forging of many friendships. For some it became more than friendship; at least three of them eventually married Cretan girls. As for the work itself, Sandy Rendel believed that: "without exception all the British who took part in it, found it the most exhilarating work they had ever done." (AMR)

Along with the officers came a string of wireless operators, often tough and hardened sergeants with a wealth of military experience, unfazed by the rough-and-tumble existence in which they found themselves. Sgt John Lewis was asked by his Cretan guide one day what he was going to do after the war. "Gangster," he replied. It was just as well that they were a tough breed because frequently they would be holed up in a damp cave for days on end with nothing but lice for company before being obliged to trudge for miles to another dark cave when danger approached.

It was often a monotonous existence, compounded by faulty batteries and charging engines which habitually failed. However, with a fine command of British invective and an equally fine sense of humour, they were able to survive their torment and were treated as comrades-in-arms by their Cretan colleagues. Sgt Alec Tarves, Xan Fielding's wireless operator, managed to learn Greek in his spare time and was apparently: "anxious to resemble the Cretans as closely as possible in every respect," so that "he washed even less than they did, and was soon so indescribably filthy and vermin-ridden that everyone referred to him in tones of admiration and affection as 'The Tinker.'" (XF)

The natural choice to head this British clandestine group of agents on Crete was an Englishman by the name of John Pendlebury. A notable archaeologist who had assisted Arthur Evans at Knossós, he became curator there for a while in March 1930 before travelling, mostly on foot, across the length and breadth of the island, recording virtually all the archaeological sites in his 1939 publication: *The Archaeology of Crete*. In doing so he came to know the landscape of the island in detail, and being a Greek speaker he got to know all the Cretans whom he encountered on his travels. Before the Battle of Crete took place, it was he who organised bands of Cretans to prepare defences and it was he who would make contact with the famous Cretan *Kapetans* of the mountains so they knew what was coming.

Jack Hamson and Terence Bruce-Mitford worked with him, but as Hamson later explained in a tribute to Pendlebury: "It was by virtue of his knowledge, of his power, and in his name that I was enabled to do in the hills whatever I succeeded in doing. And his name was indeed one to conjure with in those hills. 'I am sent by Mr John, Mr John says, Mr John suggests, Mr John requires': Those were my infallible passwords… I was to them a casual stranger; he had lived with them and knew them. It was to the echo of his voice that they listened and could respond;" (IG)

Pendlebury Street, near the Haniá gate in Iráklio

My Wife Suggested Crete

In the heat of the battle, on May 22nd 1941, John Pendlebury was killed in action near the Haniá gate at the western end of Iráklio, on his way into the hills to make contact with one of those Cretan *Kapetans*. In 2019 I heard the name of John Pendlebury still being mentioned with great affection in the village of Tzermiádo on the Lasíthi plateau, a place and a village people whom he had greatly treasured in his pursuit of archaeology. On one of our visits to Iráklio we found the small side street near the Haniá gate which has been named after him. Beneath the street sign bearing his name we read the simple epitaph: "English archaeologist who fell in the battle of Crete."

In time the role which should have been Pendlebury's, as head of the mission, was given to an Australian, Tom Dunbabin – as it happened another archaeologist and Greek speaker. This knowledge of the Greek language, combined with a highly intelligent and purposeful mind, soon earned him the respect of his Cretan guides and colleagues, perhaps especially in the Amari valley where he was simply known as O'Tom.

Presumably though, if you have heard the name of any of these British Liaison Officers it will be that of the great travel writer, Patrick Leigh Fermor. A self-confessed philhellene and Greek speaker, Philedem or Michali as he was known by one or other of these codenames became a firm favourite amongst the many Cretans who crossed his path, and of course his fame increased when he successfully kidnapped the German General Kreipe and removed him to Egypt in 1944. I must also mention the name of Xan Fielding who was to become a close friend of Leigh Fermor. The wild west of Crete was set to become his territory, the most difficult area in which to exercise any real control or to have any significant influence.

For all these mavericks, life was undoubtedly tough and supplies hard to come by. Most of their food was generously provided by the Cretans who scarcely had enough for themselves, although there were occasional night time air drops and even less frequently some supplies arrived by motor launch or submarine. My own uncle, Alan Fernyhough, found himself at GHQ Middle East and the Central Ordnance Provision Office in Cairo during these Cretan resistance years. I therefore hope, although I have no proof, that he played some part in supplying these airdrops and sea landings. This is my own tenuous link with the island's struggle at this time, and sadly I left it far too late to ask Alan all about it.

As for the relationship between these Brits and their Cretan colleagues, bonds of friendship and trust developed, and according to one officer "…to a point where difference of race meant little." (PLF) Sometimes it would take time for a good relationship to develop. This was certainly so in the case of Sandy Rendel. It was Tom Dunbabin who eventually noticed the beginnings of an *esprit de corps* in Rendel's group, while in reverse roles Rendel, on a visit to the Amari Valley – Dunbabin's base – found that his boss was both well-known and well-liked: "It was delightful to see the enthusiasm which greeted him everywhere;" (AMR)

This camaraderie was also experienced sometimes by members of the SBS groups who occasionally appeared on the island for sabotage operations. A certain Aristeides Christophakis was detailed to assist an SBS Sergeant in blowing up an oil dump. A few days later, a boat returned to evacuate the SBS party. "They still could not exchange two coherent words in the other's language" explained Sandy Rendel (AMR) who witnessed their smiling handshake as they parted. "I don't suppose they will ever meet again, but each, it was clear, would always share the happiest of recollections of the dawns, and days and nights when they marched and crept and crawled around their oil dump together." (AMR)

Alexo Kokonas, a schoolteacher in the Amari valley at that time, has been described by Leigh Fermor and others as a saint for all the unquestioning help and succour that he gave them. Alexo's son, Niko, although a youth at the time, also took part in local resistance activities. Years later he wrote this tribute: "In the battle of Crete, British and Commonwealth troops fought alongside us, and for them and for those British officers and NCOs who shared with us the rigours of the Resistance, we have the sincerest affection and respect." (NK) This 'affection and respect' continued long after this chapter of the island's history was concluded. Xan Fielding experienced an abundance of warm hospitality when he returned to the island some ten years after he had first set eyes on the White Mountains. Much later, while attending the 50th anniversary commemorations in 1991, he was, by all accounts, still greeted with genuine affection by those village people with whom he had been acquainted half a century earlier.

The memorials which are clearly visible in many towns and villages serve as reminders of the horrors of the resistance years. In the Viánnos district at the village of Amirás near the south coast, a prominent sign advertises The Holocaust Museum, accompanied by a set of modern sculptures. You may think that this name is overly dramatic, but the villages in this area were all burned or blown up by the Nazis and an estimated one thousand villagers were killed. A young couple were looking after this small museum when we visited. The man spoke little English but we soon discovered that his grandfather had been one of the victims shot by the Nazis. As his wife explained so well: "The next generation know all about it. They grew up with the consequences."

WWII history in this part of the island is still clearly remembered with much sorrow and a degree of bitterness. It must be said that the actions of one or two of the more boisterous Cretan *Kapetans*, who controlled resistance gangs based in the hills and mountains, prompted some of the Nazi reprisals but, in the Viánnos district at least, these leaders are still held in high regard and blame for the reprisals was often shifted towards the British. Certainly the sabotage operations conducted by those SBS groups from time to time – blowing up fuel dumps, disabling some Luftwaffe aircraft and killing a few Germans in the process – brought little if any benefit to the Allies and sadly resulted in horrendous and savage reprisals on the civilian population. These British operations may have contributed to some Cretans becoming German collaborators, although many of these were hunted down by other Cretans. A grisly death would follow. Ralph Stockbridge (senior ISLD officer on the island) surely concluded correctly that: "The collection of good intelligence was nearly always of far greater value." (NK) Foreword by RH Stockbridge).

Memorial in the village of Pefkos, Viánnos district

Political allegiance also played its part in events at this time. Certainly the party known as EAM (and its military wing ELAS), allied to the KKE

Fighting for Freedom - Again

Road sign near the village of Amiras, Viánnos district

(the Greek communist party), was highly suspicious of the British and of their post-war intentions. "Indeed, from mid-1943 onwards, EAM initiated a vicious anti-British propaganda campaign in Crete…asserting that the British government's post-war intentions were to reduce Greece to subservience." (NK) Sandy Rendel found a chilly and antagonistic attitude in the village of Amirás, where the Holocaust Museum is today, when he met a communist group there, and several of the SOE agents had a difficult time trying to keep the political peace between the various factions. In the end they relied only on non-communist resistance fighters in their work, because these were the people they felt they could trust.

It was these Cretans who, in providing all their loyal help and protection, ensured – with few exceptions – the survival of these British officers and their wireless operators. The Official British Report of 1945 suggested that: "The success of the Mission depended on the presence of a population 90% pro-BRITISH." (NK) Whether this is an exaggerated figure is prone to speculation. In the years of occupation, it ought to be remembered that those Cretans in the pro-communist element of the population were still very much patriots, intent on liberating their island. As a result of these circumstances, a highly effective spy network developed throughout the island and John Pendlebury's initial work should not be underestimated in this achievement.

I want to emphasise that it was the people of Crete, or at least the vast majority of the population, whose efforts ensured the efficient gathering of intelligence – at great personal risk to themselves. As a result, if the Allies had decided to open a counter-offensive in this part of the Med, Crete would have been well placed to effect success. This 'great personal risk' very much equated to risking their own lives, and for some this meant the ultimate sacrifice. Patrick Leigh Fermor's wireless operator, Apostolos Evangélou, was captured and shot in prison. One of the sons of the Alones village priest, Siphi Alevizakis, was arrested and executed. Antoni Zoídakis from the Amari Valley, having been captured by a German patrol, was tied to the back of a vehicle and dragged for several kilometres until he was dead. Sandy Rendel painfully remembered sending a young man into Haniá only a week or two before the final German surrender. "He had left me with a smile, knowing gladly that he was trusted to carry out a dangerous job…". (AMR) He didn't return – he was arrested and shot.

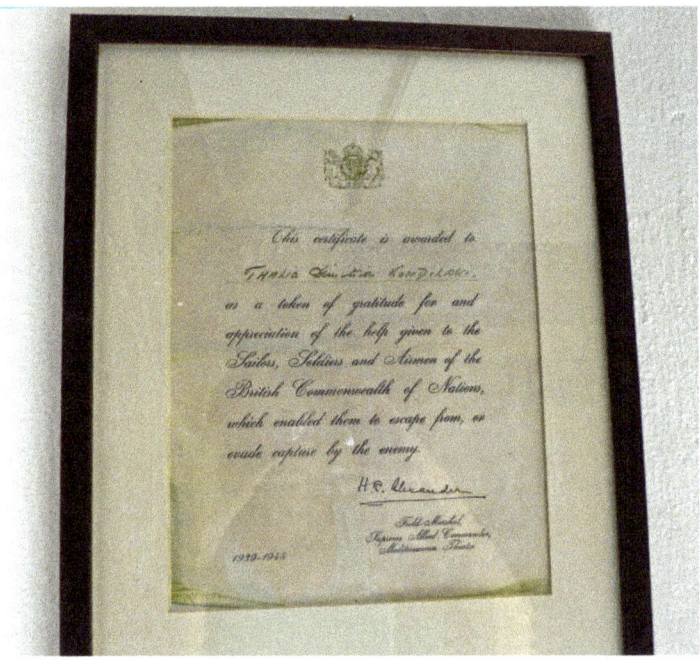

Certificate presented to a Cretan civilian by a grateful British commander

Fighting for Freedom - Again

Singling out individual Cretans may well be unwise. A good number are praised in the published accounts of British officers and in the Official British Report of 1945 including abbots, priests and women – for their phenomenal courage and support. However the vast majority have remained unsung heroes to this day. The three Cretans I am about to mention – all three being wonderful characters in their own right – provide classic examples of those who offered their selfless support to the British at this time. It is from the pens of Patrick Leigh Fermor, Sandy Rendel and Stephen Verney that I have learned about them.

Firstly, George Psychoundakis, a shepherd boy, who had been given a limited education and yet undoubtedly yearned to learn and later told the story of his experiences in his own book *The Cretan Runner*. In SOE circles, his code name was 'the Changeling', and later on: 'the Changebug'. However, to his fellow villagers he was known as *Bertódoulos-the Jester*, as a result of his rather mischievous comic humour. George was Xan Fielding's first guide when he (Xan) arrived as an SOE agent in January 1942. But he also worked – mainly in the west of the island – for Leigh Fermor, Dick Barnes, Jack Smith-Hughes and Tom Dunbabin. "This youthful Kim-like figure was a great favourite of everyone's, for his humour, high spirits, pluck and imagination and above all the tireless zest with which he threw himself into his task. If anybody could put a girdle round Crete in forty minutes, he could". (PLF)

Kosta Lubounes from Neápoli worked for Sandy Rendel in the east. "Kosta was one of the most likeable of men. No one seeing the kindliest of many wrinkles at the corner of his eyes as he smiled, would ever have guessed that he was the highly intelligent centre of a spy network. With his cap and trim white moustache and swinging an old walking stick he reminded me, as we strolled along the cliffs, of a rather meditative country squire or perhaps an ex-officer ruminating quietly in retirement at Eastbourne." (AMR)

Lastly, from the pen of Stephen Verney who arrived as an SOE agent in August 1944, comes the story of another shepherd boy: "...after a short rest, Tom [T. Dunbabin] introduced me to Markos Drakakis who was to be my Cretan guide. He was a shepherd boy from Así Goniá, a nearby village. We were about the same age, and from that moment on, he came with me everywhere, by day and by night, and risked his life for me many times over. Through him I came to know the courage and generosity of the Cretan people, who, almost without exception, were ready to give everything, including themselves, for the freedom of their country." (SV)

George Psychoundakis wrote about some of the horrors which they had to face and how they felt about it all: "Crete had to resist, and she resisted with all her might. And these [German] strangers, strutting now in the guise of brave swashbucklers, should have been begging forgiveness for all the evil they had done to Crete; for their cruel attack upon the island and for all the barbarity that typified them; for their 'vengeance', as they called it. Now people beheld their brothers shot with their hands tied behind them, their houses burnt and their fortunes destroyed. Children were killed in their mothers' arms, and men and women, both young and old, fell together before the German bullets. Whole villages, with their churches and their schools and all that was sacred, were burnt and blown up; yet they talked of a New Order. What a monstrosity!" (GP)

Jack Smith-Hughes, SOE agent on Crete and one of the earliest to make contact with the Cretan resistance, presided over the Cretan Office in Cairo for almost all of its duration and was fully aware of the quite outstanding efforts of the people of Crete in defence of their island and their Allies. In March 1945 in Cairo he wrote his report: "In time SOE officers will be leaving Crete and others will be replacing them; they will be responsible for paying a great debt of gratitude to the Cretans, who have put up such a magnificent performance." (JS-H in Appendix K to the Official British Report on SOE missions in Crete 1941-1945. (NK)

The naked truth of the consequences of their resistance to invasion and loyalty to their British allies is this: over 3,700 civilians – men, women and children – were killed. Some were killed in the battle, others were caught in their resistance work, tortured and shot. In reprisals, civilians were rounded up and executed *en masse*. At the village of Kali Sykia women were thrown into burning houses and burnt alive. Forty villages were blown up or burned to the ground. By May 1945 there was an appalling shortage of housing, food and clothing for the survivors.

~ ~ ~ ~

So when I laze about on the beach at Hióna, breathe in the cool air of the White Mountains, smell those wild herbs as I amble through my favourite gorge, or listen to the haunting sounds of the lyra – or whatever it is that I am enjoying at a given moment on this island – I don't think it will do me any harm to pause for a minute or so and reflect on what happened here in the 1940s. Michael Morpurgo was indeed correct: "Horrible things do happen in beautiful places".

C: THE AFTERMATH - CIVIL WAR

"So in an atmosphere of warm friendliness, ended an episode that, though intensely interesting from a purely military point of view, was for us a tragic and deeply disturbing experience. We had seen the fierce hatred that springs up in a country involved in civil war, and we had seen, too, how inevitably heavy are the civilian casualties after nearly a month's fighting in the heart of a capital city."
BRIGADIER GS THOMPSON, CO 1ST FIELD REG RA ATHENS, DECEMBER 1944/JANUARY 1945. FROM *THE ROYAL ARTILLERY COMMEMORATION BOOK 1939-45*. (GST)

Greece suffered appalling civilian losses during the Nazi occupation: an estimated half a million Greek civilians died of starvation during the severe winter of 1941-2; by the autumn of 1944, as the Germans withdrew, as many as 130,000 civilians had been killed by Hitler's forces.

During the occupation, the Germans had recruited right-wing Greeks in order to establish 'security battalions' to supress communist ideology. In spite of the eventual German retreat, one of Churchill's overriding objectives was to prevent Greece from being swallowed up by Stalin's communism. He therefore insisted on backing the monarchist and right-wing politicians, even though British Intelligence had suggested that EAM/ELAS (the communists) were the only logical group able to maintain order. Hence the security battalions – the former German collaborators – and other extremist forces of that ilk remained powerful and threatening. Apart from the hatred and disgust which many Greek citizens felt towards them, fear of what was to come was understandably of great concern.

So then another tragedy began. Fighting broke out between left and right-wing groups in Athens prompted – although it was going to happen anyway – by police opening fire and killing 16 EAM supporters on December 3rd 1944. British forces sent by Churchill to prop up the government had arrived in October and became embroiled in the ensuing conflict. In the two months of December 1944 and January 1945, 11,000 Greeks were killed. This was the "tragic and deeply disturbing experience" that Brigadier Thompson had witnessed.

Thompson's report highlighted this appalling death toll. Arriving at Pireás on December 10th, he was shocked by the intensity of the fighting so early in the conflict. The catalysts for civil war - distrust, resentment, anger and hatred - had been brewing for some time. This situation was compounded by the British. Four British destroyers and three corvettes were supporting infantry and artillery. Meanwhile, ELAS fighters were well organised and equipped.

A ceasefire, signed on February 12th, was short-lived. Democratic reforms promised by the British-backed government had failed to materialise. Fearsome right-wing vigilante groups moved about at will. Left-wingers were always excluded from public office, and often persecuted, resulting in a huge exodus of ELAS supporters: 80,000 of them withdrew to mountainous areas and regrouped. ELAS underwent a metamorphosis and became the Democratic Army of Greece (DSE). Accordingly in 1947, full-scale civil war became a dreadful reality, the horrors of which continued until 1949. Circumstances over which the DSE had no control eventually forced them to abandon their struggle. Thus the carnage on the Greek mainland came to an end.

~ ~ ~ ~

Above the village of Thériso, near Haniá, a peace accord was signed in November 1943 between nationalists and communists. Nikolaos Skoulas and General Mandakas, of the opposing sides, were both present. Many people believe that this agreement to a large degree prevented Crete from becoming immersed in the violent civil war which afflicted the mainland. In terms of scale I could probably get away with that statement. Crete retained her feeling of individuality, partly I suppose, because the island is geographically detached from the landmass of eastern Europe. Therefore the people were less influenced by the doctrine of Russian communism and took less notice of Stalin's successes which fuelled the hope of many Greeks on the mainland.

It must also be remembered that SOE officers had rarely, if ever, offered supplies let alone weapons to the communists. In one incident in the last months of the war, Stephen Verney and his guide had to stand guard outside warehouses in Kastélli Kissámou to prevent the communists from taking a cache of Italian weapons.

There are other reasons for the difference between the plight of the mainland and what happened in Crete. Any collaboration with the Germans in occupied Crete had been minimal compared to the mainland. Thieves and other convicted criminals had sometimes offered their services to the Nazi occupiers. However, "Accusations of collaboration against Cretan conservatives and the centre-right fell flat because so few were tainted." (AB) Antony Beevor, in his book *Crete. The Battle and the Resistance,* advanced a further theory as suggested by John Stanley, an ISLD agent who arrived on the island in 1943. Stanley's rather startling hypothesis reasoned that the ever present threat of Cretan family vendettas must also have curtailed, if not prevented, a devastating civil war: "The blood feuds engendered would have been so appalling that the very idea acted as a primitive equivalent of nuclear deterrence." (AB) The other important fact was that the Cretan communists could not hope for nor did they receive any support or supplies from their political friends on the mainland – the logistics were just impossible.

So most historians seem to have concluded that civil war in Crete was largely avoided as a result. Nevertheless, in any society it has always been the case, and sadly still is, that extreme political ideologies usually lead to violence. It was always clear during the resistance years that the opposing political post-war aims of nationalists and communists might produce violence in Crete too. Although George Psychoundakis enjoyed witnessing ecstatic scenes on the day of liberation in Haniá, (23rd May 1945), he had also heard the whispers: "that the two sides might come to blows." (GP) Even in October 1944 when the Germans had retreated from Iráklio, Sandy Rendel realised "that some of our best friends were in trouble with the communists." (AMR)

The peace agreement between the two sides at Thériso in November 1943, was followed by another agreement in September 1944 above the village of Zoúrva. A further accord was signed in February 1945 at Fres. It is to the credit of the Cretans themselves that they managed to come to these arrangements. However, the fact remains that even by May 1945 there had already been fifty deaths resulting from politically motivated conflict. For the 10 years between October 1944 – with the death of Yanni Bodias, leader of the communist guerrillas in eastern Crete – and October 1954, over 300 people from both sides of the political divide were killed. Many more were wounded.

As often happens in civil wars, families were split apart because of opposing ideological views – in Crete to a point where on at least one occasion father was killed by son. Not only that, but a former member of ELAS by the name of Anagnostakis murdered his uncle. Many Cretan citizens lived in fear for their lives, either because they helped the communists and therefore were liable to be arrested, or because they were known nationalists and therefore potential targets of the communists. The brutality of the killing was at times extreme. Many of the communists who were killed were then decapitated and their heads paraded through villages before being displayed prominently in Haniá. While the authorities claimed that this was to prove that these guerrillas had been killed, the guerrillas claimed that it was to terrify them and frighten their supporters. No wonder that some of them took their own lives rather than surrender.

My Wife Suggested Crete

As I write, the only two books in English specifically concerned with this Cretan civil war are those written by Colin Janes: *The Eagles of Crete* and *The Guerrillas of Crete*. It is mainly from these two sources that I have gleaned the information included in the previous paragraph, and also from which I can provide the following résumé.

The Cretan version of the DSE or Democratic Army was unofficially formed on the 28th October 1946. For an idea of numbers, no more than 500 communist guerrillas joined this Democratic Army throughout the whole of the conflict, although on top of this number it ought to be remembered that there were plenty of sympathetic relatives and friends. In eastern Crete there were about a hundred at most, but by May 1947 most of these had been killed or captured. The surviving dozen set off to walk westwards, two of them being killed on the way. Hence the authorities became aware of their plans to join up with the main nucleus of guerrillas in the west.

Here, the guerrilla army reached a peak of about 300, but with neither support nor supplies from mainland colleagues these people lacked arms, food, clothing and footwear: numbers dwindled. Amnesties by the Greek government led to the surrender of others.

A change of leadership led to a recruitment campaign and numbers increased again close to the previous peak. In March 1948 the communists organised the ambush of a visiting Greek minister – Sophocles Venizelos. The ambush took place near the village of Maheri not far from Haniá; although the minister's driver was wounded, everyone else survived unscathed. As a result of this attempted ambush Lt Colonel Vardoulakis – a Cretan from Anópoli – was given sole military command in the war against the communists. A new battalion of 150 *gendarmes* soon arrived from the mainland. Their arrival "… and the appointment of Vardoulakis as military commander finally signalled the beginning of the end for the guerrilla army." (CJ)

The new leader of the guerrillas decided that the Omaló plateau would become their base, but having eaten their way through a stockpile of seed potatoes they had to start raiding villages for food which naturally decreased their popularity further. Eventually they retreated into the Samariá gorge where the last major action of this conflict took place in June 1948. Great care was taken by the military authorities to guard all known exit routes out of the gorge. After three days the communists were holding out in an area just north of the village of Samariá. Rather than surrender they followed a local shepherd up the steep mountainside at night – an almost impossible feat even in daylight.

Fighting for Freedom - Again

The Omaló Plateau, a bleak temporary home to communists
in the winter of 1947-1948

Between April and June 1948, 25 guerrillas were killed, 18 arrested and 107 surrendered. By January 1949 only about 50 communists continued to hold out as fugitives.

In October 1949, the communist leaders on the mainland were forced to declare a cessation of hostilities. By the summer of 1950, 16 fugitives remained on the run in western Crete; by 1959 only eight of these fugitives remained at large. The story of this last group of eight, which included two women, is detailed in Colin Janes' book: *The Guerrillas of Crete*. Six of them including Nikos Kokovlis who became leader of the banned communist organisation in 1949, with his wife Argiro, eventually felt forced to make the long and tortuous journey via Athens and Italy to Tashkent in Uzbekistan. From Athens it took them five months to reach Tashkent. In Uzbekistan they joined 17,000 other Greek communists who had left their homeland. After initial joy, disillusionment soon followed: "This was not the utopia the six had expected to find in the USSR." (CJ)

There remained two other fugitives at large in Crete – they had refused to leave their island when the other six left. Not until 22nd February 1975 did these last two communist guerrillas receive an amnesty from the government. They came out of hiding the following day.

My Wife Suggested Crete

Unbelievably George Tzobanakis from the village of Kókkino Horió and Spiro Blazakis from neighbouring Gavalohóri on the Dhrápano peninsula had evaded both death and capture for 30 years. They had come to be known as the Eagles of Crete and their first night as free men was spent in a modern and comfortable hotel in Haniá. In contrast to their years of hiding in damp caves along the coast or in the mountains, the noise of the town's traffic kept them awake for almost the whole night. The story made the headlines in the foreign press with a photograph of the two survivors as they finally emerged from their secretive life appearing on the front page of the *Guardian* newspaper. These two men are now firmly established as legendary figures in Cretan folklore.

Kokovlis and his wife Argiro were granted amnesty in April 1976, together with the four others who had left Crete with them in 1962. They all returned to Greece. Courtesy of Colin Janes, I was directed to a documentary about these six Cretans who had left the island for Tashkent. Called *There Was No Other Way*, it had been filmed when only three of them were still alive: Nikos Kokovlis, his wife Argiro, and Yanni Lionakis. The documentary showed Argiro Kokovli and Yanni Lionakis on a return trip to visit Italian friends who had helped them in 1962 as they made their way to Tashkent. It was a day full of emotion. Nikos Kokovlis was too frail to travel to Italy. However, towards the end of the documentary film, Nikos and Argiro are seen being driven high into the White Mountains. The old man, visibly moved, admits that he burst into tears as he got out of the car. He had never expected to see these mountains again. "They are lifeless", he said, "but they have soul".

Colin Janes has been quoted as saying: "all these guerrillas in Crete deserve the title 'Eagles of Crete'". Yianni Lionakis, one of the other 'six', died in his home village of Gavalohóri in January 2012. Kokovlis lived on until August of that year, surviving to the ripe old age of 92. The last of the Eagles to pass away was Argiro Kokovli. She died in March 2019 at the age of 94, thus bringing to an end this extraordinary chapter in Cretan history.

~ ~ ~ ~

Politics in Crete has rumbled on uneasily with some occasional fiery violence attached, although this has been more noticeable on the mainland. Any lingering anti-British sentiment – although I stress that you are very unlikely to witness it – has often been linked to the events on the Greek mainland. Here, at the end of WWII, those former German collaborators became highly influential as they were allowed to take on powerful roles in national affairs. Christopher Somerville, a British journalist who walked across the island a decade or so ago, was reminded by an ex-mayor of Argyroúpolis of how the Greeks perceived this: "The English supported the Greek government, the King, all the forces of reaction. The Greeks saw some people who had collaborated with the Germans given positions of power, given influence and opportunities. ELAS, that was our pro-Communist party, it was defeated, and many good patriotic wartime andartes were killed or discredited. And the people saw the British supporting this. They remembered how at Yalta, Churchill had carved up the world with Stalin and Roosevelt, and Britain had taken Greece as part of its sphere of influence. Lots of Greeks didn't like that, and they didn't like the English very much." (CS)

However, any animosity towards the British would also have been stoked by the attitude and actions of the British government when the Cyprus crisis erupted. With tense beginnings in the 1950s, fighting between Turkish and Greek Cypriots in 1963 was followed by the attempted toppling of the Makarios government and subsequent Turkish invasion in 1974. This was all too much for Greeks and Cretans to bear. In 1999 the bombing of Yugoslavia by NATO was considered outrageous to many Greeks, Cretans included – Serbia had been a historical ally of Greece for many years.

In recent times, any hostility towards Germany has usually been associated with the Greek financial crisis and the cost, in terms of further economic hardship, of EU bailouts, as Germany is seen as controlling European coffers. Isolated incidents have included a couple of German tourists refusing to pay a Greek taxi driver for their journey on the basis that the Greek nation owed Germany an awful lot more. With regard to the battle of Crete and the occupation bitterness may remain but it is not directed at anyone in particular these days. "As for the Germans," wrote Adam Hopkins, "the Cretans seem to bear little resentment." He went on to say: "What lingers is the memory of death, destruction and hardship, bitter to think about but accepted without blame, much as a natural cataclysm, an earthquake, say, or a tidal wave." (AH)

In 1979 Patrick Leigh Fermor attempted to find a suitable spot in Crete for a memorial plaque in memory of fallen comrades during the resistance years. His request to site this plaque firstly at Moní Arkádhi and then at Moní Préveli was eventually refused. A car with four 'journalists' had turned up to dissuade the abbot at both monasteries from allowing such a thing. (I recently discovered that this bronze plaque, although still intact, remains hidden away at a well-protected military installation). Shortly after this thwarted project, a huge explosion blew up PLF's car in Iráklio: "There it was indeed, with the whole front scattered for acres all round, 10 yards of burnt, slow-burning fuse underneath, and a red poster with hammers and sickles." (PLF from *Dashing for the Post*). The communist party in Iráklio had been at work. In complete contrast, Leigh Fermor received plenty of embarrassed apologies from his many Cretan friends. "The CP are only a small minority in Herakleion: but it shows what hatred and organization can do." (PLF from *Dashing for the Post*.) I was not surprised to learn that when other former SOE officers visited long after the war, they were not welcomed back so warmly by families of the communists: they were seen to have been on 'the wrong side' in the conflict.

In June 2020 I wrote to Nikos Kokonas, a lecturer in the department of economics at the University of Bath. His great-grandfather, Alexandros (Alexo) Kokonas, schoolteacher in the Amari village of Yerakári in the 1940s, had been – together with the village priest of Alones, Father John Alevizakis – at the top of the list of those Cretans consistently described by the British soldiers and secret agents as 'saints'. Nikos's grandfather and namesake had also – as a boy – run errands for the British, had been captured by the Germans, but had managed to escape. I felt that I wanted to say my own thank you to the current Kokonas family for all those saintly deeds. My new friend, in typical Cretan style, gave his time and knowledge freely and willingly and thanked me for my words about his family as we spoke one Sunday afternoon. My mind briefly turned to my own father as I hoped that he would have approved of my small gesture of appreciation.

Today's Cretans still know all about the battle, the resistance and the civil war, but as Nikos reminded me: "We live in the modern world now." It will be the current social, political and economic problems – local, regional and global – which will dominate the lively and heated debate at many a *kafenion* and taverna on a Sunday afternoon. In the remote hill villages, with an occasional upward glance, there may be a sighting of the Golden eagle or Bonelli's eagle, both threatened species, flying high above as these famous raptors hunt for their own Sunday lunch and continue the struggle for their own survival.

~ ~ ~ ~

The fog of war and internal conflict produce a multitude of human issues, no more so than in this particular Cretan saga. I recognise that many Cretan attributes had risen to the fore during these years: the pride in their cultural heritage and the need to emulate their forefathers; their sense of honour and self-respect; their vitality and courage and, of course, their kindness to friends and allies. They were fighting for

Fighting for Freedom - Again

freedom once again, and for their beliefs. I have discovered so much and yet I could, no doubt, occupy the rest of my days in the study of this remarkable period of Cretan history. What I have learned so far has been a humbling experience.

At the end of that documentary film *There Was No Other Way*, I watched as the frail old guerrilla leader focused his eyes on the high desert scenery, long after the curtain had been drawn over his particular struggle. The camera traced the contours of the White Mountains, and the credits rolled to the sound of a mournful yet beautiful musical composition by Vangelis Fampas; a fitting end to the bitter ravages of ideological strife.

Chapter Eleven

Rummaging about in Réthymno

"The General's behaviour was most friendly and helpful throughout and he put up with the hardships of mountain travel and living rough with fortitude".
FROM WAR REPORT NO. 8. SHORT REPORT ON CAPTURE OF GEN. KREIPE MAY 1944. (PLF)

I am about to mention one more war-time story – in truth I have already mentioned it in passing - and I do so with the promise of no further lengthy or gruesome details. If I need to provide an excuse for its inclusion here, then it is simply because most of the action associated with this extraordinary coup, as it turned out to be, took place within the province of Réthymno. This was the kidnap and abduction of the German Commander General Heinrich Kreipe by Patrick Leigh Fermor, William Stanley Moss and a cast of willing Cretan helpers on Wednesday 26th April 1944. It was an event which has naturally prompted the writing of several books and the making of a classic black and white movie, the story enduring as a symbol of Cretan resistance to occupation and Boy's Own derring-do. Some 18 days after the kidnap, the abduction party managed, courtesy of Captain Brian Coleman and the motor launch ML842, to set sail for Egypt and safety with their captured German general.

Having brought the general's car to a halt, disarmed Kreipe and given his driver a good thump, and then with Billy Moss at the wheel – Kreipe being sat on by two Cretans in the back seat – driving daringly through numerous German checkpoints in Iráklio, they eventually abandoned the car. Setting off on foot they trudged through the hills and mountains of the prefecture of Réthymno, avoiding German patrols by the skin of their teeth, before Captain Coleman took them off the lonely beach of Peristeres a kilometre or so west of the village of Rodhákino on the south coast. This was a beach I wanted to find. On a fine October day Jennie and

Rummaging About in Réthymno

I drove to Rodhákino, down to Koráka beach, along the narrow coastal road to the hamlet of Polyrízos, and after the tarmac had petered out a rough and dusty track led us to Peristeres.

This turned out to be a sand and shingle beach accompanied by a seasonal *kantina* – a snack shack. It still felt isolated and I tried to visualise the scene late in the evening of the 14th of May 1944, as the loyal Cretan *andartes* and the hardy Rodhákiniots gathered to watch proceedings: "The place was filling up like a drawing room: groups were lounging about in the rocks or strolling with slung guns quietly conversing;" (PLF) Jennie took photographs of me as I imagined it all happening, and she teasingly chastised me for allegedly standing to attention in admiration and respect for the participants of this adventurous plot that had somehow reached such a successful conclusion here so many years ago.

Most package tourists, I hazard a guess, will not have been to this part of Réthymno as they will usually be staying somewhere like Balí on the north coast or end up for a week at Plakiás on the south coast, but the prefecture of Réthymno has much more to offer. This October visit had taken us back to Lena's villa and some happy times with our friends at Mixórrouma. However, travelling will always produce the odd hitch at some point and for us this meant that Lena's previous guests had stayed on an extra day. So for one night Lena booked us in with a friend of hers whose fortunes had taken a turn for the worse.

The Rastoni Hotel, perched on a hill on the outskirts of Spíli had been listed in the 2013 version of the RGC, but by the time of our visit it was virtually derelict; the swimming pool and its surrounds had seen no action for some time. Our room was fairly basic and not to Jennie's liking. On the plus side the views west from here towards the White Mountains were magnificent and my wife consoled herself with a large chunk of *baklava*. We survived the night and I smiled as I saw the sign advertising the Rastoni – which was the only part of the place still in good condition – describing itself as: "making holidays interesting."

Because there were no facilities at the Rastoni, we travelled the short distance into town to find some breakfast. Spíli has a pleasant central *platía* complete with the replica of a wonderful Venetian fountain with 25 water spouts, surrounded by several tavernas and cafés. We went into one of them. A combination of sitting in the morning sunshine under giant plane trees, listening to the water from the fountain, being fortified by a delicious omelette, fresh fruit, yoghurt and tea, was enough to lift us from the drudgery of the dilapidated Rastoni. The town is a great centre for walkers with the E4 path close by and opportunities for challenging hikes in all directions: to the Amari valley via Mount Kédhros or to Moní Préveli, with many more choices available from the village of Mixórrouma, home to our friends and eventually the base for us in the shape of Lena's villa for a few days. Spíli itself can also claim to have a spiritual centre at its heart, as here is a large Greek Orthodox teaching academy for prospective priests. Perhaps it was with this knowledge that we accepted our experience at the Rastoni with good grace!

~ ~ ~ ~

The village of Argyroúpolis in the foothills of the White Mountains is full of surprises. To reach it we drove up through the narrow Kotsifóu gorge in full view of still more of this dramatic Cretan landscape before passing through rural villages such as Kali Sykia (which had suffered terrible horrors in October 1943 at the hands of a Nazi Jagdkommando). We journeyed on through Vilandrédo. In 1944 a Vilandrédo family had produced a sumptious meal for the Kreipe kidnappers. Nearby caves had concealed them from their pursuers. Yet now it was peaceful and fertile country as we exchanged a waving hello with a local farmer. Argyroúpolis, a name which I find most difficult to pronounce, really deserves a full day – if not more – to appreciate.

The sound of fast-flowing water can be heard in many parts of the village. This natural resource was acknowledged as far back as Dorian times when Lappa, as this settlement was then called, was an ally of Lyttos. We saw fenced-off remains when we parked the car in the upper village. The great mix of old waterworks, a Venetian fulling mill, and remnants of other Venetian buildings show that the Romans and Venetians had a big influence on the area. Lappa's necropolis with hundreds of tombs is still visible, too.

We strolled through the village and found a Roman mosaic floor protected by a canopy, apparently part of a Roman bath house, before lunching near a skilfully-constructed stone archway at Bar Maria. Avocados are grown locally, utilising the plentiful water supply, and all sorts of homeopathic remedies made from the fruit were available for purchase next door. This area is also walking country although I was content to cast my eyes up to the next village of Así Goniá, home to the late George Psychoundakis and which lies in the mist above the slopes of the Gipari gorge. Other historically important villages such as Alones and Kalikrátis remain out of sight in the hills further away. For us, exploration here would just have to wait.

Rummaging About in Réthymno

We circled back to the villa via a less dramatic route, stopping at a roadside cheese shop with the cheese factory tucked away behind. Here all manner of different types and styles were available from sheep or goat, hard and soft, salted and unsalted, mild and strong-flavoured, one matured in oil, another ricotta in style. Thus, armed with some good cheese and a glass of Cretan wine, we looked back at the photographs we had taken of Argyroúpolis, ancient Lappa and the avocados.

~ ~ ~ ~

The Venetian fortress of Frangokástello is officially just in the prefecture of Haniá, lying in the district of Sphakiá. The easiest way to get there, unless of course you are staying in this locality, is to approach from Plakiás in Réthymno province. So off we went, passing through my favourite village of Selliá and then through Rodhákino, on a twisting hilltop road that eventually descends to a wide almost triangular plain where this impressive fortress suddenly comes into view. Originally built in 1371 to deter pirates, it is now just a shell. In spite of this you can still climb up one of the corner towers from where you have fabulous views of

The Venetian fortress of Frangokástello

My Wife Suggested Crete

the mountains and coastline to the east and west. Pirates would have been spied approaching from a good distance away.

For some reason, as I admired the views, I suddenly remembered the garden shed of one of my former customers who had doctored a well-known advertisement for an animal charity so that the sticker on his garden shed window read: "Her Majesty's Revenue and Customs is for life, not just for Christmas." Whether – perched as I was on top of the Frangokástello tower – I was beginning to hallucinate or to suffer from some minor dehydration I do not know, but I was convinced that I detected through the heat-haze a band of HMRC officials riding on horseback swiftly across the plain towards me.

Even without this uneasy vision I had read that this place is not without its ghostly stories. In 1828 a Greek adventurer by the name of Daliani had attempted to spread the War of Independence from the mainland to Crete. His forces were vastly outnumbered, resulting in his death and the massacre of at least half of his men in the castle fortress. It is claimed that to this day, around May 17th, the ghosts of Hadzi Michali Daliani and his followers appear in the mists around dawn. They are known as the *dhroussoulites* or dewy ones. We walked down to the soft

Mountain view from one of the corner towers

sandy beach below and a good swim in the calm shallow water was enough to dispel any myths and ghost stories from my mind.

A word of warning comes from the RGC if you intend to stay overnight here. This time the trouble appears to be mosquitoes rather than ghosts. Looking around I noticed some small freshwater ponds formed from a stream which heads this way from the mountains above, thus creating in the warm atmosphere a natural breeding ground for the little perishers. So there may be some justification for the advice given by the RGC, which strongly recommends that you arm yourself with mosquito repellent.

On our return journey, we stopped off at a café perched high above the sea which provided panoramic views of the coast below. A combination of ice-cream and mountain tea completed my rehydration process even though photographic evidence shows me smiling profusely, something that I normally find very difficult to do when a camera is pointed in my direction. Perhaps the rehydration process was still incomplete, and the eerie phantoms of Frangokástello were not entirely banished from my mind.

~ ~ ~ ~

The prefecture of Réthymno is not short of historic places of import in Cretan history. Among the favourites must be the sizeable monastery of Moní Arkádhi, a shrine to Cretan independence. In 1866 the abbot, who was trapped inside with local people with no possible escape route, deliberately set off an explosion that killed both Cretan defenders and many of the enraged Turkish attackers. News of this horrific event soon spread throughout the island. JEH Skinner, arriving on the island the following spring when corpses were still visible within the monastery grounds, saw: "scores of bodies unburied, half-buried, sun-dried, and mangled...Anything would be better than to shrivel and blacken in this ghastly fashion." (JEHS). He described how the news had been received: "When the monastery of Arkadi was besieged and taken in November 1866, its tragic fate sent a thrill of emulation, rather than terror, from end to end of Crete" (JEHS). Moní Arkádhi thus became this huge symbol of defiance against Turkish occupation, arousing sympathy throughout Europe, although the island's independence and eventual union with Greece took another 40-odd years to achieve.

From November 7th to November 9th thousands of Cretans turn up for the annual remembrance. We sensed on our visit that this highly venerated monastery was beginning to be spruced up in anticipation of the

My Wife Suggested Crete

The church at Moní Arkádhi

pilgrimage, although the resident cat population took no notice – nothing was going to disturb their happy slumber in the flower beds. These cats probably rank as amongst the most fortunate felines on the island, judging by the piles of cat food which the monks leave here and there for their four-legged friends.

We are glad that we have seen Moní Arkádhi. It really is an impressive sight even from the outside as you first arrive, befitting of its significance in the island's history. The church, built in 1587, has a grand façade and is reason enough for a visit, while the arched cellars and the row of monks' private quarters evoke a sense of solemn importance to this holy Cretan place. Of course when we saw the still-blackened walls of the former wine cellar, it was obvious where the 1866 explosion had taken place. On the way out we climbed the steps up to the monastery's former windmill. Don't do this if you are squeamish because what you then see are the skulls of some of those who perished in 1866, as this is now an ossuary. We didn't linger long.

Our historian friend, Stelios, had informed us of a brand new archaeological museum and excavated site at Eléftherna which had been recently opened to the public. You need to allot a full day to have any hope

Rummaging About in Réthymno

Entrance to Moní Arkádhi

of seeing this extensive Dorian and Roman city, mainly because it is spread over a large area. The footpaths which lead to the various points of interest are punctuated by confusing signposts which optimistically indicate that whichever path you choose to take, will lead you to where you want to go.

We began with the necropolis, housed under a giant modern roof structure, where at least 20 cremations have been discovered, along with gold jewellery and pottery offerings. Jennie became irritated by the rather overbearing custodian who constantly told us not to stand too close to the excavations, although gradually he concentrated on consuming his packet of crisps and therefore took less notice of us. The museum in Néa Eléftherna, a short drive away, was excellent and all those offerings from the necropolis and items from the acropolis and town were nicely displayed. The block on taking any photographs irritated my wife.

Both the museum and the necropolis demand modest entrance fees, but the rest of Eléftherna can be explored without charge (as I write). So on our second visit we spent a good three hours negotiating various footpaths and deciphering the illogical signposts. Eventually we came out of the valley and reached the Roman tower which we had seen from below; it must have acted as their gatehouse. Then we found their giant

The Eléftherna necropolis

cisterns that had been carved out of the rocky hillside. Soon after the far older Dorian acropolis appeared. Nobody was there so we explored this hilltop citadel by ourselves. It was great fun.

Suddenly, over the other side of this hill we spotted the well-advanced excavations of the Dorian town below. This turned out to be the best way to see the town as it was securely fenced off. We never saw another soul on our walk but as time was marching on we decided to leave the venerated church of Ayia Ánna and a stone built Hellenistic bridge for another day. We needed to get back to our car before it got dark. To achieve this, we sought out a direct route which involved a bit of undergrowth bashing, crossing an almost dry riverbed to find a rough track which eventually took us back to the tarmac road. En route near the riverbed we chanced upon an orange grove complete with a tiny ruined house and its own deep well nearby. It was quite an Alice in Wonderland moment and will always remind me fondly of our rambles and explorations in Eléftherna.

Not far from Eléftherna is the village of Margarítes which has a long history of pottery making including production of the famous giant *píthoi*, some of which have found their way into the UK to adorn the gardens of the rich and famous. Also within Réthymno prefecture several caves are worth

Rummaging About in Réthymno

The Eléftherna acropolis

the consideration of a visit: the Melidhóni cave (with another atrocity story), the Sfendóni cave, the Idean cave above the Nídha plateau and the Kamáres cave – I hope to see them one day and learn about the myths and legends which are no doubt attached. For relaxation you could head for the tranquillity of the Amari valley, which I have mentioned elsewhere in this book, or perhaps to one of several yoga retreats on the south coast, notably at Áyios Pávlos and Triópetra, both of which look extremely tempting in their isolated locations.

I expect by now you have noticed that one of the ways we relax on this island involves visiting necropoli and ossuaries. I therefore understand if you firmly believe that I have a seriously abnormal tendency to roam about in graveyards. Reinforcing your belief is rather simple as we have also visited the extensive Minoan cemetery at Arméni, located just off the main Spíli-Réthymno road. Some of the 200 rock-cut tombs were really quite spectacular and we briefly went into one of the chambers, much to the horror of our friends, Yanni and Eleni, who watched from above. An additional asset of this cemetery comes from the upper branches of numerous mature oak trees. These provide cool shade to escape the heat of a summer's day.

My Wife Suggested Crete

Above all else the province of Réthymno is – for us – synonymous with spending happy times with our German friends, Yanni and Eleni, at their Cretan home in Mixórrouma. They have a new edition to their family of dogs in the shape of Sophia – another rescue case – although my favourite of the three remains the mischievous Pontikos or 'little mouse', who is sometimes teased as his belly is tickled with the German words: "Pontikos! Was machen die Mädchen auf Paris?" (What do girls do in Paris?) For us Réthymno also means further visits to favourite tavernas: the kind and spritely Agamemnon and his taverna nestling under the mighty Mount Kédhros; the Taverna Gefyra and its shady terrace by the Megalos Potamos river bridge near Palm Beach; at Niko's on the outskirts of Spíli, run by a most competent chef who used to cook for the budding priests nearby – they must have eaten very well; and perhaps my favourite spot in my favourite village of Selliá, at a little restaurant called Elia with the most mind-boggling views, mouth-watering food and equally memorable Cretan wine.

In complete contrast to the culinary delights of Elia, I also fondly remember sitting at the table of our friends in Mixórrouma one day when old Manoli from the village turned up. We sat happily munching walnuts and apples washed down with a glass or two of local *raki*. This too was a perfect autumnal feast.

We have been fortunate to have been invited on two other occasions to noteworthy feasts in the Mixórrouma area. The first was to the *kafenion* of young Manoli, the word 'young' being used to distinguish him from old Manoli rather than to flatter him. Young Manoli is still a lively character even if he is no longer a spring chicken. The occasion was to celebrate the successful distillation and quantity of the current year's *raki*, as well as to adjudicate on his new red wine. The general consensus amongst the noisy gathering of 10 villagers was that the wine would mature nicely.

Jennie tried a few words of Greek which were widely acclaimed although Manoli had no hesitation in correcting her mistakes. He then proceeded to deliberate on the choice of my new Greek name since Hugh was not an option. Pieces of barbecued chicken and pork, potatoes, bread and salad were liberally distributed among the guests and the local welder noticed that I was gulping down the wine in good Cretan style, which appeared to lift my status somewhat. It was a raucous gathering, but we were made to feel most welcome.

Our other feast was of a more formal nature. At 9am one morning Yanni and Eleni picked us up to drive the short distance to the village of Lambini and once there, to the tiny chapel of St. George. Around 60 or

70 villagers of all ages had turned up for this blessing of the wine from the year's grape harvest. The Papa also appeared to be blessing the bread and all manner of solemn intonations emanated from him from within the chapel – which could barely house more than half a dozen worshippers at any one time – before he continued his work alfresco.

My new friend, the welder, arrived to kiss the icon of St George, which had been hung outside the chapel for the day's proceedings, and to light a candle. As these formalities were taking place, the women of the village began appearing with trays of home cooked food including enormous pots of *pilafi* – a rice and meat concoction. It also became obvious that the villagers attached particular importance to the piece of bread handed out to everyone by the Papa. So, by 10.30am everyone was indulging in a hearty stand-up meal and as we left I detected the menfolk beginning to get serious about the wine and *raki*. I felt honoured to have been allowed to witness and take part in a traditional Cretan religious festival at this isolated spot in the Réthymno hills.

~ ~ ~ ~

In 1972 Patrick Leigh Fermor and Heinrich Kreipe, former captor and prisoner in April 1944, were reunited in Athens – together with some of the Cretan participants of that wartime plot – during the making of a documentary for Greek television. There is in existence a wonderful photograph of the two men clinking glasses together with happy smiles on both faces as they reminisced. PLF wrote: "We had both drunk at the same fountains long before; and things were different between us for the rest of our time together." (PLF *Words of Mercury*.).

Jennie and I have often raised a glass or two of some local nectar in celebration of discovering the hills and valleys and ever-changing coastline of this prefecture of Réthymno. Relaxing on the patio of their house in Kato Mixórrouma, gazing across at the village church of St Nicholas nestling in typical Réthymno countryside, we too have happily clinked glasses together with our own German friends on many an occasion – which is of course the way it ought to be.

Kato Mixórrouma

A Cretan Interlude

"The Katzphur People"

August 1944 was a desperately sad and horrific time for the people of the Amari valley in Réthymno province, where many villages were systematically destroyed by the Nazi occupiers. Yet, even in these dark days, Cretan humour remained alive and well. Shadowed by Mt. Ida, the village of Fourfourás sits on a ridge roughly midway down the eastern side of the valley, and, incidentally, was the birthplace of another member of the Kreipe abduction team – George Tyrakis. All the villages of the Amari were given their own wartime codenames by the Allies. Fourfourás was called Katzphur. Tom Dunbabin, head of clandestine operations in Crete at the time, and who had a winter shelter near this village, related the following story about the Katzphurians.

"The Katzphur people were a merry folk, perhaps above most other Cretans. The village is a big one, and rich; it has sheep-walks and corn-lands, gardens and vineyards, above all vineyards. I never met a Katzphurian, whether in the village or in the fields, in forest or on the mountain, who had not wine with him; in the most improbable places one would turn up unexpectedly and produce from his knapsack a flask of wine, and some bread and cheese and a knuckle of mutton to eat with it. A story relates that two Katzphurians, old friends of the bottle, decided after one debauch to reform. To be out of temptation's way, they walked out of the village, lay down in the scrub at the edge of a field, and went to sleep in the early morning sun. Towards afternoon one of them woke, feeling something hard under his head. Putting his hand under the bush on which he was lying, he drew out a wine-flask which the owner of the field had hidden there in case he should feel thirsty while working. Such a sign from heaven should not be rejected, so after finishing the flask the two cronies went back to the village and began again." (TD) (From *Tom J Dunbabin. An Archaeologist at War.* Society of Cretan Historical Studies, Testimonies 6, edited by Tom Dunbabin).

Chapter Twelve

The Lasíthi Plateau

> *"To have stood on Ida, on Dikte and on Aphendes-Kavousi in the clear shrill wind and to have toiled through the hot little valleys with that unforgettable smell of herbs is an experience the memory of which nothing can ever take away from you."*
> JDS PENDLEBURY. THE ARCHAEOLOGY OF CRETE. (JP)

While Ida stands proudly in the centre of the island, the other two mountain peaks mentioned by the archaeologist John Pendlebury are very much in Lasíthi prefecture, with Mount Dhíkti standing on guard above the fertile upland Lasíthi plateau, some one thousand metres above sea level. Ever since Mr Maniadakis – our taxi driver in 2011 – had pointed out the road junction where one of the three routes up to the plateau begins to ascend, I had been itching to discover what it looked like. It is not an especially large area – perhaps encompassing thirty or forty square kilometres – but it is handily placed to be on the tour operator's list for touristy days out. I was however encouraged by the opinion of the RGC which suggested that if you stay overnight up here, it really can be a magical experience once the coaches have negotiated the hairpin bends back down to the coast.

Our magical experience took the form of a three-night stay at Maison Kronio on the outskirts of the village of Tzermiádho, a settlement where John Pendlebury and the Tzermiadhians had developed their mutual respect and admiration in the 1930s. It was above this village where Pendlebury had excavated the important Minoan site of Karfí as well as several caves in the area and had also trekked up to the peak of Mount Dhíkti. It took us about 45 minutes from the coast road to reach Maison Kronio in Tzermiádho's neighbouring hamlet of Marmakéto. We felt it was rather a strange name for this small apartment complex, but all soon became clear when we met up with the owners, Christine of French origin

The Lasíthi Plateau

– hence the *maison* – and her husband Vassilis who also owned the Taverna Kronio in the village. Kronio refers to the legend of the birth of Zeus.

Zeus' father, Kronos, had been warned that he would be overthrown by a son and decided to eat all his offspring. However, Zeus was saved as his mother gave Kronos a stone to eat instead. On a hillside near Tzermiádho is a cave where John Pendlebury discovered remains and tombs dating back to Neolithic times, and hence this cave was used by humans far earlier that the more famous Dhiktean cave on the other side of the plateau where finds were dated merely (!) from Minoan times, but also where allegedly Zeus was born. The villagers of Tzermiádho were apparently delighted to learn that their cave had been found to contain far older human remains than the Dhiktean cave and hence they named it Kronos after the father of Zeus. Just to complicate the picture yet more, archaeologists know the Kronos cave by the name Trápeza. I might as well add further confusion by announcing that we have named it 'the snake cave' because, on the steps leading up to the entrance when we visited, a snake was endeavouring to strangle a lizard for supper. Two Pakistani tourists turned up at this moment, and I guess the snake was as

On the steps leading to the Kronos cave

My Wife Suggested Crete

surprised as we were to see our fellow travellers from a distant land appearing on this remote hillside, as it immediately let go of its prey and each reptile departed at speed in opposite directions.

Once inside the Kronos cave, there was in fact little to see: we should have brought a torch, but even so I am told that should you venture further inside this cave, the footings become more and more precarious. The great joy for us was being able to walk to it from our apartment along a leafy lane lined with mature walnut trees which, at the end of May, were bearing vast quantities of swelling nuts. They provided welcome shade for us as we perused fields of young vegetable plants and potatoes. Wheat is grown up here too and there are plenty of fruit trees, but in sharp contrast with most of the island there are no olive groves – the Lasíthi plateau is set at too high an altitude and in winter has snow and frost to contend with.

In one of the fields, as we walked by, a herd of goats had been allowed to demolish what remained of a crop already harvested. We wandered along a track halfway up the hillside before choosing a couple of boulders in the shade of a thorny tree on which to rest and look down upon this great expanse of level farmland framed by a circle of wild hills and mountains. Mt.Dhíkti towered above at 2,148 metres above sea level.

Walnut trees line the lane leading to the Kronos cave

The Lasíthi Plateau

Now, by mid-afternoon, a delightful aura of peace had descended onto the plateau as the tourist coaches and cars had all retreated to sea level.

There had been a lot of rain in the preceding winter and through the month of April, according to Christine. Now the vegetation had perked up, and seemed to be benefitting from the late spring sunshine. Consequently we were able to enjoy the wild flowers, alpines, pink cistus and yellow phlomis. It was clear to me that Christine took a keen interest in the many roses which adorned the entrance to their property. To the rear they had built a pleasant swimming pool, the views from which led directly onto the fields of the plateau, while behind, the mighty Mount Dhíkti still retained a little snow in sheltered clefts. This was a variation of an infinity pool which I found much to my liking. After my refreshing dip I took a photograph of Jennie sitting by the pool with a cup of tea and the now almost obligatory wedge of *baklava*, enjoying the hazy sunshine. There was not another living soul in sight.

Having negotiated your way uphill from the coast, guidebooks tend to exclaim about driving through the dramatic pass of Séli Ambélou, either side of which you will see abandoned stone windmills – traditional grain mills of old. Electric or petrol-driven pumps have replaced most of the windmills, but the old-fashioned mills are still visible here and there and are well advertised by tour companies in the coastal resorts in order to attract business. Apart from the windmills, the reason most tourists take the day trip to the Lasíthi plateau is to visit the Dhiktean cave, reached after about a 20-minute climb from the sizeable car park on the edge of the village of Psykhró.

We joined our fellow tourists for the steep climb which soon induced heavy breathing and required a few halts to regain our strength. I was secretly pleased – to my shame – to see a few much younger visitors also finding the climb difficult, although a furtive glance at their waistlines usually provided the answer for their struggle. The reward for all of us when we arrived was that we could claim to have visited the birthplace of Zeus. A slight technical hitch then arises if you read about another Cretan cave – the Idean cave above the Nídha plateau further west – where the locals there will inform you that their cave was undoubtedly the birthplace of Zeus and where he was brought up.

The Dhiktean cave is dramatic enough, Zeus or no Zeus, with plenty of stalactites and stalagmites and green moss and algae and eerie ponds in the deep interior. Good lighting effects not only enhance the atmosphere, but also, together with steps and railings, make it a reasonably safe cave to visit. Another good reason for staying overnight on the plateau itself is that providing you reach Psykhró before about 10.30am, you will miss the coaches and although it may still be quite busy, you can have a pleasant time. The other big bonus which guidebooks don't seem to mention, is that from the cave entrance and café there are tremendous views down and across the fields of this fertile area, another reason to suffer this cardiovascular exercise.

Inside the Dhiktean cave

The Lasíthi plateau is also great walking country, the E4 path traversing the Dhíkti mountains before descending to, and then crossing, the plateau. If you are really fit, there are organized walks up to the summit of Mount Dhíkti. Rather less strenuous walking opportunities include wandering across the plateau on several tracks that connect the various villages. Minoan Karfí, the important archaeological site excavated by John Pendlebury, is the hilltop settlement whereto the Minoans had retreated in about 1200 BC. It occupies a dramatic position about six kilometres up from the village of Tzermiádho. We drove up a paved road from the village and then along a dirt track to the tiny Chapel of Ariadne on the Nissimos plateau where the Minoans had pastured their animals and grown their crops.

A further 45-minute walk uphill took us past old terracing, one of two springs which emerge from underground aquifers, some sizeable clumps of flowering yellow phlomis amongst the maquis, battered way markers,

The Lasíthi Plateau

The fields of the Lasíthi Plateau

and, overhead, prowling birds of prey. The remains of Minoan Karfí, difficult enough for us to make any sense of, can be found on a saddle between the two peaks of Karfí, an ancient peak sanctuary, and Mikrí Kopránа, which is easily identifiable by its modern concrete trig point. Walkers often take the more arduous ascent from the village of Kerá, but whichever way you do it the views from the top are worth waiting for, fully justifying our efforts to reach this hilltop settlement.

Of the remainder of our brief time in this distinctive part of Crete, we took the circular drive around the rim of the plateau taking in the half a dozen villages which form the community. We bought strawberries at Pinakianó and passed by the Natural History Museum at Moní Vidianí. If time allows one day, I would like to investigate as apparently this museum has information on the bearded vulture and other birds of prey which can be spotted here. Apartment neighbours came rushing over to us one afternoon pointing at a great flock of vultures flying away above us. Quite a sight! Hand-loom weaving and embroidery are traditional skills on the Lasíthi plateau and the end results are for sale in the old village shops. We contemplated buying a piece to take home, but the practical difficulties in terms of luggage allowance loomed larger.

My Wife Suggested Crete

**From Mount Karfi, 1141 metres above sea level,
Limin Hersónisou just visible on the coast**

Our apartment had been a comfortable place to stay: there was no need for an air-conditioning system as we could safely rely on the coolness of the nights, and there are no mosquitoes up here either. It was as peaceful as the RGC had led me to believe it would be. Christine and Vassilis had been welcoming and generous hosts; Vassilis had turned up each morning with gifts of fresh bread, yoghurt and fruit. Jennie finds the skins of many fruits difficult to digest, but she found no difficulty with the sweet red cherries which Vassilis produced one day. We took our evening meals at their taverna and came to realise that Vassilis was a unique if complicated character who was not averse to criticising his government's austerity measures and the sudden and enormous tax burden laid on him as a result. A German woman told him in no uncertain terms that she had always had to pay tax in her country and Vassilis countered this by saying that he understood, but it was the manner in which his government had suddenly depleted his income which he found difficult to bear. It was an interesting conversation conducted with the help of some *raki*, while we sat a few tables away where Christine quietly and discreetly pointed out to us in her French accent that: "'E 'as a good 'art!" – and so he does.

The Lasíthi Plateau

On the final morning of our stay I produced a book, the biography of John Pendlebury, and asked Vassilis about Pendlebury and the plaque which marks the spot where the other spring emerges on Mount Karfí. "I have this book too", he said and became quite animated, scolding me for not having mentioned this before. He knew all about it. Pendlebury had named this spring Vitsilovrysí, literally 'the spring of the eagle vultures.' The plaque had been Pendlebury's idea and had been made by none other than Vassilis' grandfather.

A Cretan Interlude

"Stories from the Lasíthi Plateau"

Having just described to you our own experience on the Lasíthi plateau, it seems appropriate at this moment to add the stories of two other Englishmen whose path took them here. As with the rest of Crete, the Lasíthi plateau was not spared from the cruelty of the Nazi occupiers in the 1940s. The name of the Englishman John Pendlebury was one they knew well from their intelligence reports, and they knew too that Tzermiádho had been his archaeological stronghold. Furthermore, after the fall of Crete in 1941, British agents did operate in this area of the island, notably in the shape of Sandy Rendel, whose name was well known to our host Vassilis at Maison Kronio.

The first of these two short stories, which could be more accurately described as a brief encounter, comes again from Richard Clark's *Crete - A Notebook*. I simply summarise it as 'searching for cigarettes,' which is what Mr Clark was looking for. On a cold spring day he had taken his family up to the Lasíthi plateau, and with cigarettes in mind he stopped at a traditional house which doubled as a village shop. The three elderly men whom he encountered were apparently suspicious of his nationality; they were "of an age to have fought as resistance fighters during the war and to have witnessed the atrocities committed by the occupying army". (RC). Having had our own experience at the village of Thrónos in the Amari valley concerning our nationality, I was astonished to read Richard Clark's experience in this small village on the Lasíthi plateau:

"Mustering my best Greek I asked if they sold cigarettes. One man, who I took to be the shop owner, stood up and stared me in the eyes. 'Are you German?' he growled. 'Ochi, ee-meh apo teen Angleea' I stumbled. A clap on the back almost winded me as all three opened wide smiles and said in unison 'English, katsee' pulling up a stool for me around the fire. As requested, I sat down, and each of them offered cigarettes and raki was poured. They spoke no English, but I was made to feel

A Cretan Interlude

extraordinarily welcome and my halting attempts at Greek were widely praised and treated with some amazement… More than an hour later I had managed to get a packet of cigarettes that my new-found friends refused to let me pay for."

(RC) From Crete - A Notebook, by Richard Clark.

The second story comes from the pen of Sandy Rendel who was operating as a British secret agent in 1943, mainly in Lasíthi. In reality therefore, he was working as a spy in German occupied Crete, suffering the hardships and deprivations which came with the job. Nevertheless this is a light-hearted tale, the setting for which, I now know, was the village of Psykhró at the southern end of the Lasíthi plateau in the home of the Markogiannakis family. I summarise this story simply, if rather unexpectedly, as 'An English Tea Service.'

"By coincidence I went late one afternoon to the house of Manoli Markogiannakis who had been for many years a servant of Sir Arthur Evans, the archaeologist who had conducted the excavations at [K]nossos. There he had built the Villa Ariadne which had long been an offshoot of the British School of Archaeology, but which at that time was serving as General Kreipe's sleeping quarters. Manoli was a cheerful soul. He and his wife, Ourania, after many tribulations had settled, as it were, in temporary retirement in his native village, but clearly, they were really living for the day when British students would once more come flocking back to the villa.

Manoli beamed all over when I was led in by my guide. We had not met before. At the time I was dressed in a shirt buttoned at the neck, which had been both shirt and pyjamas for some ten days at least, a very old jacket patched in most places, and frayed at the edges, some muddy breeches, puttees dyed black, and boots that flapped about where the soles were loose. At once he hastened to relieve me of my Sakkouli with the assurance of a pre-war British butler relieving a guest of his great coat. 'Excuse us, Mr Alexis,' he said, 'I am afraid that everything' – pointing to his extremely tidy sitting room – 'is in great disorder, and we have many shortages, but please be seated'. Then after a momentary pause to lend some solemnity to words, which he knew would sound suddenly enchanting, he added: 'If you will just wait a moment, Ourania will bring in the tea'. It was all exactly as if he had been referring to a parlour-maid in pre-war Wimbledon.

I must have smiled in astonished amusement, for I saw Manoli beam again. But I checked myself from exclaiming about 'the tea', for I knew by then that when Cretans speak of tea, they mean a form of camomile made from a local herb. In a few moments, however, Ourania swept in bearing, sure enough, a tray with a spotless teacloth, a china teapot complete with tea cosy, a milk jug, a sugar bowl, cups, saucers, and dessert plates to match, and a plate of astonishingly thin bread and butter with a pot of crab-apple jelly. At the moment after a day's walk I could have done better, perhaps, with half a loaf, but the spirit behind the gift was delightful. Manoli and I had some fun explaining to the guide how to manipulate an English tea service, and I think Manoli and Ourania were as pleased to be providing an English tea once again, as I was to be given it."

(AMR) From Appointment in Crete by AM Rendel.

Pendlebury, Rendel and Clark all had their fond memories of the Lasíthi plateau, and as Jennie and I have now discovered, it is a part of Crete which really should not be missed.

Chapter Thirteen

Heading back East - our Second Home

"This remote corner of Crete is not mountainous and on a calm sunny day with the sea never far away round three sides of it, it seems as utterly quiet and peaceful as any place on earth. It was a bright clear day, when we came over a hill in sight of the village. Below we could see the whitewashed houses gleaming in the sunlight with the red tiles of the roofs as neat and bright as the illustrations in a fairy story."
(AMR) AM Rendel, *Appointment in Crete*.

I have often mused in my sentimental ways as to whether this eastern village, as described above, was Palékastro, nowadays a small town but nevertheless possessing all the attributes which Rendel highlighted in those words which he wrote in the early 1950s. Perhaps my curiosity will lead me to the answer one day. Certainly Palékastro and the small village of Angathiá nearby and their inhabitants have now found a place in my heart. I did not plan it – how can you? But as a dear cousin said to us recently: "It must feel like going home now." Her particular Palékastro lies, I know, somewhere in the wilds of the Pyrenees, many miles away.

Luckily for me, Jennie has also developed a soft spot for the far eastern seaboard of Crete where Palékastro and Angathiá can be found. The natural beauty of this area has not been blighted by mass tourism and fortuitously for us the road which takes day tourists to the famous beach at Vai, and often to the monastery – Moní Toploú – nearby, bypasses Palékastro; and I doubt whether the coach drivers would relish the challenge of the narrow streets even if they chose to come this way. Public buses from Iráklio take three-and-a-quarter hours to reach Palékastro; we allow about two and a half hours by car, another reason I guess for the low-key tourism which exists.

We are not alone in hoping that this situation will remain unchanged. On a recent visit we talked briefly with an Austrian man who had been

My Wife Suggested Crete

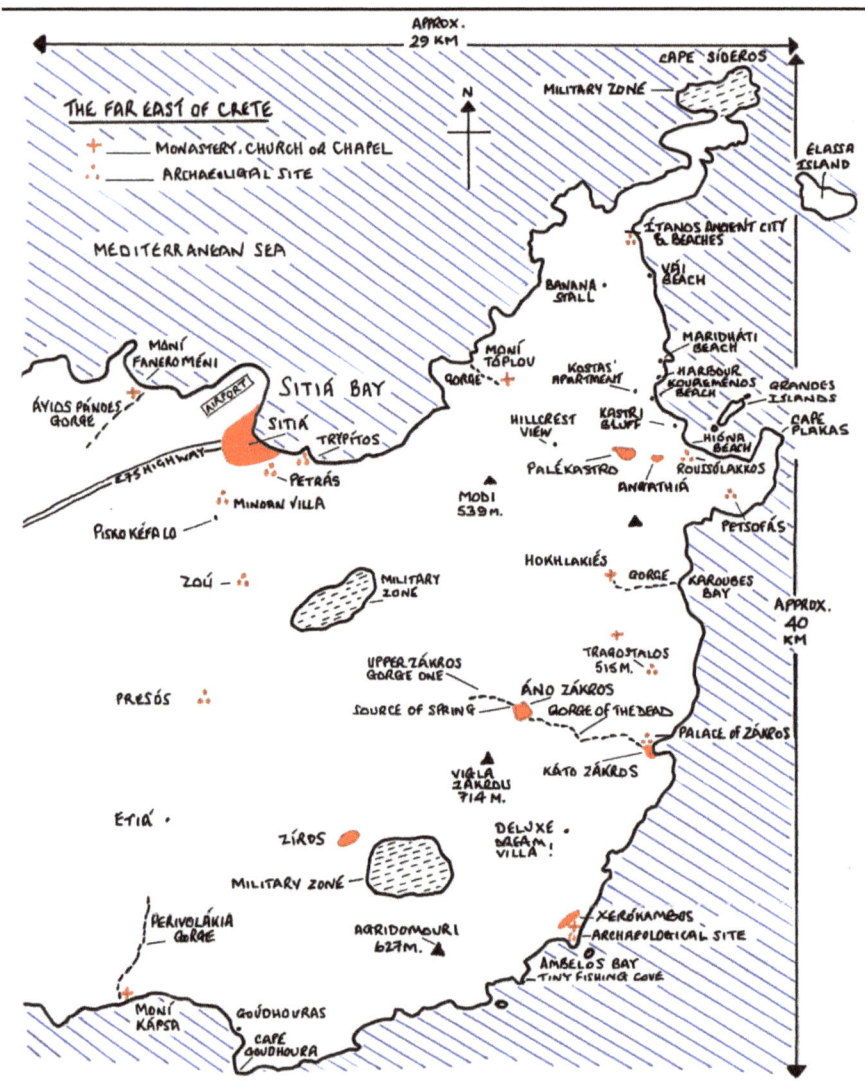

The Far East of Crete

taking his holidays in Palékastro for 20 years. Now married with two small children, he appears to have found no difficulty in convincing his new family that the tradition should continue. At home in Vienna his friends and neighbours often ask him why he persists in making this annual pilgrimage, to which he replies that he doesn't really know. It must have become a habit, he says, and always adds that it is a long and winding road journey from Iráklio, and anyway there isn't much to see once you eventually arrive. "If I was you, I wouldn't bother!" is apparently his standard response. He and I smiled over a glass of *raki* as we both hope that this corner of the world will remain sheltered from the excesses of mass development.

We have not been to Palékastro as many times as our Austrian acquaintance, but we are catching up. I often wonder as I drive over the hill, after leaving behind the town of Sitía, and the now familiar panorama comes into full view, whether the same magic will be rekindled. I have really no idea why I should doubt my feelings about the place, and perhaps ought to seek advice from a psychoanalyst. We now stay in an apartment owned by Kostas – also owner of the minimarket and the first Palékastro resident we met back in 2013. It is a little way out of town nestling among the olive groves with a view towards Koureménos beach. It was to Kostas that I offloaded my feelings of uncertainty which come over me whenever I reach the crest of that hill. I detected a smile from the man which told me that he had heard this all before and that any uncertainty would quickly fade and disappear. Nothing needed to be said, and nothing was. His smile sufficed to provide the answer. No psychoanalyst was needed after all.

There are more easily identifiable reasons for our continuing desire to spend time in the far east of the prefecture of Lasíthi: "Crete is the land of a hundred gorges" (OR & JM) and while I have referred to one or two in preceding pages they deserve more than a brief word because they are such an important part of Cretan landscape. "The key to Cretan gorges is tectonics." (OR & JM) In *"the making of the Cretan Landscape,"* Rackham and Moody explain their significance. "They are part of the island's personality: the orange and grey of their walls, the wonderful plants which are found only in Cretan gorges, their great trees, the part which they played in legend and song, and the deeds of valour and blood enacted in them." (OR & JM) The greatest gorge of them all, the Samariá gorge in the west, was for instance the scene of that last battle between communist rebels and government forces in 1948. Today thousands of tourists walk that walk, the most photographed of all the gorges.

Lasíthi prefecture has its own great selection, with Káto Zákros gorge or 'Gorge of the Dead' being perhaps the most well-known. It marks the beginning of the E4 path which traverses the island from east to west, a further reason for its popularity. The caves in the cliff walls were used for burials in Minoan times, hence: Gorge of the Dead. At Upper Zákros (or Áno Zákros) the E4 path diverges from the gorge, while the gorge itself continues uphill but now splits into two. We have had the pleasure of hiking up through Upper Zákros Gorge One, as described on the geotourism map which we picked up in the town's small natural history museum. Upper Zákros, although hardly more than a large village, is a wealthy agricultural centre blessed with a major underground spring, and climbing up through the narrow streets and alleyways it was clear that the water was being put to good use even if some of the old mills now merely function as museum pieces – relics of a past life. As we passed by, gardens were brimming with fruits and vegetables as eventually signs guided us to the source where the spring water emerges from underground into a pool shaded by big plane and oak trees. From there it is channelled into the town's water system before being allowed to supply and irrigate the entire Zákros region.

From the source we followed a path which took us into Upper Zákros Gorge One. The path soon became a track lying parallel to the winter torrent bed, where water cascades down over the boulders after deluges of rain. These torrent beds are easily identifiable by the mostly pink-flowering oleanders, shrubs which seem to particularly like this habitat and provide a constant floral display through the summer months. In early June, apart from the oleanders, we found phlomis, thyme, sage and the white flowers of oregano, some fennel, purple thistles and a mass of verbena. Herbal aromas dominated the air as we strolled on through this natural rock garden. We also found *rudites* – alpine fossils – on some of the larger rocks and our only company on our two-hour walk took the form of a couple of wary goats whose colours blended so well with the orange and grey of the rock that only their bleating confirmed their presence nearby. We sat at the end of the track, sheltered from the wind by prickly oaks, and devoured a packed lunch in total peace before wandering back down to the museum's car park far below.

Jennie and I have also tackled the gorge that begins to descend from the church at the village of Hokhlakiés, a few kilometres south of Palékastro, and ends at the isolated pebbly beach of Karoúbes Bay. It is six kilometres there and back with some boulder scrambling to master en route, so we found it a bit tough in places but managed it and took a swim at Karoúbes Bay. Some rucksack refreshment fortified us for the return journey, but clambering back up actually seemed easier than the descent. We were therefore better able to appreciate the size and colours of the cliffs and rocks of this particular gorge, before we triumphantly re-emerged at the village church.

The gorge of Moní Toploú provides an easier walk. We made it even easier by using a track which runs along the hillside before descending into the gorge. Here we spied some natural caves which must have been

Heading Back East - Our Second Home

Oleanders in Upper Zákros Gorge One

used as shelter in troubled times, before eventually the gorge reaches its destination on the north-east coast.

Lasíthi province has its share of peak sanctuaries too. These mountain or hilltop shrines are sometimes associated with a cave and have often been in continuous use from Neolithic through to Roman times. From Angathiá, Yanni (Mr Bee) had kindly signposted the way to Petsofás, a Minoan peak sanctuary about an hour's walk above the village. When his signs ran out the path was supposed to be obvious, but we took a goat trail instead and found ourselves perched precariously on a cliff edge on a windy day before we eventually managed to clamber up to re-join the path. Only then could we laugh about the error of our ways as we continued up the hill. The views from the top encompassed all of our favourite haunts in the area. We braced ourselves against the wind as it howled across this open wilderness. These days, a few broken walls and a scattering of pottery shards are the only remains at Petsofás, but in the past these peak sanctuaries served a purpose. The clay pottery offerings which have been found here often took the form of hands or arms or legs; the real body parts needed mending and the people were asking their gods for help. At the time Senór Osteo Arthritico had been causing a nuisance with my left

My Wife Suggested Crete

Inside Hokhlakiés Gorge

hip, so Jennie decided to make a pencil drawing of my offending limb and tucked it into the ancient Minoan wall. The question of whether this offering helped, rests between me and the gods.

On another occasion, in need of a good walk, we attempted the climb on a zig-zag track up to the peak sanctuary of Tragostalos. This, I have no doubt, would have been linked with the palace and town of Minoan Zákros down on the coast below. We left our car next to a roadside church and started walking. About two hours later, having dodged the flight path of two colonies of honeybees feasting on the wild thyme and two enormous billy goats accompanied by their personal harems, a weather-beaten sign announced our arrival at Tragostalos. This peak

Heading Back East - Our Second Home

View from Petsofás: Hiona beach, Kastri Bluff and Koureménos Bay.
Cape Sídheros is just out of the picture, top right

sanctuary had been plundered many centuries before our visit and there wasn't much left to see, but the views from up here provided more than adequate compensation. I could make out Cape Sídheros in the far northeast and in the opposite direction there was our beloved hamlet of Xerókambos in the far south-east of the island. The Minoans who had trudged up here to ask their gods to heal one of their relatives could at least claim that they had made a big effort. As ever on this island, and Lasíthi is no exception, history, religion, landscape and people are all inextricably linked.

~ ~ ~ ~

In the hills above Xerókambos, having driven through the substantial village of Zíros where wine-making is a serious business, you will suddenly encounter a restored Venetian mansion at the otherwise derelict village of Etiá. The mansion is perhaps more impressive from a distance and when we visited it was locked, but this fact did not deter my wife from trying to gain entry by climbing a wall with an upward shove from me. The resultant bruises on her legs still did not gain her access to the interior and resigned disappointment followed.

The Turks had had far greater success in gaining access in their time and had occupied this Venetian mansion for administrative purposes, although the local Cretans had vented their rage by causing considerable damage to the building. It was rather sad wandering through the small ruined houses of the abandoned village; once there had been 500 villagers

Venetian mansion at Etiá

living here. The old church and even older chapel had survived and were both open for us to inspect.

Five or six kilometres west of Sitía, but still very much in our eastern comfort zone, we found the monastery of Moní Faneroméni in an isolated position looking down on another gorge, this time the Áyios Pándes gorge. Confusingly there is another monastery quite close to Áyios Nikólaos, further west, which bears an identical name. En route to the version near Sitía you will encounter olives and occasional farmhouses, hairpin bends and a tiny cove where the gorge ends, before climbing up the other side to find the small community that unlike Etiá still houses permanent residents.

We found difficulty in locating the monastic church so we stopped to ask directions from an old lady dressed in traditional widow's black, whose distinguishing feature was the complete loss of all of her teeth. Whether she was laughing at our poor use of the Greek language or the fact that we were so close to the church without realising it – as it was just around the corner – we will never know. It was worth the visit to see this fine old church set in a courtyard of flowers and surrounded by the mostly empty quarters of the monks, perched at the edge of another magnificent gorge. In 1829 it had been looted and burned by the Turks and the frescoes inside are blackened and graffitied, further proof of those violent times. There is a small cave behind and below the church where offerings had been hung on the icon of the Virgin, in the same kind of way as the offerings at the peak sanctuaries of more distant times. It was here perhaps that I should have hung my own ex-voto – the depiction of my dodgy left

A multitude of taxímata (ex-votos) in the cave behind Moní Faneroméni

leg – which I had purchased in Haniá. It would have blended in rather nicely with all the others hanging here.

At Ítanos, five kilometres north of Palékastro, we had already viewed the remains of the ancient city including basilicas with fallen pillars and masonry. We soon realised that Ítanos, which is sometimes called Erimoupolis Bay, is also a good place to swim especially from the northern of the three small beaches, this sandy stretch being reached by walking over a headland – and in June complete with clumps of flowering thyme. It is especially sheltered here and swimming is therefore possible even when the wind is up. As long ago as the 1850s, the learned Captain Spratt had agreed that the bay here was:

"So commodious and safe an anchorage ... to shelter and invite the navigator during the prevalent northerly gales of summer ..." (TABS)

Here, too, is a lesson in geology as there are some curiously twisted folds of rock which were formed millions of years ago. They really are quite an extraordinary sight at both ends of this beach. I have seen photographs of similar folds located near Áyios Pávlos in Réthymno prefecture, which look equally startling. Between Zákros and Xerókambos are great patches of purple limestone and at some of the Minoan settlements you can still see how craftsmen used this stone to great effect to create a pathway or courtyard. There is in fact an enormous variety of geological formations, including the great walls of the gorges, to wonder at throughout the island.

Beautiful but curious rock formations at the northern beach of Ítanos

Unlike Vai beach down the road, Ítanos has no facilities, but a 10-minute drive finds us back at our Palékastro apartment unless we decide to top up on our supply of local bananas en route, which is frequently the case. On a calm day other isolated coves near Hióna beach have beckoned us, as here we often find that we have one of them entirely to ourselves. Although there is plenty of sand, there are occasional rocks on which to perch and here I have frequently experienced a free and gentle foot massage courtesy of the accompanying shingle which has been smoothly manicured by the waves over many years. For me this is yet another Cretan treat.

Whichever beach we return from, having washed off the sea salt from our bodies, a cup of tea on the balcony is usually the next requirement as we take in the beauty of our surroundings once again. Two or three fishing boats begin to leave the small harbour at Koureménos from about 5.30 in the afternoon, providing the wind allows. It seems to take them about half an hour to reach the Grandes Islands out in the bay before they are lost from our view as they head out to sea beyond Cape Plakas.

By now the young windsurfers have called it a day so then, as we sit on our balcony, my attention is usually drawn to the mixture of pink hues and gathering shadows in the hills, including Petsofás – as the sun begins to set. At this time of day the wind sometimes eases too, the odd barking dog welcomes the return of his owner amidst the olive groves, and Mr

Balcony view: A corner of Koureménos Bay, the Kastri Bluff and Petsofás

My Wife Suggested Crete

Rotavator begins his journey home. The cicadas, or at least the vibration of their tymbal membranes, give us their evening performance as the light fades. The finale is left to the magnificent stars in the heavens as light pollution is not an issue here.

I suppose I must appear rather weird to many modern people; why should they understand that this list of evening entertainment is more than enough to satisfy my soul? These days I do indeed find it difficult to leave "this remote corner of Crete" (AMR). The last day is always full of emotion as we say goodbye to Mr and Mrs Banana, to Toula at the bakery, Mr Milk and his brothers, Yanni and Maria at their village shop in Angathiá, Georgia and young Costas at the Hióna fish taverna, Manoli, Rula, Mama and her husband at the Mythos taverna, together with Mrs Frenetic, and of course our apartment hosts and minimarket owners, Kostas and Maria. They are all wonderful people and we miss them dearly when we leave and remember all their kindness and hospitality and affection towards us.

On our last visit we went to find a Minoan farmhouse set on a hillside overlooking the village of Zoú near Sitía. We were not surprised to find ourselves alone amongst the ruins, and still intact was a remarkable stone bench some 3,500 years old where I sat taking in the surrounding countryside. I noticed a patch of wild blue scabious as Jennie searched in vain for farmhouse pots and pans of old. Here I had time to think again of all the people we have been so privileged to meet in this eastern corner of Crete.

In 1928 John Pendlebury travelled to Palékastro. "John loved the wildness and isolation of the place." (IG) He and his colleagues bathed in the sea at Hióna beach as we have done many a time. As he did, we have tried to imagine the long-lost harbour: "It is thousands of years since the merchant princes of Palaikastro vied with the High King of Knossos in the possession of the finest painted frescoes and the most magnificent pottery; thousands of years since the Egyptian traders came creeping in with their fine spices and their proud tales of conquest." (IG) Nowadays this is still a place where you can let your imagination run riot, and yet where all is calm as the walls of the old Minoan city of Roussólakkos gather dust amongst the scrub nearby. As in Rendel's day, it still seems to me "as utterly quiet and peaceful as any place on earth." (AMR) If ever a fairy story became a reality, I guess for me this has been it.

Heading Back East - Our Second Home

The author at an isolated cove,
near the old Minoan port city of Roussólakkos

Chapter Fourteen

Saying Goodbye - a Conclusion is Required

"It was the Greeks who gave to the world the term 'philoxenia', while leaving other races to construct out of the elements of their language the word 'xenophobia'; and nowhere is this "love of strangers," which they universally preach, practised with more conviction and intensity than in Crete".
XAN FIELDING, THE STRONGHOLD. (XF)

Crete is always difficult to leave, and this I know was the case for the great Hellenophile, traveller and author: Patrick Leigh Fermor. He said just that in one of his books. For me leaving Crete towards the end of a year, which happened mid-December recently, seemed especially emotional. We had left our apartment on the south coast of the island on a warm sunny day with the temperature at 20°C and the Libyan Sea had calmed down from the previous stormy 24 hours. As we left I turned to feast my eyes on Mount Dhíkti which had been given a first dusting of winter snow courtesy of the storm. From a distance it appeared to have been sprinkled with icing sugar, and when we reached Iráklio we saw too that Mount Ida now had been crowned with the first snow of winter. Down below the snowy peaks and throughout the island, the olive harvest gathered pace. The pick-up trucks laden with hessian sacks full of this most important and precious commodity were speeding off to the local olive press at the pre-arranged hour; an annual harvest and pressing which is so important and quintessentially part of Cretan life.

December finds few tourists on the island. The large tourist hotels, apartments, villas and tavernas mostly close and in these towns and villages the people can enjoy some welcome peace and perhaps even some rest although I would not recommend suggesting to them that this is the case: "Rest?! Ha! We have to harvest the olives and the trees will need pruning and repairs need to be done now. Rest?! Ha!" Here and there plastic Christmas trees, lights, wreaths and baubles appear, even

Saying Goodbye - A Conclusion is Required

sometimes in the town square, although thankfully not until mid-December as opposed to the crazy practice adopted in the UK when Christmas apparently has to begin in October if not before. In Crete I sense that the celebrations to commemorate the birth of Jesus Christ are more restricted to the day itself. Our friend Kostas admitted to having a family feast on the 25th in celebration but by the 26th it was all over for another year.

For the few brave tourists who do visit at this time of year there are benefits. The museums remain open, as do many of the historical sites, and by and large you can have them to yourself. Monasteries and churches by their very nature continue to welcome visitors providing you respect their opening hours and their dress code. The sea can still be warm enough for swimming; even a 66-year-old Englishman can enjoy it and stay in for some time without feeling cold – on December 9th as I remember it! It was a great treat. Of course the weather is more unpredictable now, but the temperature is consistently warmer than the UK. Some tavernas remain open all year – particularly in the towns and cities so that eating out and being able to sample the delights of Cretan cuisine is still possible, and Cretan hospitality remains unbroken by the change of season.

As December brings another year to an end, it is perhaps appropriate to attempt a closure to my story. Even from the memories of a December visit, this island and her people can induce in me a nostalgia, a longing to return to revisit places and people we know and continue to explore new corners of The Big Island. Having enjoyed reading the tales of other travellers I thankfully realise that I am far from being the first to be affected in this way and I cannot emphasise enough that the size of the island means that there is always going to be something new to see. Consequently, there remain considerable swathes of this land which I still yearn to explore. As one of those travellers put it: "One could spend a very long time in Crete without managing to see every place of interest or natural beauty." (AH)

How can I analyse or explain my feelings? The landscape must play its part. I was well into my 40s when I first had the chance to visit islands of the Caribbean. I remember being taken up into the hills of Jamaica and marvelling at the jungle, the coconut palms and fields of pineapples: I was overwhelmed by this lush beauty. Another great treat was to venture well over 2000 kilometres away from any other human habitation to encounter the enormous Moai statues of Easter Island and listen one evening to rhythmic sounds emanating from the island's annual music festival as Pacific waves came charging in before breaking up on the shores of this

My Wife Suggested Crete

fascinating place. I concede that I have been so fortunate in my travels, and I can still fondly recall vivid memories of many extraordinary landscapes.

Having now spent more than seven months of my life on the island of Crete you might think that I would treat the Cretan landscape as a given, something so established in my mind that I take each vista for granted. Not so. I still derive enormous pleasure when I spy the panorama of the White Mountains, Mount Ida, Mount Dhíkti or the Thriptí range. I still find a lovely tranquillity in the Amari valley and up on the Lasíthi plateau. The coastline – especially the southern – can be dramatic and the ever-changing mood of the sea still draws me into some kind of other-worldly trance. Of the many beaches, plenty can rival the best which this planet has to offer with their powdery white sand; and yet here in Crete I have often found beaches which are so peaceful that they feel as if they were meant for Jennie and I alone. The gorges provide their natural breathtaking magic and the flora and fauna, the thyme, and the smells of all the wild herbs continue to hold their place in my sensory memory. The pines and cypress, planes and oaks, and simply the scrub – the maquis, phrygana and steppe on which the sheep and the goats feed and over which the vultures and eagles prey – all add to the natural treasures of this land.

The purple flowers of wild Cretan thyme.
this particular patch near the town of Sitía

Saying Goodbye - A Conclusion is Required

Colourful wilderness in the Lasíthi hills

The history of the island must also contribute to my personal longing to return. In the bustle of the major towns and cities elements of former times and reminders of past rulers and empires remain to tell the story. Out in the countryside it is perhaps simply the vast quantity of ancient ruins which has amazed me, as well as the astonishment that I feel when I stumble on fallen pillars dotted about in olive groves and the remains of palaces which were built more than 3,000 years ago. In the museums I have then perused the great mountain of magnificent treasures that the archaeologists have gradually unearthed. What an extraordinary wealth of history this island owns; and with this immense history come the myths and legends of courage and tragedy, and with the natural tendency of the islanders to exaggerate, great heroes are born and the tales live on in an ever expanding form. Theatre comes to life.

Do the flavours of the Cretan kitchen actually make me want to return? I have at least to concede that nowhere in the world have my taste buds enjoyed themselves so much; nowhere has my digestive system been so at ease; nowhere have kitchen knife-sharpeners been so redundant as the island's fruits and vegetables are so fresh and ripe that they cut as easily as gliding through butter; and yes, their olive oil is outstandingly

My Wife Suggested Crete

**The central staircase of the Palace of Festos,
at the eastern end of the Messará plain**

good. In other parts of the world, here and there, I have been fortunate in sampling exceptional food. Thinking of Thailand, my senses recall the lime and lemongrass, the coconut and chilli in their great soups and curries, flavours which seemed to me to blend perfectly with the heat and humidity of the jungle as we consumed them on a seashore while cameras clicked away to record another heavenly sunset.

In Portugal I remember the wonderful simplicity of freshly grilled fish and wrinkly potatoes washed down with that zingy white wine, Vinho Verde. In Sicily a plate of fresh anchovies and juicy slices of orange was a glorious salty/sweet combination. In Chile, a delicious *pastel de choclo*, a pie made with sweetcorn and sugar, washed down with a glass or two of their magnificent Sauvignon Blanc will always bring back happy memories. In sharp contrast the food of northern Europe, including the UK, rarely finds a home in my memory of culinary triumphs.

In Crete it is, I am sure, the freshness and quality of the ingredients which are so outstanding. The food may often be simple but it has been enriched once again by the island's history of invasion by people who have arrived from all points of the compass. Hence occasionally I express surprise at the combination of herbs and spices which are sometimes used

Saying Goodbye - A Conclusion is Required

before discovering that it does of course all blend beautifully. Grandma's old recipes have thankfully survived together with a whole host of those fresh ingredients produced on the island. So it is that I often yearn for another visit to a Cretan taverna to savour my favourites once again or to try something different, and I must therefore conclude that the delights of Cretan cuisine do indeed contribute to my abiding nostalgia.

Happy culinary memories

Even with all of this to tempt me back, I have no doubt that many can argue similar excuses which lure them back to their own particular idyllic location where the landscape, the history and the cuisine – and not forgetting the climate – provide all that their bodies and souls require. Consequently, I can find no good reason to argue about that. I accept that we are all different and therefore so are our needs and dreams. Dear friends of ours have loved nothing better than to roam about in the French countryside searching for old bits of furniture which they then restore back in Devon before their classy workmanship provides the welcome return on their investment. They have, I know, enjoyed mulling over their triumphant purchases with a glass or two of good wine, accompanied by chunks of rustic pâté and pungent cheese in some quiet backwater of rural France. "It's what we do," they told me.

There is however one subject which I am happy to debate with anyone wishing to challenge my views, and that is the nature and spirit of the Cretan people. I have had the good fortune of visiting 'the land of smiles' as Thailand is often affectionately described. I have witnessed and received kindness and courtesy from many Europeans, and I fondly remember the polite dignity of the people of Oman, the warm affection shown to me as a young Brit travelling in Canada, and perhaps above all the smile-inducing humour, kindness and sociability of the Irish. For me though, at the top of the human tree sit the Cretan people whose extraordinary hospitable welcome to strangers from a foreign land is in my opinion both unique and quite exceptional, and therefore, in the end, I judge that it is the people of Crete – notwithstanding their occasionally fierce and bewildering ways – who drive my desire to return as soon as I have left.

To reinforce this thesis, my mind is drawn to some of the British wartime agents, whose feelings for the Cretan people on whom they so heavily relied shine through in the words which they have penned. Sandy Rendel, thinking about the best of his helpers felt that: "I have no hope or wish ever to work again with better men or women" (AMR) and, some years after leaving the island and on reflection he felt that his time there, "still seems real to the point of intensity and romantic to the point of melodrama." (AMR) Xan Fielding attempted to put it all down to sentimentality but admitted that he would never really be "permanently exorcized" from the spirit of the island and its people. In the end, he had to conclude: "The island's most important exclusive feature of all" was indeed "the Cretan people." (XF)

If I need further support then I merely have to quote the lyrical words of the maestro, Patrick Leigh Fermor, who summed up the Cretans so perfectly: "the flair for friendship, company, talk, fun and music; originality and inventiveness in conversation and an explosive vitality that seems to recharge itself from the high voltage of the air…Their glance and their speech were equally unguarded; there was something both patrician and bohemian in their attitude to life and their sense of the comic drew a thread of humour through everything …". (PLF)

These authors, you could argue, were writing at a time when the heroic age of yester year had once again appeared. Yet in 2012 Richard Clark assured his readers in *Crete - A Notebook* that the people: "are as welcoming as ever; their generosity of spirit towards the stranger remains unabashed". (RC) Even the RGC has been forced to mention the

Saying Goodbye - A Conclusion is Required

hospitality that forms part of traditional Cretan life. Yet I fear that, once again, I am prone to the accusation of painting too glamorous a picture of Crete and her people.

In spite of that, however, I have been heartened by two sources of encouragement. Firstly, Oliver Rackham and Jennifer Moody, in their book *The Making of the Cretan Landscape,* insist that: "It is a uniquely glamorous island, but the majority of tourists ignore the glamour and remain on an unexciting and tideless beach." (OR & JM) Secondly, my own dear wife has added her thoughts: "The island and its people give me the feeling of a 'glamour'. That's a force field, magic, magnetism, seductiveness, witchery, spell-binding delight, mesmerisation and enchantment. It holds all of that for me and beguiles me! The people are alluring and the whole island has such a magic about it."

After that I probably ought to say: "I rest my case!" and return to the fields where I have often attempted to hit little white balls into a hole, and then make another 17 attempts to do the same thing at a location known as Downes Crediton Golf Club. I have derived both pleasure and frustration from this game throughout my life, not only in the wilds of Devon but at some classic and manicured courses in Scotland, in Thailand and the Algarve region of Portugal. For any golfing colleagues brave enough to be reading this, there are now two golf courses in Crete, although one is owned by an enormous hotel complex at Eloúnda in the east. The other is situated in the low hills south of Iráklio and close to the neighbouring north-eastern coastal tourist strip. To me, even as a hardened golfing enthusiast, it looks incongruous with its lush green fairways contrasting awkwardly with the Cretan scrub, and I hope it is not the forerunner of others to come. No doubt it will appeal to some tourists staying close by and I suppose it sits better here, along with a couple of theme parks, than it would elsewhere on the island.

A myriad of opportunities for activity and entertainment beckon the visitor, even though I would feel a tinge of sadness if the preceding pages had not provided enough ideas for all. For the adventurous there are mountaineering and caving and even bungee jumping to look forward to, while on the coast scuba diving and sea fishing can be added to the list of things to do. Boat trips to some of the offshore islands are widely available during the summer months; and if you crave real isolation you can get a ferry for the 50-kilometre journey to the most southerly island in Europe – Gávdhos. Beware though as you may get stuck there when the seas get too rough for ferries to operate. On Crete, whatever it is that you

My Wife Suggested Crete

find to do, at whatever speed, rest assured that it will be enhanced by the kindly and generous nature of the Cretan people.

~ ~ ~ ~

It was on the last day of September, two or three years ago, that our plane took off in a westerly direction (as they usually do) from N. Kazantzákis International Airport. Almost immediately I knew we were roughly speaking above our favourite Ippokampos or Seahorse taverna down on the Iraklion seafront promenade. Here the family would be continuing to serve delicious food in their customary charming, efficient and friendly way. It was always fun to watch them expertly dodging the ever-present seaside traffic, deftly carrying trays of 'goodies' at shoulder height across to their terrace overlooking the sea. Soon we were away, flying over other Greek islands on our journey home, and sure enough my inevitable nostalgia was triggered and I felt the moisture welling in my eyes as I remembered the most recent Cretan treasures that we had discovered, and the newest batch of Cretan people whom we had been privileged to meet.

On this particular visit we had found another Minoan site called Lyttos, in the midst of modern nowhere, and enjoyed poking about amidst the ruins in complete solitude save for two local farmers who were quietly attending to their vines. The wild herbs had by now been truly parched by the long summer days, but some had still managed to scent the air. We had driven along empty roads and I remembered marvelling, once again, at the majestic mountain ranges that made the villages which perched at their feet or clung to their sides look so tiny in comparison.

As I sat shackled to my seat high above the Mediterranean sea, a backward glance through the window confirmed that the coastline of Crete was now lost from view. It was then – inevitably – that my mind began to reflect on some of the extraordinary Cretan people we had met.

In particular, I thought about two old men from the village where we had been staying. Both had sported long, ruggedly handsome beards. The first of these two was, I believe, suffering from some kind of Parkinson's type disease and yet still managed to push an old pram slowly along the narrow village streets with scraps of food for the local stray cats and dogs, every morning and every evening. On passing by one morning he had offered Jennie two sweet-smelling flowers which he had just picked, accompanied by a big toothless smile and a "Kalimera!" (Good morning). The second old man, almost blind, used to sit outside his house trying to

Saying Goodbye - A Conclusion is Required

The village of Mýrthios nestling below the Kouroupa hills, Réthymno province

make out the friends and strangers who passed his way. As I had headed towards my regular morning swim, we had always exchanged a hearty "Kalimera!" and in spite of his disability, my version had always been acknowledged by a stout wave of his hand and an expression of profound welcome to his little side street in his little village.

~ ~ ~ ~

In the end, the only way to experience this extraordinary feeling of human warmth is to set foot on the island yourself. Here you will meet your own new friends, your own Kostas and Maria, Manoli and Rula; your own Nikos and Yiorgios and Yanni, and I have no doubt that you will feel enriched for having done so. So, while I am aware that anyone who has waded through these pages may have found their own favourite and special part of the world, I fervently hope that I have provided enough encouragement or provoked enough curiosity to consider a visit to the island of Crete.

If I were to use the word 'addiction' to describe my fascination for the island and my own particular feelings for her people, this would at least imply a strong and constant attachment, which is true, but it is too harsh a word to use and does not sit comfortably here. Another admirer, Adam Hopkins, decided that: "The island has a way of taking people by the throat and refusing to let go." (AH) I smiled as I first read those words because they conveyed to me this sense of fierce magnetic attraction from which I cannot escape, and yet again this may be a sentiment which is a trifle severe. Once I was asked by a friend what it was that I liked about Crete. On the spur of the moment I replied that I found great difficulty in recognising anything about the island that I didn't like. This feeling cannot be mine alone and I have noticed that several travellers have described the island as being 'enchanted' which implies that it exudes some kind of mysterious charm which, although difficult to encapsulate in words, is in fact – for me at least – unavoidable. I feel it every time I visit as if the island casts a powerful spell over me. So in the end I can keep my final analysis quite simple and just freely admit that I have succumbed to the magic of the big Greek island.

Captain Thomas Spratt's appointment to explore Crete as part of a wider Mediterranean survey in 1851 was unexpected. It came as a result of the death of his predecessor – Captain Graves. His several journeys to the island were interrupted as his surveying skills were needed elsewhere – particularly in the area of the Black Sea. Due largely to the Crimean War, his absence from England and 'a long indisposition' – as he described it – there was a lengthy delay in publishing his two hefty volumes of *Travels and Researches in Crete.* Not until 1865 did they appear in print.

In the penultimate chapter of his work, he began to eulogise about the significance of Crete and its inhabitants "in the archaic times, from their having been the stage in the progress of civilisation and art…..". (TABS) He left his readership in no doubt that this island was worthy of investigation. I quote his words heartily now as a suitable conclusion to my own deliberations: "…. and so I leave the reader to his reflections upon the scene before him and upon Crete in general, hoping that my humble narrative and descriptions may have had the happy fortune in some way to excite his interest, or to awaken in his mind scholastic reminiscences connected with one of the most classic and important islands in the East". (TABS)

It was early in 2011 - 160 years since Captain Spratt had commenced his work - as daffodils and primroses heralded the arrival of an English spring, that Jennie and I began to discuss holiday destinations. Where might we go next? At that time I could not have anticipated what a wonderful idea it would turn out to be, when my wife suggested Crete.

Postscript

On the third of January 2019 we received a message from our friends Kostas and Maria that a few days before on the 28th December, their first baby had been born in their home town of Palékastro in eastern Crete. The news arrived with an attached video showing mother and daughter in fine fettle. Jennie promptly flooded our kitchen with tears of joy. Had I been a gun owner I know that I would have shocked and horrified our nice new neighbours, throwing open our French windows and celebrating Cretan-style, by firing several shots into the air in a traditional *feu-de-joie*.

On a sadder note our German friends phoned to tell us of the death of their dear Pontikos, the mischievous little dog of whom I had become so fond. However, he died peacefully and had been given a wonderful life by his owners.

Family tragedies continue to beset human beings wherever you happen to live and Crete is no exception. In this year of 2019 we witnessed the grief of an old lady in Angathiá who continued to cry every day for the husband whom she had lost six months earlier. In Palékastro one day as we sat in the Mythos taverna, we watched as Manoli and Rula both rushed into the street to comfort another woman who, clutching the crucifix hanging around her neck, looked mournfully towards them with an air of uncomprehending sadness. Rula quietly told us later that the father-in-law of the lady's daughter had shot himself. No-one knew why. As ever on this island, when needed, people come together; family rifts and village arguments are cast into the shadows and human warmth and compassion rise quickly to take their place.

By and large our travels in Crete in 2019 gave us wonderfully happy and fulfilling times and provided us with equally wonderful memories to treasure. I believe we treasure them even more than ever as events of 2020 have unfolded. In the introduction to this book I rashly proclaimed that I was: "well aware of all the horrors yet to come." 2020 has proved me utterly wrong, as of course I was totally unaware of the impending crisis as the world attempts to cope with the COVID-19 virus. As I write, friends in Crete have encouraged us that there are relatively few cases there and that they believe that the situation is under control. I sincerely hope so – the islanders have had more than their fair share of misfortune and misery to cope with in recent times. On the sitting room window sill of our Devon home, stands an exact replica of a handsome ceramic bull. The original had been discovered in the Palace of Zákros where archaeologists decided it had been made in the golden Minoan period of the island's history in about 1600 BC. We purchased our version from a talented artist cum sculptor in Áyios Nikólaos and our bull stands proudly on display, a symbol of fierceness, beauty, unpredictability, courage and strength. In my view these qualities are also shared by the people of the island who will no doubt rise to the challenge of defeating this new and particularly virulent enemy.

The bull of Zákros

Glossary

Andartes Cretan resistance fighters or guerrillas in WWII
Andesites There appear to be a cluster of these volcanic rocks in the Tripitos area east of Sitía (as identified in figure 7 (1.1) P.87 of the Field Guide to the Geology of Crete)
Appelation Contrôllée A French system of guaranteeing that a particular wine was produced in a named region
Baklavá A filo pastry cake made with honey and nuts
Bougátsa A Cretan creamy pie, often made with cheese, and always topped with sugar and cinnamon
Briám A vegetable dish usually consisting of courgettes, tomatoes, onions and potatoes. Aubergines and peppers are sometimes added. There is a similar dish called Imam
Dhroussoulites Dewy ones, dewy shades, or dewy shadows. These ghostly apparitions only appear (allegedly) when early morning dew remains. Foreign visitors have had little success in experiencing this phenomenon. Locals have sometimes contacted the hapless ghost hunters (once they have returned to their native land) to report that the *dhroussoulites* had eventually turned up, albeit a little late
Ernie The computer that randomly selects the prize winning numbers of premium bonds
Esprit de corps Literally translated "spirit of the body" from the French words. This is a feeling of pride and loyalty, which Dunbabin detected in Rendel's group
Estiatório Usually a modern form of a traditional taverna, serving plenty of oven baked dishes
Exedra A seating area or display area found at some archaeological sites on the island
Feu–de–joie In a French dictionary I have seen this translated as 'bonfire', but it can be literally translated as 'fire of joy', and this is the meaning as it relates to Crete – a celebration
Gendarmes Paramilitary police officers

My Wife Suggested Crete

Kafenío   Café/bar
Kalderimi   Ancient paved road, sometimes described as a mule track
Kantina   Guide books generally refrain from mentioning this simple form of catering. In Crete, a *Kantina* usually takes the form of a lock-up cabin or mobile unit, where the choice of refreshments varies considerably
Kapetan   The leader of a group of Cretan resistance fighters in the 1940s. Among the more influential were Bandouvas, Xylouris, Petrakoyiorgis, Grigorakis (Satanas), Dramountanis, and Petro Petrakas from Asi Gonia
Katastrofi   Demands for Smyrna to become part of Greece led to a disastrous Greek military campaign and a withdrawal of military support by her allies. As the Turks counter-attacked, they massacred thousands of Greek and Armenian residents. (Circa 1919 – 1922). The word *Katastrofi* is often used to describe these harrowing events
Kolokythokeftedes   Courgette fritters or courgette balls, deep or shallow fried. They often contain onion, potato and herbs but their consistency varies from taverna to taverna. As usual arguments can rage as to the correct ingredients and cooking method
Malotíra   A bushy plant which grows in mountain areas, hence the name 'mountain tea'. It can be combined with other herbs such as sage or Cretan dittany, and honey is often added
Mantinades   Cretan rhyming couplets, sometimes combined with a musical arrangement
Metamorphic   Rock which has been transformed by heat, pressure or other natural forces
Mizíthra   Goat or sheep's cheese in the style of ricotta
Oikoyeniaka   Family matters. A polite way of describing a feud between two families which often ended in violence
Olivine   A green or brown silicate mineral found in many igneous rocks
Oúzo   A spirit distilled from grapes but with an aniseed flavour. More generally Greek rather than specifically Cretan
Papa   A priest in the Greek Orthodox church
Pentozalis   Energetic Cretan dances requiring great skill
Pithoi   Large storage jars, often decorated, used as long ago as the Minoan age
Pilafi   The broth from cooking the meat (usually lamb or chicken) is utilised to create this risotto-style rice. The lamb or chicken is usually served separately but when it was offered to us, it was all mixed together

Glossary

Platía A plaza or square, often the centre of a village. They are more numerous in the towns and cities

Raki Officially known as *tsikoudiá*, this spirit is distilled from the remains of the grape harvest

Retsina As the name suggests, this is a resinated wine; not to everyone's taste

Sakkouli A Cretan rucksack made of cloth with criss-cross cords instead of modern day straps

Serpentine A dark or olive green mineral consisting of a silicate of magnesium

Siganos Much slower that the *pentozalis,* these dances can be enjoyed by everyone

Spartium Junceum Commonly known as Spanish Broom, with fragrant yellow pea-like flowers

Tavli A form of backgammon, a game often played in bars and cafes

Taxímata (ex-voto) An offering which is left at a religious or other sacred place

Thimárisio Thyme honey

Zaharoplastía A patisserie or cake shop

Permissions and References

I am most grateful to the following authors, publishers, institutions and copyright holders for granting me permission to use quotations and extracts, as follows:-

Denise Harvey for *Edward Lear The Cretan Journal*. Third edition. 2012. Copyright © Denise Harvey (Publisher).
Imogen Grundon for *The Rash Adventurer A Life of John Pendlebury*. Libri Publications Ltd. Copyright © Imogen Grundon 2007.
Peter Trudgill (author) and John Chapple (publisher) of Lycabettus Press for *In Sfakiá*. Copyright © Peter Trudgill 2008 and 2015 (revised edition).
David MacNeil Doren for *Winds of Crete*. Copyright © David MacNeil Doren. 1974. (Published by John Murray).
Adam Hopkins for *Crete Its Past, Present and People*. Copyright © Adam Hopkins. 1977, 1989. (Published by Faber and Faber).
Richard Clark for *Crete A Notebook*. Copyright © Richard Clark. 2012.
Paul Dry of Paul Dry Books Inc., for *Hide and Seek* and *The Stronghold*, both by Xan Fielding. Copyright © Paul Dry Books Inc. 2013. (*The Stronghold* first published in London 1953 and *Hide and Seek* first published in London 1954, by Secker & Warburg).
Penguin Random House UK as follows:- from *The Colossus of Maroussi* by Henry Miller published by William Heinemann. Copyright © 1941 Henry Miller. Reproduced by permission of the Random House Group Ltd.
New Directions Publishing Corp as follows: excerpts from THE COLOSSOS OF MAROUSSI by Henry Miller. Copyright © 1941 Henry Miller. Reprinted by permission of New Directions Publishing Corp.
Robert Rendel and the Rendel family for *Appointment in Crete* by A M Rendel. (First published in July 1953 by Allan Wingate Ltd, London).

Permissions and References

Alexandros Kokonas, the Kokonas family and Mystis Publications (Manouras G-Tsintaris A. Co) for *The Cretan Resistance 1941 – 1945* by N A Kokonas, MD. Copyright © "Mystis" 2004.

Marilyn Sadleir for *The Road to Prevelly* by Geoffrey Edwards. Copyright © E G Edwards. 1989.

Rhys Ferguson for *Flowers of Rethymnon Escape from Crete* by Lew Lind. Copyright © Lew Lind. 1944 and 1991.

Extracts from *Abducting a General* by Patrick Leigh Fermor © The Estate of Patrick Leigh Fermor 2014, reproduced with permission of Hodder and Stoughton Limited through PLSclear.

James Angelos (author) and Penguin Random House LLC (US) for *The Full Catastrophe* Copyright © 2015 by James Angelos, published in the United States by Crown Publishers, an imprint of The Crown Publishing Group, a division of Penguin Random House LLC New York.

Granta Books of London and Penguin Random House LLC (US) for *Dinner with Persephone* by Patricia Storace. Copyright © 1996 by Pat Storace.

Quotation from *The Villa Ariadne* by Dilys Powell, reproduced by permission of Peters, Fraser and Dunlop on behalf of the Estate of Dilys Powell.

Cassandra Verney for *Snakes and Ladders* by Stephen Verney, copyright © 2016, Stephen Verney.

The Royal Logistic Corps (which now incorporates The Royal Army Ordnance Corps) for *A History of the Royal Army Ordnance Corps 1920 – 1945* by Alan Fernyhough. Copyright © Royal Army Ordnance Corps 1967.

Quotations from *Official History of New Zealand in the Second World War. Crete* have been reproduced with the permission of the New Zealand Ministry for Culture and Heritage. Author D M Davin. Published 1953.

The Society of Cretan Historical Studies, The Historical Museum of Crete, and Assistant Director of HMC, Agisilaos Kaloutsakis for *Testimonies 1 To Have and to Lose* by Reg Spurr, © Society of Cretan Historical Studies 2005-2007; *Testimonies 3 Freedom and Glory (Memoirs 1939-1945)* by Georgios Aristides Tzitzikas, © Society of Cretan Historical Studies 2012; and *Testimonies 6 Tom J Dunbabin An Archaeologist at War* by Tom Dunbabin © Society of Cretan Historical Studies 2015.

Jol Wiren for *Captive Kiwi* by R H Thomson Copyright © 1964 R H Thomson, (published by Whitcombe & Tombs).

My Wife Suggested Crete

Alexandria Publications for *Crete 1941 Eyewitnessed* by C N Hadjipateras and M Fafalios. Copyright © Alexandria Publications 2016 (also published in 1991 by Random Century New Zealand Ltd).

Dr Roderick Bailey, for his Foreword and Notes © Roderick Bailey 2014 to *Abducting a General* by Patrick Leigh Fermor (see above).

Extracts from *THE CRETAN RUNNER* by Copyright © GEORGE PSYCHOUNDAKIS 1995. Published John Murray 1995, Penguin Books 1998, 2009. Reproduced by permission of Penguin Books Ltd. ©

Extracts from *The Royal Artillery Commemoration Book 1939-1945* reproduced by kind permission of The Royal Artillery Institution.

Extracts from *Crete The Battle and the Resistance* by Antony Beevor © Antony Beevor 1991, reproduced with permission of Hodder and Stoughton Limited through PLSclear.

Colin Janes for *The Eagles of Crete* copyright © 2013 Colin Janes, and for *The Guerrillas of Crete* copyright © Colin Janes 2017.

Christopher Somerville (author) and Haus Publishing Ltd for *The Golden Step* copyright © Christopher Somerville 2007, 2012.

Extracts from *Dashing for the Post The Letters of Patrick Leigh Fermor* selected and edited by Adam Sisman, © The Estate of Patrick Leigh Fermor. 1940-2010, reproduced with permission of Hodder and Stoughton Limited through PLSclear.

Extracts from *Words of Mercury* by Patrick Leigh Fermor © The Estate of Patrick Leigh Fermor. First published in 2003 by John Murray, reproduced with permission of Hodder and Stoughton Limited through PLSclear.

W W Norton & Company, Inc., for *The Archaeology of Crete* by J D S Pendlebury. Originally published by Methuen in 1939; first published by the Norton Library in 1965.

I am indebted to Seán Damer and Ian Frazer for allowing me to extract information, figures and statistics, from *On the Run* Copyright © Seán Damer and Ian Frazer 2006. Published by Penguin Group (NZ) 2006, 2007.

I also acknowledge the use of various quotations from the following books:-

Travels in Crete Robert Pashley (John Murray, London 1837).
Travels and Researches in Crete Captain T A B Spratt (John Van Voorst, London 1865).

Permissions and References

Roughing It in Crete in 1867 John Edwin Hilary Skinner (Richard Bentley, London 1868).

I also thank Meredith Carroll, Senior Commissioning Editor at Manchester University Press with reference to *The Making of the Cretan Landscape* by Oliver Rackham and Jennifer Moody. I understand that the quotations I have wished to use fall under Fair Use / Fair Dealing. Hence I do not require formal permission, as I have cited the original source in each case.

I have tried my utmost to source all necessary permissions from the relevant copyright holders. Should any omissions come to light, I would of course be delighted to include these in any future edition of this book.

All quotations are fully referenced below.

Introduction

OR & JM "Crete is a miniature continent,…". *The Making of the Cretan Landscape.* Oliver Rackham and Jennifer Moody. Page 33.

EL "Little sleep: rats …" *The Cretan Journal.* Edward Lear. Page 31.

EL "wonderful view of Suda Bay …". ibid. Page 30.

IG "Some talk of being bitten …". *The Rash Adventurer. A Life of John Pendlebury.* Imogen Grundon. Page 55

PT "…in rural Crete, dogs are not pets…" *In Sfakiá.* Peter Trudgill. Page 107-108.

Chapter One

DMD "For us, it was one of those magic centres..." *Winds of Crete.* David MacNeil Doren. Page 42.

AH "The scale is intimate,…". *Crete. Its Past, Present and People.* Adam Hopkins. Page 100.

TABS "The site and ruins are certainly …". *Travels and Researches in Crete.* Captain TAB Spratt. (1865). Vol I Ch 13. Page 136-137.

A Cretan Interlude: "A walk up to Knossós".

RC "Getting up at dawn …". *Crete - A Notebook* Richard Clark. Pages 36-38

Chapter Two
RC "There is so much to discover …". Richard Clark. Page 4

Chapter Three
XF "as we emerged ..." *The Stronghold.* Xan Fielding. Page 230

Chapter Four
DMD "Crete, with its infinite variety …" David MacNeil Doren. Page 124

HM "God, it's incredible!" *The Colossus of Maroussi* Henry Miller. Page 140

HM "Below me, stretching away …" ibid. Page 141

TABS "in no part of Crete …" *Travels and Researches in Crete.* Captain TAB Spratt. Vol I Ch. 27. Page 331

AMR "The days at Máles …" *Appointment in Crete.* AM Rendel. Page 144

NK "he was le beau chevalier …" *The Cretan Resistance 1941 – 1945.* N A Kokonas. Appendix K. Major Jack Smith-Hughes. Page 162

DMD "I am hypnotised by it … by indescribable impulses." David MacNeil Doren. Page 76/77

Chapter Five
DMD "Cretans live close-packed …" David MacNeil Doren. Page 97

TABS "on the last day of May …" Spratt. Vol I Ch 1. Page 5

TABS "Enthusiasm is however …" Spratt. Vol I Ch 1. Page 7

GE "…and what true friends …" *The Road to Prevelly.* Geoffrey Edwards. Page 54

LL "I looked down upon…" *Flowers of Rethymnon. Escape from Crete.* Lew Lind. P 80

LL "kindness, you might say …" ibid. Page 81

LL "…there was a lot of weeping…" ibid. Page 82

Chapter Seven
PLF "Crete differs…" *Abducting a General.* Patrick Leigh Fermor. Page 89

DMD "Ferocity and generosity co-exist…" David MacNeil Doren. Page 105

RC "What makes so many people…" Richard Clark. Page 3

Permissions and References

JA	"Tax evasion in Greece …" The *Full Catastrophe, Travels Among the New Greek Ruins.* James Angelos. Page 56
JA	"Scamming the state…" ibid. Page 35
HM	"an enthusiastic, curious-minded …" Henry Miller. Page 7
HM	"Not only passion …" ibid. Page 7
AMR	"there is much about the country…" Rendel. Page 15
PS	"Every nation has its cross …" *Dinner with Persephone.* Patricia Storace. Page 37
PS	"Someone recently asked …" ibid. Page 159
HM	"Marvelous things happen …" Henry Miller. Page 15
OR & JM	"Cretans are descended …" *The Making of the Cretan Landscape.* Oliver Rackham and Jennifer Moody. Page 88
JEHS	"Cretan priests were expected …" *Roughing it in Crete in 1867.* J E Hilary Skinner. Page 93
JEHS	"When there was a battle …" ibid. Page 94
AMR	"Well, Mr Alexis …"Rendel. Page 210
DP	"highly coloured accounts…" *The Villa Ariadne.* Dilys Powell. Page 135 (quoting Cumberlege)
XF	"their friendship has infected …" *The Stronghold.* Xan Fielding. Preface Page 4
IG	"Over time they began …" Imogen Grundon. Page 323
DMD	"Above all there was a sense …" David MacNeil Doren. Page 171
OR & JM	"Nobody, not even the Turk, …" Rackham and Moody. Page 214
DMD	"Freedom is the only ideal…" David MacNeil Doren. Page 152
PT	"We hear you've had snow … for at least an hour." Peter Trudgill. Page 217
RC	"More than any other place …" Richard Clark. Page 2
SV	"their outstanding national …" Stephen Verney. Page 80
JEHS	"There is stuff …" JE Hilary Skinner. Conclusion -Page 271

Chapter Eight
TABS	"In looking towards the south .."." Spratt. Vol II Ch. 13. Page 149
TABS	"There sprung up from the south-east …" ibid. Vol II Ch. 15. Page 188

Chapter Nine
RP "Again and again do I …". *Travels in Crete.* (1837). Robert Pashley. Vol II Ch 39. Page 272

Chapter Ten A: The Battle of Crete

PLF "…to the great astonishment …" *Abducting a General*. Patrick Leigh Fermor. Page 89

XF "went out of fashion …" *Hide and Seek*. Xan Fielding. Author's note xxv

AHF "Throughout the operations …" *History of the Royal Army Ordnance Corps 1920-1945*. Brigadier A H Fernyhough. Page 135

DMDavin "the concrete conditions of the battle …" *Official History of New Zealand in the Second World War. Crete*. DM Davin. Page 463

DMDavin "No men ever held positions …" ibid. Page 463-464

IG "I judged them to have been …" Grundon. Page 282-283

IG " …the nastiness, the sloth, the nullity …" ibid. Page 283

IG "so cossetted by the colonial life …" ibid. Page 281

GAT "I've always believed that …" *Freedom and Glory. (Memoirs 1939-1945)*. Georgios Tzitzikas. Testimonies 3. Society of Cretan Historical Studies. Page 42

RHT "Dysentery and kindred tummy troubles…" *Captive Kiwi*. R H Thomson. Page 22

PLF "In a way, of course …" *Abducting a General*. Patrick Leigh Fermor. Page 90

RS "I can say quite honestly …" *To Have and To Lose*. Reg Spurr. Testimonies 1. Society of Cretan Historical Studies. Page 271

RHT "I was deeply disappointed…" RH Thomson. Page 12

CH&MF "I shall never forget the silence …" *Crete 1941 Eyewitnessed* CN Hadjipateras and M Fafalios. Quoting Ralph Stockbridge. Page 264-265

Chapter Ten   B: The Cretan Resistance & The British Secret Service 1941-1945

NK "if anything of any value…" *The Cretan Resistance 1941-1945*. NA Kokonas. Forward by RH Stockbridge. Page 15

XF "their splendid new aerodrome …" *Hide and Seek*. Xan Fielding. Page 38

XF "I recognised in the offer…" ibid. Page 9

TD "I liked it because it was …" *Tom J Dunbabin An Archaeologist at War*. Testimonies 6. Society of Cretan Historical Studies. Page 101

TD "little appeal in the tediousness …" ibid. Page 101

AMR	"and yet the more I thought of it ...". Rendel. Page 14
RB	"Leigh Fermor does not submit..." Quoted by Roderick Bailey in the Foreword to *Abducting a General*. (Patrick Leigh Fermor). Page xx
AMR	"without exception all the British ..." Rendel. Page 14
XF	"Anxious to resemble the Cretans... as The Tinker". *Hide and Seek*. Xan Fielding. Pages 118-119
IG	"It was by virtue of his knowledge ... could respond". Grundon. Page 300-301
PLF	"to a point where difference ..." *Abducting a General*. Patrick Leigh Fermor. Page 88
AMR	"It was delightful to see..." Rendel. Page 102
AMR	"They still could not exchange..." ibid. Page 188
AMR	"I don't suppose they will ever meet..." ibid. Page 188
NK	"In the Battle of Crete," Kokonas. Introduction. Page 21
NK	"The collection of good intelligence...". Kokonas. Foreword by R H Stockbridge. Page 14-15
NK	"Indeed, from mid-1943 onwards..." ibid. Introduction. Page 21
NK	"The success of the Mission ..." ibid. Page 135
AMR	"He had left me ...". Rendel. Page 229
PLF	"This youthful Kim-like figure..." *Abducting a General*. Patrick Leigh Fermor. Page 68
AMR	"Kosta was one of the most ..." Rendel. Page 158
SV	"after a short rest ..." *Snakes and Ladders*. Stephen Verney. Page 73-74
GP	"Crete had to resist..." *The Cretan Runner*. George Psychoundakis. Page 45.
NK	"In time SOE officers ..." Kokonas. Appendix K, Major Jack Smith-Hughes. Page 171

Chapter Ten C: The Aftermath. Civil War

GST	"So, in an atmosphere of warm ..." *The Royal Artillery Commemoration Book 1939-1945*. Brigadier G S Thompson. Page 176
AB	"Accusations of collaboration ..." *Crete. The Battle and the Resistance*. Antony Beevor. Page 340
AB	"The blood feuds engendered ...".ibid. Page 336
GP	"that the two sides ..." Psychoundakis. Page 313.
AMR	"some of our best friends..." Rendel. Page 230
CJ	"... and the appointment of Vardoulakis ...". *The Eagles of Crete*. Colin Janes. Page 105

CJ	"This was not the utopia ..." *The Guerrillas of Crete.* Colin Janes. Page 132	
CS	"The English supported the Greek government..." *The Golden Step.* Christopher Somerville. Pages 147-148	
AH	"As for the Germans ..." Adam Hopkins. Page 160	
AH	"What lingers is the memory of death ..." ibid. Page 160	
PLF	"There it was indeed ..." Dashing for the Post - The Letters of Patrick Leigh Fermor. Page 329	
PLF	"The CP are only a small minority ..." ibid. Page 329	

Chapter Eleven

PLF	"The General's behaviour was ..." *Abducting a General.* From War Report No 8. Patrick Leigh Fermor. Page 160	
PLF	"The place was filling up ..." ibid. Page 92	
JEHS	"scores of bodies unburied ... in this ghastly fashion". Hilary Skinner. Page 75 & 77	
JEHS	"When the monastery of Arkadi ..." ibid. Introduction Page xxiv	
PLF	"We had both drunk ..." *Words of Mercury.* Edited by Artemis Cooper. Patrick Leigh Fermor. Page 96	

A Cretan Interlude: "The Katzphur people".

TD	"The Katzphur people were a merry folk ..." *Tom J Dunbabin. An Archaeologist at War.* Tom Dunbabin. Testimonies 6. Society of Cretan Historical Studies. Page 78 & 79

Chapter Twelve

JP	"To have stood on Ida ..." *The Archaeology of Crete.* JDS Pendlebury. Introduction. Page xxix

A Cretan Interlude: "Stories from the Lásithi Plateau".

RC	"of an age to have fought ..." . Richard Clark. Page 153
RC	"Mustering my best Greek ..." ibid. Page 152
AMR	"By coincidence I went late one afternoon ...". Rendel. Page 160 & 161

Chapter Thirteen

AMR	"This remote corner of Crete ..." Rendel. Page 239
OR & JM	"Crete is a land of hundred gorges ..." Rackham & Moody. Page 25
OR & JM	"The key to Cretan gorges ..." ibid. Page 26

OR & JM	"They are part of the island's personality ..." ibid. Page 25
TABS	"so commodious and safe an anchorage ..." Spratt. Vol 1. Ch.18. Page 196-197
AMR	"This remote corner of Crete ..." Rendel. Page 239
IG	"John loved the wildness ..." Grundon. Page 56
IG	"It is thousands of years ..." ibid. Page 56
AMR	"as utterly quiet and peaceful ..." Rendel. Page 239

Chapter Fourteen

XF	"It was the Greeks ..." *The Stronghold.* Xan Fielding. Page 295
AH	"One could spend a very long time ..." Adam Hopkins. Page 195
AMR	"I have no hope or wish ever ..." Rendel. Page 15
AMR	"...still seems real to the point ..." ibid. Page 16
XF	"permanently exorcised ". *The Stronghold.* Xan Fielding. Page 293
XF	"The island's most important ...the Cretan people" ibid. Page 296
PLF	"the flair for friendship ...through everything." *Abducting a General.* Patrick Leigh Fermor. Page 90
RC	"are as welcoming as ever". Clark. Page 254
OR & JM	"It is a uniquely glamorous island..." Rackham & Moody. Page 210
AH	"The island has a way of taking people ..." Hopkins. Page 14
TABS	"in the archaic times ..." Spratt. Vol II. Ch. 22. Page 273
TABS	"...and so I leave the reader ..." ibid. Vol II. Ch. 22. Page 273

Bibliography

General History
Theocharis Detorakis *History of Crete* translated by JC Davis (1994)
Chris Moorey *A History of Crete* (2019)
Nikos Psilakis *Byzantine Churches and Monasteries of Crete* (1994)

Archaeology and Ancient History
Leonard Cottrell *The Bull of Minos* (1984; first published 1953)
Sinclair Hood *The Minoans* (1971)
JDS Pendlebury *The Archaeology of Crete* (Norton Library 1965; first published 1939)

WWII History: The Battle of Crete; The Resistance Years and the Aftermath
Antony Beevor *Crete: The Battle and the Resistance* (1991)
Christopher Buckley *Greece and Crete 1941* (Efstathiadis Group 1977; first published 1942)
Alan Clark *The Fall of Crete* (1962)
MG Comeau *Operation Mercury* (1991; first published 1961)
Geoffrey Cox *A Tale of Two Battles* (1987)
Seán Damer & Ian Frazer *On the Run* (2006)
DM Davin *Official History of New Zealand in the Second World War 1939-1945: Crete* (1953)
Wes Davis *The Ariadne Objective* (2014)
Geoffrey Edwards *The Road to Prevelly* (1989)
Murray Elliott *Vasili, the Lion of Crete* (1987)
Alan Fernyhough *A History of the Royal Army Ordnance Corps 1920-1945* (1967)
Xan Fielding *Hide and Seek* (Paul Dry Books 2013; originally published 1954)
C. Hadjipateras & M. Fafalios *Crete 1941: Eyewitnessed* (2016; originally published 1989)

Bibliography

Hugh Hodgkinson	*Before the Tide Turned* (1944)
Imogen Grundon	*The Rash Adventurer. A Life of John Pendlebury* (2007)
Colin Janes	*The Eagles of Crete* (2013)
	The Guerrillas of Crete (2017)
GC Kiriakopoulos	*Ten Days to Destiny: The Battle of Crete* (1985)
NA Kokonas	*The Cretan Resistance 1941–1945* (2004)
Patrick Leigh Fermor	*Abducting a General* (2014)
Lew Lind	*Flowers of Rethymnon: Escape from Crete* (1991)
Gavin Long	*Australian War History, Greece, Crete and Syria* (1953)
Callum MacDonald	*The Lost Battle* (1993)
William Stanley Moss	*Il Met by Moonlight* (2014; originally published 1950)
Yannis Prekatsounakis	*Crete. The Battle for Heraklion 1941* (2016)
George Psychoundakis	*The Cretan Runner* (Penguin Books 2009; originally published 1955)
AM Rendel	*Appointment in Crete* (1953)
Adam Sisman	*The Letters of Patrick Leigh Fermor. Dashing for the Post* (Selected and edited by – 2016)
I McD Stewart	*The Struggle for Crete* (1991)
Society of Cretan Historical Studies	*From Mercury to Ariadne* (Costas Mamalakis 2010)
	Escape from Crete (J de Mole Carstairs 2016)
	Tom J Dunbabin. An Archaeologist at War (Tom Dunbabin 2015)
	To Have and to Lose (Reg Spurr 2007)
	Freedom and Glory (Georgios Tzitzikas 2012)
David A Thomas	*Crete 1941. The Battle at Sea* (1972)
WB Thomas	*Dare to be Free* (1974; first published 1951)
G S Thompson	*The Royal Artillery Commemoration Book 1939-1945* (Edited by WE Duncan 1950)
RH Thomson	*Captive Kiwi* (1964)
Stephen Verney	*Snakes and Ladders* (2016)
Mathew Willingham	*Perilous Commitments* (2005)

Modern History

James Angelos	*The Full Catastrophe. Travels Among the New Greek Ruins* (2015)

Topography and Geology
Charalampos G Fassoulas *The Field Guide to the Geology of Crete* (3rd edition 2004)
Oliver Rackham & Jennifer Moody   *The Making of the Cretan Landscape* (1996)

Travel Writing
Richard Clark   *Crete - A Notebook* (2012)
Deborah Devonshire & Patrick Leigh Fermor *In Tearing Haste* (Edited by Charlotte Mosley 2009)
John Ebdon   *Near Myths. A love Affair with Greece* (1989)
Xan Fielding   *The Stronghold* (Paul Dry Books 2013)
Adam Hopkins   *Crete, Its Past, Present and People* (First published in 1977)
Edward Lear   *The Cretan Journal* (2012; first published in 1984)
Patrick Leigh Fermor *Roumeli. Travels in Northern Greece.* (1983), *Words of Mercury.* (2003)
David MacNeil Doren *Winds of Crete* (1974)
Henry Miller   *The Colossus of Maroussi* (1971)
Robert Pashley   *Travels in Crete* (1837)
Dilys Powell   *The Villa Ariadne.* (1999; first published in 1973)
JE Hilary Skinner   *Roughing it in Crete in 1867* (1868)
Christopher Sommerville *The Golden Step* (2012; first published in 2007)
Captain TAB Spratt   *Travels and Researches in Crete* (1865)
Patricia Storace   *Dinner with Persephone* (1997)
Peter Trudgill   *In Sfakiá* 2015   (1st Edition 2008)

Travel Guides
John Fisher & Geoff Garvey *The Rough Guide to Crete* (June 2016: 10th Edition; 2019: 11th Edition)
Jonnie Godfrey & Elizabeth Karslake *Landscapes of Eastern Crete* (2003)
Nick Edwards, John Fisher, Rebecca Hall, et al
    The Rough Guide to Greece (April 2015: 14th Edition)
Paola Pugsley   *Blue Guide. Crete* (2010: 8th Edition)

Cooking and the Cretan Diet
Marianthi Milona   *Culinaria Greece* (2007)
Mystis Editions   *Cretan Cuisine*

Bibliography

Maria and Nikos Psilakis *Cretan Cooking* (Revised Edition 2000)
Barbara Roberts *The Truth about Statins* (2012)

Fiction
Nikos Kazantzákis *Freedom or Death* (1983; first published 1955. Translated by Jonathan Griffin)

Index

A
Agiós Ioánnis peninsula 29, 37
Agrilés 131, 132, 135, 139
Akrotíri peninsula 126
Akrotíri Spanda 125
Allied War Cemetery 144
Alones 172
Amari valley 82, 172, 179, 183
Ambelos 76
Amirás 155, 157
Angathiá 37, 38, 43, 45, 73, 78, 195, 199, 206, 219
Ánidri 130
Ánidri gorge 130
Ano Sými 68
Áno Zákros 42, 75, 197
Anópoli 138, 164
Anóyia 80, 106
Apodoúlou 82
Áptera 118, 119, 120, 121
Arádena 138
Argyroúpolis 167, 172
Arhánes 98
Arméni 179
Arvi 62, 63
Así Goniá 159, 172
Assiderato hills 56, 81
Axós 80
Ayia Ánna 178
Ayiá Ekateríni 96
Ayiá Ekateríni Museum 96

Áyia Galíni 56
Áyia Iríni gorge 130, 132
Ayía Marina 127
Ayía Paraskeví 81
Ayiá reservoir 126
Ayía Rouméli 137
Ayiá Triádha 57
Ayías Ekaterínis 96
Áyii Apóstoli 127
Áyios Ioánnis 138
Áyios Mínas 96
Áyios Nikólaos 19, 22, 24, 28, 91, 122, 202
Áyios Pándes gorge 202
Áyios Pávlos 179, 204
Ayíos Títos 58

B
Balí 171
Bay of Pigs 134

C
Candia 90
Cape Plakas 205
Cape Sídheros 41, 201
Chaniá 8

D
Dedhálou street 95
Dhamnóni 60
Dhia 19

Dhikeosinis street 95
Dhiktean cave 185, 187
Dhíkti mountains 67, 70
Dhoukos Bofor 93
Dhrápano peninsula 126, 166
Doriés 29
Dríros 26, 28, 30

E
E4 path 171, 188, 197
El Khandak 90
Eléftherna 176
Eloúnda 29
Elyrós 131, 135
Erimoupolis Bay 203
Etiá 201, 202

F
Faistos 57
Falásarna 115, 116, 120
Férma 65
Festos 57, 91
Flória 128
Fódhele 97
fountain of Idomeneus 97
Fourfourás 183
Fournés Botanical Park 126
Fournoú Korýfi 64
Frangokástello 173
Frati 88
Fres 163

G
Galatás 146
Gavalohóri 166
Gávdhos 87, 215
Gdohia 68
German War Cemetery 146
Gipari gorge 172
Gorge of the Dead 197
Górtyn 58

Gortyna 58
Górtys 58
Góudhouras 63
Gournés 20
Gourniá 26
Goúves 20, 97
Graméno 129
Gramvoúsa 116
Grandes Islands 205
Gulf of Kissámou 117
Gulf of Mirabello 37

H
Hamézi 37
Hándhakos street 95
Haniá 8, 89, 123, 124, 149, 173
Haniá airport 14
Heraclium 90
Heraklion 8, 90
Hersónisos 16, 20
Hill 107 125, 146
Hióna 38
Hióna beach 43, 206
Historical Museum of Crete 97
Hokhlakiés 198
Holocaust Museum 155, 157
Hóra Sphakíon 138
Houdhétsi 69
Hyrtákina 130

I
Idean cave 179, 187
Ierápetra 64, 91
Ímbros 138
Iráklio 8, 90, 149
Iráklio airport 14
Iron Gates 137
Ítanos 41, 204

K
Kalamáki 54, 57, 60

Index

Kali Sykia 160, 172
Kalikrátis 172
Kamáres cave 179
Kamilári 61
Kándanos 128, 131
Karfí 184, 189
Karoúbes Bay 198
Kastélli Kissámou 120, 127, 162
Kastélli Pedhiádhos 14
Kastrí Bluff 38, 43
Katharó 20
Katharó plateau 32
Kato Mixórrouma 181
Káto Stalós 127
Kato Sými 67, 68
Káto Zákros 42, 197
Kavoúsi 37
Kédhros mountains 56, 57
Kendochori 60
Kerá 189
Kissamos 115
Knossós 30, 34, 47, 93, 153
Kókkino Horió 166
Kommós 57
Korai Street 92
Koráka beach 171
Kotsifóu gorge 172
Koúles 93
Koum Kápi 123
Kouremónos 43, 109
Kouremónos beach 47, 197
Kourtaliótiko gorge 82
Koussés 58
Koustoyérako 130, 131, 132, 136
Kritsá 20, 23
Kyriakosélia 121, 122

L
Lambini 180
Lappa 172
Lasíthi 20, 184, 193

Lasíthi plateau 20, 47
Lató 24, 32
Límin Hersonísou 16
Limni beach 86
Lion Square 95
Lissós 131, 134
Livadás 130, 131, 132, 136
Livanianá 138
Loutró 138
Lyttos 172, 216

M
Maheri 164
Makriyialós 65
Máleme 125, 144
Máleme airfield 146
Máles 67, 70
Malevisi 90
Mália 16, 20
Margarítes 178
Maridhati beach 47
Marmakéto 184
Martinengo bastion 100
Mátala 54
Megála Horáfia 119
Melidhóni cave 179
Messará 57
Messará plain 57
Mikrí Kopróna 189
Mirsíni 37
Mixórrouma 60, 114, 171, 172, 180
Monastiráki 82
Moní 133, 136
Moní Aretíou 29
Moní Arkádhi 167, 175
Moní Faneroméni 202
Moní Kápsa, 65
Moní Koudhoumá 71
Moní Odhíyítrias 61
Moní Préveli 84, 167, 172
Moní Toploú 41, 47, 195, 198

Moní Vidianí 189
Morosini fountain 95
Mosque of the Janissaries 124
Moulianá 37
Mount Dhíkti 184, 187, 188, 208
Mount Ida 32, 82, 208
Mount Kédhros 60, 172, 180
Mount Yioúhtas 108
Museum of Ancient Greek Technology 97
Museum of National Resistance 1941–1945 126
Mýrthios 87
Mýrtos 63, 68, 73
Mýrtos Pirgos 64
Mýthi 67

N
N. Kazantzákis International Airport 216
Natural History Museum 96, 189
Néa Eléftherna 177
Néa Hóra 114, 125
Nea Présos 48
Neápoli 20, 159
New Gate 99
Nídha plateau 84, 179, 187
Nissimos plateau 188

O
Oloús 30
Omaló plateau 137, 164
Oreioi 130
Ornó Mountains 37

P
Pahiá Ámmos 32, 37
palace of Knossós 90
Palace of Mália 26
Palace of Zákros 42, 220
Palazzo d'Ittar 97

Palékastro 38, 39, 43, 195, 206
Paleóchora 128, 130, 132, 133, 135
Palm Beach 86
Panayía Kerá 23, 26
Paximadia Islands 56
Péfki 67
Pefkos 68
Peristeres 170
Perivolákia gorge 65
Petrás 74
Petsofás 199, 205
Pezá 98
Phaistos 57
Pinakianó 189
Pireás 93
Piskokéfalo 48
Piskopiáno 20
Pláka 29
Plakiás 60, 81, 82, 171, 173
Plataniás 127
Plátanos 37, 115, 120
platía 91, 171
Platiá Venizélou 95
Polyrínia 116, 120
Polyrízos 171
Pómbia 58
Porto Rafti 143
Présos 48, 135
Préveli 84
Prevelly 86
Priouli fountain 96
Provarma 122
Psilafi 132
Psilorítis 82
Psykhró 187, 193

R
Repi 58
Réthymno 60, 80, 81, 149
Réthymno province 173
Réthymno-Spíli road 79

Index

Rimondi fountain 81
Riza 68
Rodhákino 87, 170, 173
Rodhopoú peninsula 116, 125
Roussólakkos 39, 206

S
Samaria brand 122
Samariá gorge 47, 137, 164, 197
San Marco 95
Sarakinás gorge 67, 70
Séli Ambélou 187
Sélino 130, 131, 137, 149
Selliá 87, 173, 180
Sfendóni cave 179
Sfínari 116
Shrine of Peace and Remembrance 85
Sibritos 82
Sideropórtes 137
Sísi 20
Sitía 13, 37, 73, 91, 105
Sívas 58
Skiniás 29
Skotinó cave 97
Sotiris Christós 130
Soúdha Bay 118
Soúdha Bay Allied War Cemetery 89, 118
Soúgia 131, 133
Soúyia 131
Sphakiá 102, 105, 130, 138, 173
Spíli 60, 171, 172
Spinalónga 29
St Minas 96
St Nicolas Bay Hotel 19, 20
St Títos 95
Stilianoú winery 98
Stýlos 122
Syia 134

T
Tavronitis bridge 146
Teménia 130
Temple of Apollo Delphinios 26
Temple of Pythian Apollo 58
Tértsa 64
Thériso 126, 162, 163
Thriptí mountain range 32
Thripti Mountains 21
Thrónos 83, 84, 192
Toumba 132
Tragostalos 200
Trápeza 185
Triópetra 179
Trypítos 74
Tsiskiani 133
Tsoutsouras 63
Týlissos 80
Tymbáki 150
Tymbáki airfield 56, 57
Tzermiádho 184, 188, 192

U
Upper Zákros 197
Upper Zákros Gorge One 198

V
Vai 195
Vai beach 47
Vasilikí 32
Vathýpetro 98
Viánnos district 155
Vilandredo 172
Vitsilovrysí 191
Vríssi beach 138
Vrouhás 29

W
White Mountains 32, 113, 121, 132, 172

X
Xerókambos 75, 76, 201, 204

Y
Yerakári 168
Yialaskári 129
Yialaskári beach 130

Z
Zákros 204
Zákros Gorge 42
Zíros 201
Zoú 206
Zoúrva 163

www.ingramcontent.com/pod-product-compliance
Lightning Source LLC
Chambersburg PA
CBHW061249230426
43663CB00022B/2961